Questioning the Law in Corporate America

Recent Titles in
Contributions in Legal Studies

Common Law in Southern Africa: Conflict of Laws and Torts Precedents
Peter B Kutner

A History of the Anglo-American Common Law of Contract
Kevin M. Teeven

"We Have a Duty": The Supreme Court and the Watergate Tapes Litigation
Howard Ball

The Shaping of Nineteenth-Century Law: John Appleton and Responsible Individualism
David M. Gold

Comparative Constitutional Federalism: Europe and America
Mark Tushnet, editor

Church-State Constitutional Issues: Making Sense of the Establishment Clause
Donald L. Drakeman

The Politics of Obscenity: Group Litigation in a Time of Legal Change
Joseph F. Kobylka

An Essential Safeguard: Essays on the United States Supreme Court and Its Justices
D. Grier Stephenson, Jr., editor

A "Representative" Supreme Court? The Impact of Race, Religion, and Gender on Appointments
Barbara A. Perry

State Constitutions and Criminal Justice
Barry Latzer

The Sixth Amendment in Modern American Jurisprudence: A Critical Perspective
Alfredo Garcia

Positive Neutrality: Letting Religious Freedom Ring
Stephen V. Monsma

Questioning the Law in Corporate America

Agenda for Reform

Gerald L. Houseman

CONTRIBUTIONS IN LEGAL STUDIES, NUMBER 71
Paul Murphy, Series Adviser

Greenwood Press
Westport, Connecticut • London

Dedicated to two residents of Fort Wayne, Indiana—
David B. Keller, a lawyer who sets an example for his profession, and
John Stein, an entrepreneur who sets an example for his profession

Library of Congress Cataloging-in-Publication Data

Houseman, Gerald L.
Questioning the law in corporate America : agenda for reform / Gerald L. Houseman.
p. cm.—(Contributions in legal studies, ISSN 0147-1074 ; no. 71)
Includes index.
ISBN 0-313-26341-8 (alk. paper)
1. Law reform—United States. 2. Corporation law—United States. I. Title. II. Series.
KF384.H68 1993
349.73—dc20
[347.3] 92-35554

British Library Cataloguing in Publication Data is available.

Library of Congress Catalog Card Number: 92-35554
ISBN: 0-313-26341-8
ISSN: 0147-1074

First published in 1993

Greenwood Press, 88 Post Road West, Westport, CT 06881
An imprint of Greenwood Publishing Group, Inc.

Printed in the United States of America

The paper used in this book complies with the Permanent Paper Standard issued by the National Information Standards Organization (Z39.48-1984).

10 9 8 7 6 5 4 3 2 1

Contents

Tables

Preface

SINCE THIS BOOK was written, this nation and its cities have been recovering from events in Los Angeles and other locales—the riots and the Rodney King case verdict which served as their catalyst. The delicate balances and arrangements of society, law, and civilization have been allowed to fall apart once again.

The American people and much of the world appear shocked, and words condemning lawlessness, killing, and property destruction are easily falling from the lips of citizens, mayors, community leaders, politicians, and the president. The violence and wanton disregard endemic in all riots are universally condemned; but, to their credit, the American people seem also to condemn the King trial verdict in which police brutality was sanctioned by an all-white suburban jury.

President George Bush's perspective was different. He believed that the riots could be blamed upon the indulgences of the 1960s and the shortcomings of Lyndon Johnson's Great Society programs. More important, he said nothing at all about the King verdict except that he was shocked. This fit with his political priorities.

These two events—the trial and the outbreak of riots—bring into sharp perspective the issues that are the subject of this book: the issues of human rights and the distorting effect upon these wrought by the exaggeration and overemphasis upon one of them, namely, property rights. The first two chapters demonstrate that the setting, the background, the very premises of American law provide us with two harsh realities: the education of lawyers, the most important group of practitioners in the field of public policy, which is heavily and egregiously overburdened with exaggerated claims and emphases on property rights; and the education of the American people on human rights questions, which is sorely lacking in most basic respects and all too often accepts the overemphasis upon property rights at the expense of other rights of greater or equal value.

Property rights contain a psychological dimension not found in other human rights issues. Other human rights issues tend to emphasize the equality of men and women before the law, the justice of fair treatment, and the real impossibility of stating that one person's claim to rights is somehow innately to be preferred to another's. But the arena of property rights can—and does—quite deliberately set out, often in precise dollar terms, the differences in claims made upon the legal and policy systems of this nation; and though it is not always said that one claim is innately superior to another, such an assertion is hardly unusual. Congress has decided that some banks cannot be permitted to fail, whereas others can; that Chrysler Corporation should have loan guarantees that other corporations cannot have; and that the wealthy should not pay taxes in the proportions paid by lesser folk.

Policy reasons offered for such measures are usually found to be bereft of logic when they are rigorously examined. Hard data are seldom friendly to conservative causes. It is therefore important to review the premises of policies and the institutions that benefit from them, which is the goal of Part II. The focus of Part II is the business corporation, because it is the dominant propaganda organ for, and beneficiary of, property rights considerations even when these are detrimental to the vast majority of us. Distortion and rigging of the elections process are among the results; denial of the rights of organized labor is one of the others. Behind such machinations lie the assumptions of the corporate structure itself, which should be examined and questioned, though it seldom is, and the truly excessive games that they play, such as merger and takeover mania. It is certainly the case that these chapters can be seen as part of a larger picture, one in which the corporation, continuing to operate upon the basis of archaic legal assumptions, reaches quite directly—and uniformly in an unwholesome way for the body politic—into our lives, destroying jobs and the economy through maniacal and ego-driven takeover activity, destroying the political process with an election system that is close to becoming a farce, and destroying even our chance to compete with the corporation in the economic arena by bashing unions through mostly illegal means.

There are some intellectual foundations for such excesses. Most of these can be dismissed because they are inconsistent, transparent, at odds with the facts, violative of our hopes for human justice, or, not to be overlooked, simply a badly built set of explanations hampered by a willingness to accept anything the Establishment may do. There is one school, however—known by the name of "law and economics"—that is given validity by legal and policy scholars and that seems, at least at first, to contain strong resources. These are strong enough, in fact, to reach the seats of the U.S. Supreme Court and some of the respected groves of academia. It is therefore simply not a thorough effort to focus upon institutional practices without looking at and examining their intellectual props. This, then, is the concern of Part III and the Chapter 7.

What, then, is the result? For an author, the immediate answer is that one must hope—hope that the book will be read and the arguments will be listened to, joined, and debated. In this world of many media messages, perhaps that is all that one can reasonably expect.

My hopes go further, however. I still desire deep and lasting social and political change. Many of the skeptics in my area of life, the university, will smile at this; they have long since learned that the system is quite unresponsive, and that if it is ever going to change its ways (not to mention its manners), it is unlikely that the changes that ultimately occur will take forms even remotely resembling those advocated by an academic writer.

My response is that although I would never refuse a radical label for my work—at least in the classic sense of getting to the root of problems—this is really just a call for basic decency, something that has been sorely missing from the American body politic. This is a plea for doing some of the things that are already being done, and reasonably well at that, in like societies throughout the world. Indeed, this should be regarded as a manifesto against the worn-out, stale, and out-of-touch policies and assumptions that have dominated our lives long after any possible usefulness for them has expired.

It is also hoped that the debates on these topics will contain awareness of that most political of elements, time, and its effect upon policies and, above all, upon people. Ten years ago I wrote *City of the Right* for Greenwood Press, a book in which I argued that the various conservative solutions offered for the cities would not work. And they didn't; but few, apparently, listened. So we have been doing a lot of nothing for a lot of years; how much longer do we have to begin the response to our problems?

No effort of this sort can be completed without reliance upon the insights, or sometimes of the direct help, of various friends, associates, and, in some cases, upon scholars I know only by their writings. I must therefore acknowledge strong intellectual debt to John Brigham, Eugene Hogan, Michael W. McCann, C. Herman Pritchett, H. Mark Roelofs, and Victor Wallis. In addition, the insights and support of the following people must be recognized: Elliot Bartky, Ted Becker, Donna Bialik, Leif Carter, James Jordan, Ronald Kahn, Carl Kalvelage, David Keller, Samuel Krislov, Charles E. Lindblom, Howard Margolis, John Massaro, John Modic, Kristen Renwick Monroe, Stuart Nagel, Srinivasan Narayanan, Mary Cornelia Porter, Ronald Pynn, Phyllis Farley Rippey, Kim Scheppele, Martin Shapiro, Philippa Strum, Harry Stumpf, John Taylor, Georgia W. Ulmschneider, Conrad P. Waligorski, Lettie Wenner, Paul Wice, and Aaron Wildavsky. Three students—Laura Lineback, Ardeth Maung, and Christine Platz—have assisted this project in various ways. The research papers of graduate students Bill Gaugler, Helen Heckman, John Kurtz, and Annette M. Teders also proved helpful. Finally, I must thank above all Penelope Houseman and my daughter Victoria, who is an insightful critic and author in her own right.

PART I

FORCES RETARDING CHANGE IN THE AMERICAN POLICY ARENA

1 Lawyers and the Study of Law

Whose law are we learning? What kinds of clients are we being prepared to serve?

—Philip M. Stern, muckraking journalist and former law student[1]

AN UNDERSTANDING OF THE LEGAL PROFESSION and its values is critical to an understanding of our political system. Access to the law, and therefore to the decision-making levers of society, is not only a matter of observed differentiations in what we usually describe as a democratic society; it is quite strictly a description of the workings of the system. The many questions one could ask about access to, and allocation of, justice can take up volumes. For example, we could ask *how much* law is available to the majority of Americans today? The answer might be very little indeed if we consider the availability of legal services.

A tragic paradox is at work here; for although the United States has more lawyers than any country in the world and continues to turn out thousands more of them every year, the bulk of legal services is placed only at the disposal of the business world and the well-to-do.[2] A skewing of rights, responsibilities, priorities, and public policy is therefore the result of this imbalance.

This information is hardly new; it has been commented upon many times. Law, political science, and other disciplines have been made aware of these problems through studies of such matters as the political attitudes of judges, the serious flaws found in both federal and state systems of judicial administration, and the deleterious effects of some of the socialization patterns found in the law school experience, among other concerns.[3] The bar explains that it is not happy with this. There have been repeated calls over the years for making lawyers and the law accessible to the broad public.[4] There have been urgings for the bar to provide more volunteer lawyers, public interest lawyers, legal aid work, group plans, and other reforms aimed in this direction. The American Bar Foundation has an ongoing research program aimed at improving the responsiveness of the bar to public needs.

LEGAL EDUCATION: CONSERVATIVE AND DYSFUNCTIONAL

It is a short step from the current malaise to an examination of the place of professional origin for lawyers, the law school. And this subject has hardly been neglected. The *Journal of Legal Education*, an academic periodical, is devoted exclusively to the subject; the bar foundation also promotes studies in this area; a variety of academics, not all of them from the discipline of law, searches out ways to make law schools relevant to society's needs; and, very importantly, the law schools themselves carry out programs of self-examination and improvement. The demands for reform are a continuing feature of this dialogue. There have been calls for review of the law school curriculum, of the Socratic method of teaching law courses, of the case method of study, and of the overemphasis upon appellate decisions. The latter are alleged to be only the concerns of people wealthy enough to fight appeals against trial verdicts. There are also admonitions for an awareness of the results of the socialization patterns found to dominate law school life.[5] It must be admitted that some salutary changes have been made as a result of these efforts. Courses on Poverty Law, Civil Rights, Women and the Law, and Consumer Law are now included in many curricula. Clinics are commonly established both to provide hands-on, practical legal training and to give helpful legal advice and assistance to those who could not otherwise afford it. And there are dedicated students, faculty, and administrators whose aims and, more important, accomplishments are grounded in social and political conscience.

It also should be pointed out that the history of legal scholarship is hardly a story of stagnation or purposelessness. Dynamic and encouraging trends have been beneficial not only to the profession but to our politics and the development of worthwhile public policies. The Realists used the third and fourth decades of this century to break the chains of a stodgy, mechanistic, and classist system of law that had sought to enshroud itself in something resembling a divine mystique. Later, the small but effective Law and Language movement provided more than its share of new and refreshing insights, led to a great extent by James Boyd White of the University of Michigan.[6] Behavioral social science has made its contributions as well, enabling us to look at motivational factors in the work of judges, lawyers, prosecutors, and others. The Law and Economics movement, in my view, has not given us very much at all, but even those scholars must be said to occasionally force a reexamination of premises (see Chapter 7). (It can also be acknowledged that this movement did fit in well with the social and political climate of the 1980s and the early 1990s, but this is hardly a compliment.) Certainly, the Critical Legal Studies movement has given us a feast of debunking and gray-matter provocation while it has mounted socially and politically useful assaults upon all manner of assumptions, including many associated with legal education.[7]

Among the latter is Duncan Kennedy's article entitled "Legal Education as Training for Hierarchy."[8] Kennedy believes that the Socratic method is in most instances a matter of "pseudoparticipation," and that virtually everything in the law school experience—dialogue, method, curriculum, motivations of the law school community, and assuredly the processes of legal reasoning—militates against progressive social change and in favor of privileged and status quo forces. Law school, in a word, is conservative; it is also socially dysfunctional.[9] This is a serious set of comments we might pay some heed to, even if there are elements with which we disagree. Kennedy is basically telling us that his profession is flawed from the beginning of its earliest development in the first year of required courses.

THE BAR, PUBLIC RELATIONS, AND PUBLIC OPINION

We all know that there are widely held notions about lawyers, judges, and the law that hardly speak well for the profession. An organization known as HALT—Help Against Lawyers' Tyranny—has been around for about a decade, ambitiously lobbying for nonlawyers' rights to perform a variety of services it feels do not require a member of the bar. *AntiShyster*, a free newsletter, has developed a popular following by simply chronicling how lawyers take advantage of the public.[10] A recurrent theme of the raucous *Washington Monthly* holds that we have too many lawyers doing too many expensive and unnecessary tasks, and doing them in quite ham-handed and inefficient ways. And even though many of us now believe that we have put Watergate behind us, there is no doubt that the various scandals we place under that rubric had as one of their recurrent themes the infidelity, cowardice, and greediness of lawyers, including, and perhaps especially, attorneys-general.

It is safe to assume that a segment of the public holds opinions about lawyers that may lead to reluctance to consult with one even when she/he is faced with a demanding legal issue or problem. A Gallup Poll done in 1988, the most recent available, found lawyers getting a high or very high rating from 18 percent of the sample, an average rating from 45 percent, and a low or very low rating from 33 percent.[11] This may not be a total disaster: Lawyers rate better with the public than politicians, stockbrokers, advertising professionals, or the sellers of used cars or insurance. At the same time, they are below bankers, doctors, pharmacists, television and newspaper reporters and commentators, building contractors, and funeral directors. Lawyers are also the butt of many jokes, some of which have an edge to them. And because the esteem variables of lawyers cannot be said to be too good, it follows that their educational process may be perceived to have some problems as well.

The history of legal education does not necessarily help their cause either. The abandonment of the apprenticeship system in the early decades of this century and its replacement by an almost airtight system of American Bar Association (ABA) control is a tale of many tawdry details as well as of a great and overarching concern for the development of a monopoly on certification. We are probably better off without the apprenticeship system, it must be conceded, and a better system with more public input could have been developed instead.

In all events, a major result of ABA control has been the general requirement of seven years of higher education to earn a law degree in addition to a period of qualifying for the bar examination. A shorter span of time is generally the requirement in most countries. Clearly, this has the effect of reducing access to legal education, but it should be borne in mind that this was the original intention. The intention, in fact, is even seamier than this if one looks at the history of the bar in New York, Pennsylvania, Illinois, Ohio, and many other states.[12] The major motivations, plainly put, were anti-Semitic and anti-foreigner, and this was explicitly stated by many august leaders of the bar who openly worried that the law might be spoiled by the presence of practitioners who had sprung from diverse and unacceptable roots.[13] Any serious survey of legal education must, unfortunately, take into account these loathsome deeds and their results.

THE UNCHANGING LAW SCHOOL

Putting aside history and public relations problems of the bar, it is safe to assume that law school is generally seen as a powerful socializing agent. The student learns a new language. Even more important, she or he learns a reasoning process that is accepted not only because students usually accept things, but because it appears to be practical, worldly, and satisfactory in explaining how laypersons are not conversant with the law, and how they are often to be found at odds with its logic and its balancing factors.[14] Learning this process is the essence of that which sets off a lawyer's terms of reference from the terms understood in the broader public.

A number of caveats and qualifiers is in order. It is true, for example, that law students have been subject to many socializing forces during the course of their education, and many or most of these forces are derived from education in some other context. In addition, law students are a diverse lot, and they are more diverse today than ever before. The range of ages, backgrounds, and values comes from a much larger cross-section of the public now found in the law schools. Gender alone has been a major change in recent decades, for the female law student—today representing half the student body—was a rarity, comparatively considered, just two decades ago. Finally, it must be conceded that some students—albeit a minority in the 3 to 10 percent range—come to law school with a public interest purpose in mind and remain committed through their three years of law school socialization and environment.[15]

Keeping all of these considerations in mind, it is still accurate to say that law schools have shown a marked resistance and resilience in encountering the forces of change. The Socratic method remains in place despite charges of "pseudo-participation" and, perhaps more profoundly, the very real problems of covering necessary materials in the allotted time. The case method is still overwhelmingly dominant despite the reduced role of cases as a source of law in the face of massive statutory, administrative, and regulatory activity at all levels of government.[16] The faculty remains almost totally made up of law-trained people, and in many schools, they do not have advanced degrees; there is little room, however, for historians, psychologists, social scientists, or others, even though these may have a great deal to offer to legal education. Professor Martin Shapiro of the University of California, Berkeley, for example, is one of the very few political scientists found on a law school faculty with a permanent appointment. And it is generally conceded that the curriculum has seen remarkably few changes since the turn of the century. There have been additions, of course, but the core and most of the accoutrements of this curriculum have remained the same, in place decade after decade. Much of the curriculum had to be revised—actually more enlarged than revised—after the two most active and interventionist eras of government, the years of the Roosevelt and Johnson administrations. This revision, or enlargement, whichever it may be, did not alter the basic character of legal education, however, nor did the relatively few courses (in the bulk of the law schools) that have been added to heed some of the interests of women, minorities, consumers, the poor, and other groups.[17]

CLASSIFYING THE CURRICULUM

What is the basic law school curriculum, then, and what values does it represent? A review of the courses offered in law schools will show that they tend to break down into three groups:

1. ''How to'' or ''neutral impact'' courses
2. ''Property rights'' or ''property rights emphasis'' courses
3. ''Human rights'' or ''broad social value'' courses

''How to'' or ''neutral impact'' courses are purposefully centered on the development of lawyerly skills, are practical in nature, and provide methods and factual bases for a great variety of work in other courses or fields of legal endeavor. Some examples: Civil Procedure I and II, Evidence, Federal Courts and Jurisdiction, Legal Accounting, Conflict of Laws, Remedies, and Counseling and Negotiation. These are defined here as ''neutral impact'' courses because there is nothing obviously found in the character of these courses that would enable their inclusion in either of the two more controversial categories listed above. The knowledge and skills to be gained from such courses can conceivably be put to any use considered legitimate to the ends of legal practice. It is not the case that these courses should be considered ''neutral'' in terms of their impact upon the socialization of law students. After all, they provide important tools that help to define the services of the aspiring lawyer in either of the other two categories.

"Property rights" or "property rights emphasis" courses are vital to legal education but are concerned only with that one bundle of rights pertaining to the ownership, acquisition, disposal, conveyance, and use of property. Obviously, such courses are of greatest value to those whose predilections are directed toward servicing propertied interests. Courses such as Property I and II, Trusts and Estates, Corporations, Taxation, and Securities Regulation fit this category. Naturally, it can be argued that property rights are important to all of us, propertied or not, because a convenient set of rules has been laid down that we can all rely upon as we carry out our lives; but this carries us out of the concerns of this study. The observation should be made that even those scholars most committed to property rights and who argue for their enlargement must always finally concede the recognition of other rights as well as the powers of government to regulate, control, and even take (with just compensation) property.[18] Property rights, regardless of such arguments, clearly set up a definable category, and most certainly conclusions can be drawn from the relative importance placed upon this category, for it is a truth as well as a truism that other human rights are just as valuable or even more valuable than property rights. It will not spoil any suspense to disclose that, as anyone familiar with the study of law would anticipate, this group of courses dominates the law school curriculum of today, of this century, and before.

"Human rights" or "broad social values" courses are concerned with that broad panoply of human rights and allied considerations—other than property rights and categorically independent and separable from property rights—that is found in the assumptions of free, democratic, and civilized communities of the world. Courses in this area would include Constitutional Law I and II, Criminal Law I and II, Civil Rights, Jurisprudence, and Poverty Law. The connection of law with the concept of justice comes readily to the fore in such courses; to many people, this is what the study of law is all about or at least should be all about. It is also this set of courses that most interests and excites social scientists and other lay commentators and observers of the legal system. Few political scientists, sociologists, or journalists spend their time or concerns on the matters related to the first two listed categories of legal studies.

Any number of acceptable methods and approaches can be taken to derive something resembling a standard law school curriculum in the United States. The method used here was to randomly select twenty-one law school bulletins from the great batch available to any prelaw counselor (which is sometimes one of my campus duties). Such a selection should include regional variations of curriculum as well as other considerations that might make a difference—national versus local or regional law school, prestige versus ordinary, public and private, large and small, traditional and experimental, and so forth. The schools selected appear to cover these variations in one way or another.[19] Then a simple count was made of all of the course offerings listed by the law schools. Any course that proved (sometimes under various names) to be a consensual offering—in other words, an offering of at least eleven of the twenty-one schools—was placed on the standard curriculum list (see Table 1.1). Those failing to show up in such numbers were not included.

A larger sample could have been used, but twenty-one law schools represent well over 5 percent of the total. In any event, the great uniformities of curricula —also not a surprising finding—hold little promise of turning up something different through a broader effort. In fact, there were no surprises that appeared as a result of this exercise, but it is interesting to note how the three categories numerically defined the law school curriculum with this model. Fifty-four percent of all course offerings are those with a property rights emphasis; 31 percent of the sixty-seven courses were those of the "how to" or "neutral impact" variety; and a paltry 15 percent, just ten of the courses, were in the human rights or broad-based values emphasis category.

Some of the categorizations can be questioned. Torts I and II, for example, are listed with the majority group of thirty-six property rights courses, but this area of the law, one might object, is designed for the purpose of making one whole again after a personal injury, false imprisonment, or perhaps a libel or slander has taken place. (The latter has a connection with privacy law, and privacy is a broad and generally recognized human right.) It is nonetheless the case that these injuries and wrongs are usually defined in property terms in the form of money damages. A lost arm or eye is worth so much, a reputation is valued at X dollars, and a life can be computed for the benefit of the surviving members of the family. Under these circumstances, it is difficult to fit Torts under either of the other two categories.

There may be other objections, although it is plainly impossible to anticipate all of them. Labor Law, for example, could be placed under the "human rights" rubric because the right to organize a union is something that is internationally and almost universally recognized. Simultaneously, however, it must be conceded that most labor issues are defined in economic, hence property, terms. In any event, it is fair to assume that a large number (if not a majority) of students who see this as a field of specialization is not going to be drawn to it because of some overriding fealty to unions or the working class. The chances are good that union-busting will be the aim and purpose of many potential lawyers in this field. All of the courses listed under the property rights category, then, are concerned with issues and their resolution that can be defined in economic terms. We certainly cannot exclude the possibility that idealism might show up in the practice of law in these areas, and this idealism can surely be on either side of an issue; but ideals and legal principles that can be defined in noneconomic terms are often hard to find in any of the course areas so categorized. This is the case, to cite just a few examples, with International Law, Sports Law, Energy Law, and Law and Health Care. All of these areas can conjure up visions of idealism and of occasional noneconomic issues and solutions, but these are hardly the norm.

Indeed, a greater problem with these categories is that we may end up with an understatement of the propertied and privileged values found in the law

TABLE 1.1 The Standard Curriculum Offered by Law Schools in the United States

21 COURSES OF A "HOW TO" OR "NEUTRAL IMPACT" NATURE
(31% of Curriculum)

Administrative Law
Alternative Dispute Resolution and/or Arbitration
Appellate Practice
Civil Procedure I and II*
Comparative Law
Conflict of Laws
Evidence
Federal Courts, Jurisdiction
Independent Reading/Research
Internship
Law Review
Legal Accounting
Legal Profession
Legal Research and Writing I and II*
Legal Services Clinic
Legislation
Local Government Law, State and Local Government Law
Moot Court
Pretrial Practice, Counseling, Negotiation
Remedies
Trial Practice

10 COURSES WITH A HUMAN RIGHTS OR BROAD-BASED EMPHASIS ON VALUES
(15% of Curriculum)

Civil Rights, Civil and Political Rights, Civil Rights Litigation
Constitutional Law I and II*
Criminal Law I and II*
Criminal Procedure
Employment Law, Employment Discrimination
Environmental Law
Jurisprudence
Juvenile Law, Children and the Law
Legal Ethics
Legal History, American and/or British

36 COURSES CONCERNED WITH PROPERTY RIGHTS OR A PROPERTY RIGHTS EMPHASIS
(54% of Curriculum)

Admiralty
Antitrust Law
Banking, Financial Institutions
Bankruptcy
Business Planning
Commercial Law/Transactions, Commercial Paper, Sales, Secured Transactions
Commercial Real Estate Development
Contracts I and II*
Corporate Finance
Corporate Reorganization Taxation
Corporations, Business Associations
Debtor Protection/Creditors' Rights
Energy Law, Oil and Gas Law
Estate and Gift Taxation
Estate Planning
Family Law
Federal Taxation
Insurance Law
Intellectual Property and/or Copyright
International Business Transactions, International Trade
International Law
Labor Law
Land Transactions, Land Transfer, and Finance
Land Use
Law and Economics
Law and Health Care, Law and Medicine
Natural Resources Law
Patents, Trademarks
Products Laibility
Property I and II*
Regulated Industries
Securities Regulation
Sports Law
Taxation of Corporations and Partnerships
Torts I and II*
Trusts, Trusts and Estates, Wills and Trusts

*Required first-year course

school curriculum. Much of Constitutional Law, for example, is concerned with issues such as federalism and the Commerce Clause and these are often connected to, if not controlled by, economic considerations. This is also the situation in courses like Environmental Law and Employment Law. Putting these into the human rights and related courses category is, in part, an act of faith, a faith in the more than occasional reference or concern to matters that go beyond mere economic definitions.

A further problem to the set of categories developed might be based upon the question of what courses a student *actually takes* as opposed to what is offered. This really presents no problem. It certainly is true that no law student in her or his three years can hope to take more than a small number of the total of courses that might be made available. The set of courses actually taken, however, will either reflect something like the numbers with which the totality of course listings is broken down or may *even exceed* the lopsidedness of the property category set out here. A number of factors contributes to this, including the requirements of the bar exam, which is invariably property-heavy; the relatively smaller number of courses actually offered in many law schools because of a variety of scheduling, student interest, and other considerations (and this may militate against allegedly "fluffy" human rights courses); or, quite simply, the choices of students, and we know that 10 percent or fewer of these have public interest motivations.

The matter of which courses are actually taken, then, probably militates still further against the minority group of "human rights" courses. It *is* necessary for students to take Criminal Law and Constitutional Law classes—four of this group of ten courses—because these are invariably in the required first-year curriculum and they are also on the bar exam.

The numbers derived by counting courses for this study therefore should be seen not so much as important in themselves, for they are neither surprising nor remarkable. Instead, they should be seen as simply one more of many manifestations of the skewing of values one obtains from legal education. Until the long overdue reforms of the bar, its practices, and its contributions (or lack of contributions) to society are addressed, there can be little hope for basic changes in law school curricula. Legal education for the foreseeable future will continue to be a conservative force as well as a denial of the changes and social forces thrust upon all of us by this turbulent century.

NOTES

1. Philip M. Stern, *Lawyers on Trial* (New York: Times Books, 1980), vii–viii.

2. Ibid., esp. viii, 136, 162; also read the essays in David Kairys (ed.) The Politics of Law (New York: Pantheon, 1990), and in Michael W. McCann and Gerald L. Houseman (eds.), *Judging the Constitution* (Glenview, IL: Scott, Foresman, 1989)

3. This point has long been conceded; back in 1971, Chief Justice Warren Burger wrote that "One great weakness, now being corrected, has been the lack of counsel for the large number of people who could not afford the cost of counsel and especially [is] this true of the accused in criminal cases." This is in the Foreword to L. Ray Patterson and Elliott E. Cheatham, *The Profession of Law* (Mineola, NY: Foundation Press, 1971), v. Things may have gotten marginally better, but we are still waiting.

4. Richard L. Abel, *American Lawyers* (New York: Oxford University Press, 1989), Chaps. 10 and 11; Stern, *Lawyers on Trial*; Jerold S. Auerbach, *Unequal Justice: Lawyers and Social Change in Modern America* (New York: Oxford University Press, 1976); Duncan Kennedy, "Legal Education as Training for Hierarchy," in Kairys (ed.), *The Politics of Law*, 38–58; Bertram Barnett, *Law, Lawyers, and Laymen: Making Sense of the American Legal System* (San Diego: Harcourt Brace, 1984), see esp. comments on the case method, 33–34; Herma Hill Kay, "What Is Legal Education? And Should We Permit It to Continue in Its Present Form?" *Georgia State University Law Review* 6 (Spring 1990), 349–68; George L. Priest, "The Increasing Division Between Legal Practice and Legal Education," *Buffalo Law Review* 37 (Fall 1988/89), 657–83.

5. The critical literature on law school education is far too extensive to take up here; the reader is referred as a starting point to the *Journal of Legal Education*. A set of worthwhile articles in various law journals was produced by Justin Green, John R. Schmidhauser, and Larry L. Berg in the early 1970s. Some work on legal education is also found in the useful reader by Robert Lefcourt (ed.), *Law Against the People* (New York: Vintage Books, 1971); also see Albert P. Melone, "Legal Education and Judicial Decisions: Some Negative Findings," *Journal of Legal Education* 26 (1974), 566–79.

6. James Boyd White, *The Legal Imagination* (Chicago: University of Chicago Press, 1986), and his *Justice in Translation: An Essay in Cultural and Legal Criticism* (Chicago: University of Chicago Press, 1990). The reader is also referred to White's other works as a way of getting to know this approach.

7. Critical Legal Studies essays are found in Kairys (ed.), *The Politics of Law*; other broad surveys of this literature are found in *Essays in Critical Legal Studies* (Cambridge: Harvard Law Review Association, 1986) and the *Stanford Law Review* 36 (nos. 1 and 2) (January 1984); also see Mark Kelman, *A Guide to Critical Legal Studies* (Cambridge: Harvard University Press, 1987).

8. This is found in Kairys (ed.), *The Politics of Law*, 38–58.

9. Ibid.

10. *Wall Street Journal*, February 26, 1991.

11. *The Gallup Poll 1988* (Wilmington: Scholarly Enterprises, 1989), 225.

12. Auerbach, *Unequal Justice*, Chaps. 4 and 5; this story is also available in many other places; see Stern, *Lawyers on Trial*, for example.

13. As Auerbach and others point out, the bar won control not only of the law school certification process but of a system that required the recommendation of a member of the bar in order to gain law school entrance. This had the effect of "grandfathering" law school entrance so as to favor those who were culturally, religiously, racially, and ethnically acceptable.

14. Kennedy, "Legal Education."

15. Abel, *American Lawyers*, Chap. 10.

16. Barnett, *Law, Lawyers, and Laymen*, 33–34; there are also some problems with the casebook itself and with the tendency to regard it as holy writ, according to Patricia

Woodward and Patrick Dalton, "Stuck to the Letter of the Law," (London) *Times Higher Education Supplement* 1 (February 1991), 23.

17. Abel, *American Lawyers*, Chap. 10; Duncan Kennedy, "Legal Education"; Kay, "What Is Legal Education?"

18. See, for example, the frustrations of Richard Epstein in *Takings: Private Property and the Power of Eminent Domain* (Cambridge: Harvard University Press, 1985), though few matters seem to daunt him.

19. One further possible objection to asserting a connection between the law school curriculum and the socialization of lawyers is the fact, demonstrated here and there, that lawyers, by and large, seem to understand Bill of Rights freedoms and to give support to them; but this does not mean that human rights other than property rights can be assured of their rightful place in the hierarchies of lawyers' values. The career patterns they follow certainly do not indicate that there is much to cheer about.

The schools selected for the sample are Albany Law School, Boston University, California Western University, Columbia University, Drake University, Duke University, Marquette University, University of Michigan, University of Oregon, Pepperdine University, Santa Clara University, Southern Illinois University, Syracuse University, University of Toledo, University of Tulsa, Valparaiso University, Vanderbilt University, Vermont Law School, Wake Forest University, Willamette University, and Yeshiva University.

Special thanks are in order for assistance on this chapter to Professor Albert P. Melone of Southern Illinois University, to student assistant Christine Platz, and to Professor John Massaro, who read an earlier version of this chapter in his role as panel discussant for the 1991 Meeting of the New York State Political Science Association in New York City.

2 Bill of Rights Freedoms and the American People

The very purpose of a Bill of Rights is to withdraw certain subjects from . . . political controversy, to place them beyond the reach of majorities and officials and to establish them as legal principles to be applied by the courts. One's right to life, liberty, and property, to free speech, a free press, freedom of worship and assembly, and other fundamental rights may not be submitted to a vote; they depend upon the outcome of no elections.

—Justice Robert H. Jackson[1]

If there is such a thing as justice, it could only be administered by one who knew the inmost thoughts of the men to whom he was meting it out.

—Clarence Darrow[2]

THE EXHILARATION ENJOYED BY SOME—and probably most—Americans during the Gulf War of early 1991 should perhaps be tempered by the fact that this period was not particularly good for the enjoyment of some of the civil liberties we have come to have every right to expect. The Arab-American population was subjected to a variety of indignities and occasional brutalization. This rough treatment was extended to other peoples, both citizen and alien, who appeared to be Arabs or Iranians or Muslims of some kind. Opponents of the war also had some problems imposed upon them by the more superpatriotic members of the national community, though these were by and large less severe.

The Gulf War months were also a dire period for freedom of the press. For the second time in less than a decade, media people were not allowed to join our military forces as they launched our side of the war. As in the case of the Grenada invasion and conquest of 1983, national security justifications were used to keep the press away. In addition, all coverage of the war from the Middle East was closely monitored by the Pentagon. It was not as though such reportage would be a departure from our traditions. The Fourth Estate had been a welcome firsthand witness to the military events of World Wars I and II, Korea, Vietnam, and all other conflicts. Why should these relatively small wars be different? The American people, quite shockingly, are nonetheless supportive of such Defense Department strictures.[3]

Carrying out an executive order of the president, the then War Department ordered all Americans of Japanese ancestry, citizens and noncitizens alike, to be sent to concentration camps for the duration of World War II. (''Concentration camps'' is the term used by the government in official documents to describe these places.) Though no polls were taken at the time, there is little question that the American people either supported this order with some enthusiasm or, at the least, were passive about its implementation. The Supreme Court upheld this action in a 1944 decision.[4] The World War I years had also seen a massive roundup; at that time, the victims were members of the Socialist Party, a large and consequential organization at that time. Employing his war powers and the Espionage Act, President Woodrow Wilson authorized their arrest and detention without trial for the duration of the war period. A young J. Edgar Hoover obliged by deputizing right-wing extremist members of the American Protective Association, a superpatriotic vigilante group.[5] Clearly, the American people approved, in what appeared to be overwhelming numbers, of the government's action.

ANTI-CIVIL LIBERTIES ATTITUDES IN AMERICAN LIFE

Any political observer with the smallest acuity knows that the examples cited above are but the tip of the iceberg when it comes to a description of anti–civil liberties attitudes in America. The task of interpreting what American freedoms are under various sets of circumstances is not an easy one, and a consensus of opinion is often lacking on such issues. This is true whether these be the rights of the accused; school prayer; freedom of political expression; or the equal rights of women, minorities, the elderly, the poor, the gay community, aliens, or the physically impaired. There are any number of reasons why there is so much conflict over civil liberties questions. These surely include the fact that civil liberties are considered important by their defenders; the intrusion of a vast array of controversies into the civil liberties arena, including crime control, national security, religion and its role in our lives, attitudes toward the media, and attitudes toward life-styles or certain definable groups of people;[6] and, perhaps most of all, a great amount of confusion about the principles and rules by which we decide civil liberties matters. Not infrequently, for example, the rights of a ''majority'' are invoked, or questionable assertions about ''democracy'' are made, as though the civil liberties of individuals or groups should be decided in the same way we decide elections.

Recent national experience demonstrates, moreover, that civil liberties issues are often thrust into the heat and mire of election campaigns. Constitutional law scholars had thought, prior to the 1988 presidential campaign, that the issue of requiring a pledge of allegiance in the public schools had been well settled in *West Virginia State Board of Education* in 1943; but there it was, in the middle of the campaign, being discussed as though it were a matter of first impression.

Even the membership of a candidate in the American Civil Liberties Union (ACLU) was manufactured into an issue, making the candidate ironically suspect because he belonged to an organization whose only platform, basically, is the Bill of Rights! However desirable some think it may be to inject such issues into campaigns, it seems clear that this is hardly the best or most appropriate forum for temperate discussion and consideration of such matters. Civil liberties issues must be approached in an atmosphere of reason, deliberation, contemplation, and an earnest desire to arrive at conclusions logically and humanely.

It can be seen at the outset that the achievement of civil liberties sensibility will be beyond many, perhaps even most, people. But why should this be the case? The evidence is vast. The Bill of Rights polls taken first at Purdue University in 1948 and replicated ever since; the Samuel Stouffer study on political nonconformity and its updates;[7] and a great array of data from the Gallup Opinion Index and other national polling organizations, from studies by Seymour M. Lipset and Herbert McCloskey, and from studies such as the McCloskey-Brill *Dimensions of Tolerance* show that the American people and a civil liberties sensibility are not at one. Even minority views within these opinion samplings can be startling, for anti-libertarianism does not need majority support to become threatening.[8]

Polling data, all the same, are only one measure of the lack of understanding of civil liberties problems and concerns. Overt deeds are reported in the press almost daily. The *ADL Bulletin*, a publication of the Anti-Defamation League, now annually cites more than 1,000 incidents, ranging from swastika daubings on synagogues to more threatening kinds of events.[9] Small but determined minorities of Americans join one or another branch of the Ku Klux Klan, the Posse Comitatus, the Liberty Lobby, the John Birch Society, the Aryan Nations, or other groups built around premises of hate. But even more respectable Americans join in opposition to the movement of minority groups into their neighborhoods, to the presence of some objectionable book on the local library shelf, or to the marches and demonstrations of groups they simply do not like.

It is possible that the situation today is an improvement on the past. Some polling data indicate this.[10] There is also, as we know, ample evidence for saying that Americans may be more tolerant than peoples of other nations. And we know from the McCloskey-Brill data and many other studies that level of education, region, economic circumstance, and many other factors can affect poll findings across time and space. Also, some subgroups in the population—including many academics—can generally be expected to be more liberties-sensitive in their attitudes.

Polls that deal with civil liberties topics, however, have built-in problems with frankness because, after all, bigotry and anti–Bill of Rights attitudes may be seen as respectable in one milieu but not in another. Relatively few polling subjects, it can be assumed, are willing to tell an interviewer that they hold beliefs or viewpoints that, in polite company at least, are simply not respectable. In addition, polls are merely snapshots of the views expressed at one given time;

new circumstances, such as a strong economic downturn, anxiety over wars or potential wars, or the arrival of large numbers of new immigrants who bring different customs and languages to a neighborhood, can change a charitable individual of latent anti-libertarian tendencies into a strident advocate of scapegoat measures.

DEVELOPMENT OF A CIVIL LIBERTIES SENSIBILITY

Attitudes that are intolerant, unjust, and anti–civil liberties are not difficult to learn and incorporate into one's set of values. The impulse to strike down a person perceived as a threat or, for that matter, an idea that is seen as threatening may just be visceral, requiring little thought at all. Far too often, working out differences is not a goal at all, and this is the impression often left by bumper stickers, shirts, or other media that display insensitive slogans or symbols. The development of a tolerant sensibility, however, is quite a different matter. In their study, *Dimensions of Tolerance*, Herbert McCloskey and Alida Brill tell us that

> those who become defenders rather than foes of civil liberties need to acquire a greater measure of information and intellectual sophistication about libertarian norms, a sense of relevant principles such as reciprocity, and an ability to understand the rules of the democratic game. Learning the arguments for freedom and tolerance formulated by notables such as Jefferson, Madison, Mill, or the more libertarian justices of the Supreme Court is no easy task. Many of these arguments are subtle, esoteric, and difficult to grasp. Intelligence, awareness, and education are required to appreciate them fully.[11]

Social learning and a psychological willingness to engage in this learning are therefore of paramount importance. It can be the case, for example, that white, male wage earners will see African-Americans or women as rivals in the economic arena and will therefore ascribe undesirable characteristics to such groups or develop a lack of care about their rights or treatment. But libertarianism and tolerance require an understanding in some depth of social, political, economic, and legal problems and much more than a mere "live and let live" attitude; they require a willingness to extend freedoms to those people and groups that, for whatever reason, are not liked or trusted.

This is asking a great deal. History, including certainly the history of the United States, shows that many or perhaps most people are willing to suspend or abolish freedoms for other people on a shockingly frequent basis. Libertarianism requires that we not only take a position against these tides of history but that we be farsighted enough to see that the denial of freedom to anyone can, at some future time, result in the denial of freedom to all.[12] Bad practices are imitated. Precedents are set within and without the framework of law. And neither the law, the society, the customs and practices of people, nor government is static. They are more or less continuously in the throes of change; and because of this, the fight to maintain civil liberties is also continuous.

If attitudes of libertarianism and tolerance must be learned and may even require an appreciation of abstract and difficult writings and thoughts, then the cause of civil liberties starts off with great disadvantages. If libertarian attitudes are correlated with a contemplative frame of mind, for example, we as a nation of people are probably in trouble because it seems so increasingly difficulty to obtain times and places of quiet and contemplation. I am still struck, fifteen years later, by Tom Wicker's essay on the movie *Nashville*, which addressed much more than is confined within that particular film. Wicker suggests that Americans do not even want an opportunity to sit and quietly think. Bitterly, he says that the film depicts the

> vulgarity, greed, deceit, cruelty, barely contained hysteria, and the frantic lack of root and grace into which American life has been driven by its own heedless vitality . . . the writhings of a culture that does not even know it is choking on exhaust fumes . . . a culture desperately clinging to the idea of value while vulgarizing almost every particular value . . . the American mobility culture, with its autos, obsolete and crunchable the day they're sold, its fast-food parlors, plastic motel rooms, take-out orders, transient sex and junk music.[13]

If Wicker's description of American society and of its national psyche is even approximately accurate, the cause of civil liberties has an assuredly dark future, for it will be difficult and even painful to substitute quiet, contemplation, and the development of a libertarian consciousness for the absurdities and violence he believes to be dominant.

The question remains—why are the American people seemingly so willing to forego the guarantees of the Bill of Rights, sometimes for themselves and more often for others? Or, to put the question a little differently, what are the barriers to civil liberties that have been erected in the American polity, and why are they there? Although it is probably impossible to establish or claim an exhaustive inventory, it appears that there are at least ten possible influences that help to produce such attitudes, belief systems, and causes: (1) traditions of the American political culture and system; (2) popular media; (3) leadership examples of actions that are at odds with libertarian principles; (4) a pathological obedience to authority that exists in many or most people; (5) the presence of authoritarian personalities within the populace; (6) the fears held by people of making choices, that is, a real fear of freedom; (7) privatism, which exists in many anti-civil liberties manifestations; (8) elitism; (9) the oppressions of daily life, especially those found in the workplace; and (10) bureaucratically devised and justified anti-liberties deeds carried out in the name of efficiency or of administrative convenience. Let us examine each of these in turn.

Anti-Liberties Traditions of Politics and Culture

Anti–civil liberties practices are accompanied by their own sanction. National security has been the sanction for events ranging from the Alien and Sedition Acts through the suspensions of liberties seen during the Civil War, World Wars I and II, and the recent Gulf War, and it most certainly was the excuse for such excesses as the House Un-American Activities Committee, the Subversive Activities Control Board, the Palmer raids of the post–World War I era, and the recent harassments of Arab-Americans by government officials. Convenience of administration has been offered as the basis for government impoundment of foreign-source mail and the new identification requirements wrought by recent immigration legislation. Public safety is the general and usual reason given for curfew laws or the imposition of martial law. The need to settle the West and civilize the wilderness was the rational accompaniment to the genocide carried out against Native Americans. But important as these and many other depredations are, it is probably even more vital to recognize the anti–civil liberties heritage that has grown out of the basic values of the American tradition.

These are well known. Social Darwinism, an important part of our past as well as the Pat Buchanan presidential campaign, can be blamed for a variety of justifications for inequality, and this applies not only to inequality of result but to inequality of opportunity.[14] A more important tradition, the work ethic, which may have served us better in the past, can undoubtedly be related to the gratuitous and often unjustified clamor against the rights and claims of welfare recipients and the poor generally. Our centuries-old fascination with technology, our long-held assumption that if you *can* build it or do it, then you *should* build it or do it, works to the disadvantage of those who seek to shoulder the responsibilities of our environment, who look after aesthetic concerns, who make judgments on bases other than the dollars-and-cents bottom line, or perhaps, who simply wish to point out the dangers of this or that technology. A group organized in Hanford, Washington, in 1982 challenged the continued production of plutonium and the instruments of war. Hanford did not take well to this peace group because the community produced half of all the plutonium processed in the country at that time. The wife of an engineer employed at this facility was the leader of the group. What happened in this case is instructive, but not very cheering:

> Even the most modest public dissent on the arms race was seen as an intolerable threat. The engineer's superiors soon began asking him about his wife's activity. Co-workers, fearing aspersions of disloyalty, stopped joining him at lunch. Where security personnel had once searched his car perhaps twice a year, in accordance with routine procedures, now he was inspected nearly every week. Others in the group also reported harassment; one was fired. Many were ostracized by friends and neighbors.[15]

The tradition posed here is not merely our long-term attachment to the technological answer to problems; it is the tradition, now a half-century old, of maintaining a large defense establishment in times of peace. (The term "peace" is of course not to be taken literally for the Korean War, Vietnam War, or Gulf War periods.) Large defense budgets in peacetime are unprecedented in the nation's history, and because it is axiomatic that war consciousness tends to breed conformity, it cannot be surprising that the years since 1945 have seen continuous and often excessive attention to national security and loyalty issues, often to the detriment of civil liberties and their practice.

The populist tradition, which has progressive and grass-roots features that are often commendable, also has a dark side, characterized by racism, xenophobia, and anti-Semitism.[16] Indeed, many of the better understandings we are able to derive from our national experience are those in which a populist influence can be shown to have been at work. Anti-intellectualism, dark appeals to "common sense," and fears of certain kinds of knowledge—political, social, literary, sexual, or scientific—are bound together under this rubric of populism; and it almost goes without saying that distrust of the people by elites of one kind or another can often be bound up with the populist experience. Too many Bryans, Longs, and Wallaces have been thrown up by this heritage for any of us to be very comfortable with it.

Very deeply rooted in the fabric of American beliefs—and this is especially the case since 1945—is a strong antisocialism born out of the Cold War era as well as the strong and historical attachment to private property. This tradition, not surprisingly, has made the problem of tolerance of socialist groups particularly acute, and it hardly matters whether such groups have democratic or revolutionary aims.[17] In addition to posing significant civil liberties problems for such people, problems that have included government surveillance and break-ins and other harassments, this has made it impossible to add any social democratic dimension to the country's political debates, and we are the poorer for this.

Other traditions also undoubtedly contribute to anti-libertarianism; indeed, even the very consensual values of the "atomistic" individual and private property, which come out of the Lockeian-Hobbesian-Founders tradition, have their dark side in a privatism that causes any number of problems. This is such a big topic, however, that it is treated separately below.

Popular Media

It is not necessary to proceed in a very systematic way to demonstrate that popular media undermine libertarian values. It would, in fact, be difficult to imagine this not being the case. Almost any observer possessing some discernment can tell when the network news organizations have decided to "stir up the masses" with coded presentations of features or news events. The plight of a welfare mother may be the theme of a feature; but if the mother is African-

American, has four different children out of wedlock by four different men, and has a history of little or no employment, it is not too hard to believe that such a depiction will reinforce the stereotyping and condemnations some individuals prefer to indulge in.[18] Such depictions run the gamut of the issues of the day, from taxation to narcotics addiction to urban problems.

Some people do not watch the news. The press may supply them with stereotypes, rigidities in thinking, and other concomitants of anti-libertarianism. This is particularly the case with the shrieking supermarket tabloids such as the *National Enquirer*, which, though it contains very little in the way of an overt political message, often can be seen pandering to anti-libertarian instincts. Sensationalist television programming of the Geraldo Rivera–Phil Donahue variety and radio talk shows do more than their share of damage. Perhaps the most important source of anti-libertarianism in the popular media is the crime film or the television crime show. These are replete with castigations of defendants who rely upon being read their rights, or who demand a lawyer, or who hide behind some ''trick'' embedded within the law, such as the Fifth Amendment right against self-incrimination. In the ''Dirty Harry'' series of films starring Clint Eastwood or any of the violent extravaganzas of Charles Bronson, there are no problems with these because suspects are simply murdered in cold blood.

One of the most absurd legacies of the popular media, both of the press and electronic media, is the idea of the legal technicality. It is often explained to the public that so-and-so should have been kept behind bars, and this certainly would have been the case had it not been for a ''technicality.'' These technicalities drop in from outer space and, quite irrationally, free the suspect almost like magic. What the public is never told is that these technicalities are in fact legal and constitutional protections put in place for reasons grounded in logic and historical experience. For the immediate future, however, it appears that scriptwriters, newscasters, and most assuredly the general public will continue to believe in technicalities. The obverse is also true: They will not believe in the law or the Constitution.

The popular media attack those qualities referred to earlier in the quotation from McCloskey and Brill. Contemplation, thoughtfulness, awareness of complexities, subtleties, and, indeed, the nuances of civil liberties issues—these are simply not the stuff of the popular media. Television is an action medium in which the achievement of abstract understandings of matters is quite alien. And even the day-to-day press requires the reader to look carefully at details and to dig deeply in order to find the essence of civil liberties issues.

Not to be taken up in this discussion, because it will take us too far afield, are the laxities and cowardice of the media, a matter extensively treated in informative studies like Mark Hertsgaard's *On Bended Knee*.[19] Books like this, as well as other sources, show that the post-Watergate era has seen the development of a new pusillanimity in the media that has not served us well during recent wars and other foreign adventures or during scandals and constitutional usurpations like the Iran-Contra affair. This cowardice and lax behavior of the media has created a major threat to civil liberties concerns because executive power appears to be expanding all over the place at the expense of constitutional government.

One last observation appears in order. It has quite often been noted, and accurately, that television news has brought the conflicts and issues of the day directly to the dinner table or the living room. At this close range, it has let citizen-viewers look at the tumult of the civil rights era, the Vietnam War and the protests against it, urban riots, Watergate and the Nixon resignation, and the Iran-Contra impeachable offenses. For the most part, this reportage has left the people to sort out all of these complicated matters on their own while claiming to provide "analysis" within the framework of a hurried medium. The results have been anomie, a great deal of uneasiness, and, perhaps most ominously, an ever greater demand for state action to resolve, or get us out of, these dilemmas.[20] It is hard to escape the irony that although a great deal of the chaos of recent decades was in fact caused by government, it is nevertheless government that is called upon to deal with this chaos. But that is not the important point. Most important is that the populace now looks for state, and perhaps statist, solutions to these problems, potentially posing still another problem for the civil liberties cause.

Leadership Example

It is often said that leaders can be no better than the people they represent, and this is especially the case in a democratic nation. Whether this is true or not, it seems clear that the values espoused and the tone set on civil liberties questions by political leaders and officeholders can be expected to have some effects on the general population.

If time and space are taken here to catalogue all of the horrors of recent administrations (or, for that matter, of recent legislative branch antics or court misleadership), the agenda for the remainder of this book will be set. There are so many examples to choose from. A president violates the law 370 times in carrying out vendettas and all manner of civil liberties violations before he resigns in the face of a threatened impeachment. A governor gases an entire city with a state-owned helicopter because he is worried about some protestors in a park. The Freedom of Information Act is weakened. Racist policies are implemented. In a speech to the National Association of Evangelicals, the president of the United States sets out the falsehood that the Supreme Court has said that our little children cannot pray in school at all.[21] Before resigning as attorney-general to run for the U.S. Senate from Pennsylvania, our chief law enforcement officer sides, for allegedly jurisdictional reasons, with right-to-life protestors who are engaged in violence and the blockage of entrances to a legal abortion clinic in Kansas. An important official in the Justice Department files briefs against federal affirmative action laws because these are alleged to be racism in reverse, a threat to the great civil rights movement we all fought for; but he also goes on to fight straightforward efforts against racial discrimination as well, seeking to reward right-wing and segregationist educational institutions.

The code word "racism" that has spewed forth from the lips of most of our presidents since 1968 sends a message to those who are incensed about "quotas" or about stereotyped thinking about welfare or crime. But our point is best made by simply reviewing the litany of propositions alleged to be fact by Ronald Reagan's great friend and adviser, Attorney-General Edwin Meese III. Meese's pronouncements include (1) the Supreme Court's edicts are not "the law of the land," that is, they apply only to the parties in a case that is decided; (2) the Constitution must be interpreted only on the basis of the "original intent" of the Founders (whatever that is on a given number of matters); (3) the fifty-year-old federal-state relationship is unconstitutional or at least should be repealed, but more likely it is the former; (4) the rights of aliens are not protected by the Constitution; (5) defendants should not be told their rights upon arrest; (6) those who are arrested are guilty;[22] (7) affirmative action is racism; (8) state law supersedes federal law in most circumstances; (9) segregated institutions should receive federal help; and (10) breadline and soupline people are mostly there for a free meal, not because of need.[23]

Whatever his persuasive powers may be, there can be little question that the stamp of approval of an attorney-general on this list of questionable—and, in some cases, even silly—set of assertions is likely to give credence to a mass of confusing and confused outlooks on the Constitution and the civil liberties that it represents. This does not mean that we cannot cherish and encourage debate on constitutional issues; this must be done if we are to arrive at better understandings of these complexities. It does mean that no meaningful debate is provided, or perhaps even pretended, when such flimsy or nonsensical assertions are set out by an attorney-general. There is only a debasement of constitutional values and the dialogues we entertain in our concern about these values. To add confusion to constitutional debates in this way can only help to subtract from, rather than add to, public understanding.

Obedience to Authority

The late Stanley Milgram conducted a series of experiments in the early 1970s that had a profound effect on our understanding of the phenomenon of obedience to authority. The results of his studies are well known, making it unnecessary to go over them in detail. Milgram used fake machines, actors, and the authority figure of the psychologist in the authority uniform of the white smock to demonstrate that volunteers, never remunerated for their participation, would be willing in all circumstances to administer pain to their fellow human beings because they had been ordered to do so and had been assured that the responsibility for their actions would not be theirs.[24]

These experiments, replicated several times and in several countries, tend to show that obedience to authority poses a serious problem for libertarianism. If we are all willing to administer pain upon being ordered to do so, serious questions must be raised about our psyches and the need for the gratification sought through this obedience. The essence of the behavior to be expected from enactment of a bill of rights or a set of civil liberties provisions, after all, is found in the treatment human beings mete out to one another. If a decency as basic as refraining from harmful conduct will be abandoned merely because an authority figure orders it, then we have achieved—according to Milgram—a partial answer to the question of why death camp victims met their fates, often at the hands of ''ordinary'' people who were ''only taking orders.''[25]

The monstrousness of this is staggering to contemplate. If we are to accept Milgram's findings, however, then we are all the more constrained to support civil liberties and to provide an atmosphere in which they flourish.

The Authoritarian Personality

A study of signal importance is Theodor Adorno's *The Authoritarian Personality*, published in 1950.[26] Unlike Milgram, who gives some indication of the breadth of the obedience to authority syndrome, Adorno tells us only that such authoritarian personalities exist in society in certain numbers. We all know this, but the point of Adorno's research most pertinent to our purposes is the definition he provides of this personality. Adorno determined that the measure of an individual's authoritarian side can be made by using what he called his F Scale tests. These tests can reveal specific personality traits by calling for the subjects either to respond to or to identify phenomena such as changing images.

In one case, the subject is told that he or she will view a filmstrip of a cat. Actually, what starts as the image of a cat changes after a number of frames to a dog. A subject who does not have the particular authoritarian personality traits being tested recognizes this and identifies the dog when the image changes. The subject who does exhibit authoritarian personality traits, continues to identify the image of the dog as ''cat.'' Despite the image change, this subject sees only what he or she has been told would be shown.

Adorno has been critiqued and roundly criticized for a variety of reasons related to his methodology;[27] but probably the most strident denunciation he has faced resulted from his finding that conservatives are more authoritarian than liberals.[28] We should be less concerned with this, however, than with the typology of the authoritarian personality he developed. In his view the authoritarian personality contains the following nine characteristics:

- *Conventionalism*: Rigid adherence to conventional middle-class values.
- *Authoritarian submission*: Submissive, uncritical attitude toward idealized moral authorities of the in-group.

- *Authoritarian aggression*: Tendency to be on the lookout for and to condemn, reject, and punish people who violate conventional values.
- *Anti-intraception*: Opposition to the subjective, the imaginative, the tender-minded.
- *Superstition and stereotypy*: The belief in mystical determinants of the individual's fate; the disposition to think in rigid categories.
- *Power and toughness*: Preoccupation with the dominance-submission, strong-weak, leader-follower dimension; identification with power figures; exaggerated assertion of strength and toughness.
- *Destructiveness and cynicism*: Generalized hostility and vilification of the human.
- *Projectivity*: The disposition to believe that wild, unconventional, and dangerous things go on in the world; the projection outward of unconscious emotional impulses.
- *Sex*: Ego-alien sexuality; exaggerated concern with sexual "goings on," and punitiveness toward violators of sex mores.[29]

There may well be an overlap here with Milgram's obedience to authority type in that Adorno sees individuals possessing authoritarian personalities as characteristically exhibiting unquestioning obedience to authority. It does not take the presence of many such individuals in a society to make the rest of us miserable or, most certainly, to make civil liberties concerns take on an added burden.

Fear of Freedom and Choice

"There can be no doubt that in this last quarter of a century the reasons for man's fear of freedom, for his anxiety and willingness to become an automaton, have not only continued but have greatly increased."[30] This quotation, written by the late Erich Fromm for the introduction to the 1969 edition of *Escape from Freedom*, is of interest because the original edition was written in 1941, a time when one could hardly be optimistic about the events in Europe and the world.

Fromm's concern is with the individual, found in abundant numbers, who fears not only choice and making decisions for himself or herself, but actually fears living in a free society. Fromm's psychological approach, heavily influenced by Freud, but also quite idiosyncratic, was aimed at discovering how people cope with what he calls the postfeudal world. Fromm believed that it took at least 400 years for civilization to develop to the point at which an individual can seek self-expression, at last shorn of the securities as well as the restraints of the medieval world. Inherent in this evolution is a lag between "freedom from" and "freedom to," and many—indeed most—people are still not mature enough to engage actively in a free society. The result has been a "panicky flight from freedom" into new, often totalitarian, ties or, at the least, complete indifference.[31]

Individuals deny their full emergence into a society of free women and men. They cling to myths and idols in order to endure the fact that a person is all by himself or herself; they endure the lack of authority brought about by a seemingly meaningless universe. In this atmosphere of rationality, people repress unreasoned impulses of destructiveness, hate, and revenge; at the same time, they worship power, money, the sovereign state, and perhaps their nationhood. True, there is a continued lip service to the teachings of the prophets, Buddha, Socrates, Jesus, or Mohammed, but these teachings have largely been changed into a banal jungle of superstition, idol worship, and hypocrisy. Tied closely to this tendency is an awareness of the huge discrepancy between intellectual and technical maturity and emotional backwardness.[32] The only hope for such individuals is to seek the assurance of a leader, an oligarchy, or a state by letting its choices become their choices. Freedom is an unbearable burden.[33]

Fromm's description of this state of mind appears to make sense, especially if it is slightly amended with Herbert Marcuse's findings that although choices seem to be made by individuals on a fairly constant basis, they are largely meaningless choices, such as what brand of hat to wear, what fast-food outlet to patronize, or what kind of television set to watch.[34] Because no real choices are posed by these kinds of decisions, the subject of Fromm's concern would have no trouble with them. The problem of living in a free and democratic state of existence, however, is another matter. And the problem for a libertarian sensibility and its establishment are made not only obvious but also remote.

Privatism

The contrast, or the dichotomy, of public and private is a given of American, and indeed of Western, society. Great attention is paid for example, to whether our institutions are private or public, with preferences usually being stated for the former. The insistence upon this distinction, especially in an age of large, bureaucratic organizations, is specious, according to the late C. Wright Mills and many other students of power in America. And such a distinction poses no particular relief for the many oppressions of everyday life. Fortunately, a number of theorists and analysts have provided encouraging signs that we can see past such banalities as this distinction as we look to the real issues that pertain to civil liberties and civil libertarian sensibility.[35]

One of the most notable workers against the private-public distinction, not only in terms of our views of institutions, but in terms of everyday life and its challenges, was the late Hannah Arendt. Arendt gave us a prescient study of the question that seems to have increasing application as we move through the remainder of this century and the beginning of the next.[36] Just as important—perhaps more important for the purposes of this study—Arendt has made some trenchant observations about the hard times that can be encountered by civil libertarians in the face of the dreams of ordinary men and women trying to live out their private lives with little regard for anything else. Heinrich Himmler, the SS leader, she tells us, "proved his supreme ability for organizing the masses into total domination by assuming that most people are neither bohemians, fanatics, adventurers, sex maniacs, crackpots, nor social failures, but first and foremost job holders and good family men."[37] She points out in the next paragraph that these everyday bourgeois members of society, "who worried about nothing so much as . . . private security," proved to be easy victims as well as followers of totalitarianism.[38] Nothing is easier, Arendt says, than for a government to destroy the private lives and indeed the private morality of people whose most important worry is the safeguarding of these very things.[39]

Other chroniclers of human affairs provide tremendous evidence for what Arendt says. Raul Hilberg came up with perhaps the most sobering findings of all. He was able to look into the minds of such ordinary citizens of the Third Reich as civil servants and railroad employees to show how "ordinary" events such as the construction of signals to facilitate the movement of rail cars full of Jews and other victims to Hitler's death camps are viewed. By and large, it is fair to say that these people bowed to authority and never questioned its legitimacy or morality. They built quality railroad signals, and they administered the finances of the railroad to see that it was paid for each victim transported. They went about their jobs in ordinary ways, fulfilling what seemed to them to be ordinary tasks.[40] Such people, we can assume, were worried about the maintenance of their private lives or perhaps never even thought much about the consequences of their actions. Such detachment seems certainly possible in America, a nation where privacy is valued more than most things.

The general conclusions one might draw after a reading of Fromm, Adorno, Milgram, Arendt, and Hilberg can hardly be cheering, but it is important that they not be ignored.

Elitism

It is natural to think of elitism in connection with economic issues, rather than civil liberties issues, in the United States. In a nation lacking a nobility and titles and falling back on substitutes for these, money has become an important criterion of social and political distinction. This has meant that economics and class divisions are complementary considerations in the national culture. In one sense, elitism as an attitude may have a rational basis, if one is referring to the members of the national elite. They recognize that their interests, at least as narrowly conceived, are tied to a strong support for inequality in resource allocations. It is in no sense rational, however, for those who are not members of the elite classes to identify with or support them. The broad as well as particular interests of the great majority of people dictate identification with the working class and with the progressive elements and movements of the nation in order to effect change and to lessen the ravages of inequality.

Quite clearly this is not the case; and the connection that must be made with civil liberties issues and attitudes is the fact that such issues are, often as not, issues of class and economics. The major problem addressed here goes to the socialization patterns developed by, and often imposed upon, the people. In a most naive way, many people willingly accept the basic morality tale that is played out again and again in fiction, television, film, and the news media. This story pits the police against the bank robber or rapist, the sheriff against the cattle rustlers, and, most important, us against them—us, the upstanding and hard-working, tax-paying, honest folks against the crooks, miscreants, and subversives who would threaten the fabric and order of society. In its classic form, this tale rarely tells us anything that is socially significant. It is not considered to be very entertaining to bring up awkward matters about economics or class that are terribly important variables in civil liberties and crime control in this country.

The public's perception, by and large, is that such events do not involve economic issues or issues of class or elitism. The morality tale is played out, and the social division that appears, rather than being one of separation along class or economic lines, is one that has that small gang of no-goodniks on one side and a very big group—all of the rest of us—on the other. Crime control, subversion, and national security issues are therefore never seen as class issues in any economic or meaningful social sense; the "us" and "them" message, if there is a message at all, is paramount. And nearly all of us—all but the no-goodniks—belong to that large and nonexclusive club in which morality, respectability, and honesty are the hallmarks of membership.

This large club still manages to be exclusive in one sense, however. That is because the great mass of us identifies with the good side of the tale and, most important, with the authorities. There is an elitism here that is based upon adherence to what are seen as everyday law and order principles. We are superior to the no-goodniks; what is more, we strongly believe that we are superior to those social and economic types (and Edward C. Banfield, among others, indicates that we can probably identify these)[41] who are likely to be no-goodniks, namely, the poor and members of minority groups. To say that such a broad-based elitism is misguided is a profound understatement; but the breadth and persistence of it is undeniable. It is tied to what some psychologists and social scientists have long perceived as the need that many people in society seem to have to feel that they are at least a rung or two up the ladder above other individuals and groups.[42] On the economic side, this represents a partial answer to the eternal puzzle about why working-class and relatively underprivileged or unblessed people will support, sometimes quite stridently, the inequalities and injustices perpetrated by the well-off and the well-connected. In a most unfortunate way, they have come to identify with the powerful, the rich, and the well-off. They may see themselves as potential great entrepreneurs (or perhaps, nowadays, lottery winners) caught up in the necessities and practicalities of power and privilege. They may see themselves as a future J. R. Ewing of the *Dallas* television show, revelling in his ability to push people around.

None of this, it can readily be seen, can bode well for ideas of compassion or adherence to civil liberties principles; but this elitism is surely one of the most powerful obstacles to the sensibilities and understandings necessary for a just and civil society.[43]

Workplace Psychology

A leading sociologist and feminist writer, Carole Pateman, has pointed out that most work experiences involve living under a dictatorship, an oligarchy, or some other essentially nonconsultative authority for eight hours a day, five days a week—a big part of our lives. With few exceptions, orders are given in the business world or, perhaps, in government agencies or other organizations, from the top to those who hold inferior positions. And this latter group is most of us.

What are the political and civil liberties consequences of this situation? According to Pateman, it means that a large part of our lives is spent in an environment in which most democratic values—choice, participation, certainly equality—are put aside in the name of efficiency and the traditions of entrepreneurial and administrative practice. This is bad enough, but according to Pateman, this also tends to make these hapless employees, the great majority of us, validate and support undemocratic principles and practices when we leave the workplace. Many or most of us do not adjust very well, in all probability, to employing one set of governance principles during the greater part of our day and another during our free time. Pateman is telling us, in effect, that we become inured to democratic dialogues, values, and persuasions in favor of the well-practiced cynicism and authoritarianism found in most workplaces. Pateman has touched upon a problem that has no immediate solution (although the economic reforms proposed elsewhere in this volume would go a long way in righting this). The point is that she has shown us one further and important difficulty for the cause of maintaining democratic and libertarian values.[44]

Bureaucracy and Efficiency

In one of his most famous dissents, Justice Louis D. Brandeis warned that "Experience should teach us to be most on our guard to protect liberty when the Government's purposes are beneficent. . . . The greatest dangers to liberty lurk in insidious encroachment by men of zeal, well-meaning but without understanding."[45] It is clearly within the context of Brandeis's warning that it is pointed out that benign-sounding arguments for the convenience of governmental administration, for the classifying of this or that set of documents or group of people, and for the efficiency that will be wrought by this or that approach are arguments that can lead to trouble not only for civil liberties but for the premises of civil liberties. Bureaucracy and its related needs, or alleged needs, can, in short, help in the erection of barriers to civil liberties sensibility.

A good example of this is found in the Simpson-Mazzolli Act of 1986, an immigration measure aimed at stemming the supposed tide of aliens that is engulfing us. In order to effect this, employers are fined if they hire illegal aliens; it is clear that this measure can result in employment discrimination against Hispanics and other groups. In addition, the law goes some way toward establishing a national identity system, which at the moment is safeguarded from becoming one in every detail because of certain provisions in the Act. What we have here, all the same, is a slippery slope. It is entirely within the realm of reasonable anticipation to expect further legislation in aid of dealing with the problem of illegality, or perhaps administrative rule making, and these activities could lead to the equivalent of an internal passport system for everyone, citizen or alien, who resides in the country. One reason, among others, for thinking this is that there have been various proposals made in Congress over the years in support of a national identity card system for all residents of the United States.

The current clamors for AIDS testing and drug testing are grounded in part upon genuine fears about public health. It takes little imagination, however, to see these demands growing out of proportion, if in fact this has not already occurred. The worry over crime in the workplace has brought on a flurry of requirements for polygraph testing on an occasional or even periodic basis in some places of employment.[46] And law enforcement demands for turning back the *Miranda* rule, the exclusionary rule, or other libertarian decisions of the Supreme Court are often presented in terms of the efficiency and administrative control that new rules or rule overturns would provide. The Reagan administration's weakening of the Freedom of Information Act was likewise promoted in terms of the burden this law places on administration and good bureaucratic practice.

Although we cannot assume that every slippery slope will become an avalanche, it can neither be assumed that these demands for tightening the law enforcement apparatus, for the enlargement of discretion for officials or for employers, or for the need to test all kinds of people for all kinds of reasons will not lead to grave civil liberties problems and, along the way, to a weakening of the public's already less-than-steady resolve to resist such broadenings of power. The 1990–91 term of the Supreme Court provides fair warning of this, with its decisions upholding forced confessions, sharply reducing capital punishment appeals, and reducing or abolishing other rights.

CONCLUSION

In any number of situations, public views of particular issues may be based on ignorance or on a perceived (or misperceived) self-interest. In many of the situations listed above, however, attitudes may simply be responses to coercion.

Certainly, this is the threat with testing demanded by government agencies or by employers. It was well illustrated by the unfortunate position of the Hanford peace movement cited earlier. Many communities have practiced conformity in the face of economic pressures from environmental polluters or from manufacturers of products that place consumers in positions of unguarded risk. American history is replete, moreover, with dramatic stories of community conformity and repression in civil liberties matters that undoubtedly compelled individuals to remain silent rather than face the wrath of their neighbors and co-workers. These stories include denials of voting rights, denials of the right to earn a living, violence in labor-management conflicts, and even lynchings.

Public opinion, then, must be viewed not only in the light of polling results or election results, for it is influenced by deep psychological factors, by perceived pressures of self-interest, and even by coercion. And public opinion, as much as any of the barriers erected by society or by our institutions, can be an impediment to civil liberties and justice.

In no sense should it be insisted that public opinion is *invariably* on the repressive side of civil liberties questions. The first polls taken after the Rodney King verdict was handed down on the Los Angeles police brutality case showed a marked disdain for the jury's judgment. This was, however, a very clear case of repressive excess; and in cases of great excess—the Selma, Alabama, performance of police repression during the civil rights protest era comes to mind—the public seems able to discern issues of justice and injustice. But should this sensitivity show up only in cases of demonstrated excess?

The Bill of Rights cause, then, faces two serious obstacles. On one hand, there are the multiple problems of public indifference, lack of discernment, and the great and many factors influencing and allowing these. On the other hand, those supposed sentinels of liberty, the members of the legal profession, seem to have more pressing priorities, such as addressing property rights questions and making money. Both of these major problems must be pondered when we look at the concerns faced by the cause of civil liberties in America.

NOTES

1. Quoted by J. Skelly Wright, "The Role of the Courts: Conscience of a Sovereign People," *Reporter*, September 26, 1963, 27.

2. Quoted by Arthur Weisberg, *Attorney for the Damned* (New York: Simon & Schuster, 1957), 3–4.

3. *National Journal*, December 10, 1983, 2600; Sydney H. Schanberg, "A Muzzle for the Press," in Micah L. Sifry and Christopher Cerf (eds.), *The Gulf War Reader* (New York: Random House, 1991), esp. 371–74. For an extensive and well-written account of press deference and cowardice, see Mark Hertsgaard, *On Bended Knee: The Press and the Reagan Presidency* (New York: Schocken, 1988).

4. *Korematsu* v. *U.S.*, 323 U.S. 214 (1944); *Ex parte Endo*, 323 U.S. 283 (1945).

5. Gustavus Myers, *History of Bigotry in the United States* (New York: Capricorn, 1960); Richard Polenberg, *Fighting Faiths: The Abrams Case, the Supreme Court, and Free Speech* (New York: Viking, 1987).

6. Clyde Z. Nunn, Harry J. Crockett, and J. Allen Williams, *Tolerance for Nonconformity* (San Francisco: Jossey-Bass, 1978); Michael J. Corbett, *Political Tolerance in America: Freedom and Equality in Public Attitudes* (New York: Longman, 1982); John L. Sullivan, James Piereson, and George E. Marcus, *Political Tolerance and American Democracy* (Chicago: University of Chicago Press, 1982); Herbert J. McCloskey and Alida Brill, *Dimensions of Tolerance: What Americans Believe about Civil Liberties* (New York: Russell Sage Foundation, 1983); James L. Gibson, "Political Intolerance and Political Repression during the McCarthy Red Scare," *American Political Science Review* 82 (June 1988), 511–30.

7. Samuel Stouffer, *Communism, Conformity, and Civil Liberties* (New York: Doubleday, 1955); replications of Stouffer include James A. Davis, "Communism, Conformity, Cohorts, and Categories: American Tolerance in 1954 and 1972–73," *American Journal of Sociology* 81 (November 1975), 491–513; James W. Prothro and Charles W. Grigg, "Fundamental Principles of Democracy: Bases of Agreement and Disagreement," *Journal of Politics* 22 (May 1960), 276–94; also see McCloskey and Brill, *Dimensions.*

8. McCloskey and Brill, *Dimensions.* An example of such a minority opinion is a Media General–Associated Press poll showing that 25% of the American people do not think that separation of church and state is a good idea; *San Francisco Chronicle,* October 14, 1985. A variety of the polls culled by McCloskey and Brill show that both majorities and minorities fail to grasp some very basic givens of constitutional law and the Bill of Rights.

9. Also see Gerald L. Houseman, "Anti-Semitism in City Politics: The Separation Clause and the Indianapolis Nativity Scene Controversy, 1976–77," *Jewish Social Studies* 42 (Winter 1980), 21–36.

10. Davis, "Communism, Conformity, Cohorts, and Categories."

11. McCloskey and Brill, *Dimensions,* 415–16.

12. This chapter is informed by, and supportive of, a position close to the ACLU position on most civil liberties matters; indeed, I am a member. This viewpoint is sometimes described (somewhat inappropriately, I believe) as the "fortress" model, as in Lee C. Bollinger, *The Tolerant Society: Freedom of Speech and Extremist Speech in America* (New York: Oxford University Press, 1986).

13. Quoted in *Society* 13 (January/February 1976), 93.

14. Probably the most visible Social Darwinists around today are the Ayn Randian Objectivists and the organizations they have influenced, such as the Libertarian Party, the Intercollegiate Society of Individualists, and the upper reaches of the Bush and Reagan administrations (Alan Greenspan, Martin Anderson, David Stockman, and others).

15. *Los Angeles Times*, August 5, 1984.

16. Myers, *History of Bigotry.*

17. Stouffer, *Communism, Conformity, and Civil Liberties*; Davis, "Communism, Conformity, Cohorts, and Categories."

18. Also see Michael Parenti, *Inventing Reality* (New York: St. Martin's Press, 1986).

19. See the reference in n. 3.

20. Sheldon Wolin, "The Idea of the State in America," in John P. Diggins and Mark E. Kann (eds.), *The Problem of Authority in America* (Philadelphia: Temple University Press, 1981), 41–58.

21. Remarks of President Ronald Reagan to the Forty-First Annual Convention of the National Association of Evangelicals, Orlando, Florida, March 6, 1983 (issued by the White House Office of the Press Secretary).

22. The actual quotation of Meese on this is, "If a person is innocent of a crime, then he is not a suspect," letter to the ACLU membership written by Ira Glasser, executive director, n.d.

23. *Washington Post* (national weekly edition), December 1, 1986; American Civil Liberties Union, "The State of Civil Liberties in the United States: A Special Midyear Report" (June 1986).

24. Stanley Milgram, *Obedience to Authority: An Experimental View* (New York: Harper & Row, 1974).

25. Ibid.

26. Theodor Adorno, *The Authoritarian Personality* (New York: Harper, 1950).

27. Richard Christie and Marie Jahoda (eds.), *Studies in the Scope and Method of "The Authoritarian Personality"* (Glencoe: Free Press, 1954).

28. See the essay on Adorno by William F. Buckley, Jr., *Up from Liberalism* (New York: McDowell, Obolensky, 1959).

29. Nevitt Sanford, "The Approach to 'The Authoritarian Personality,' " in Fred I. Greenstein and Michael Lerner (eds.), *A Source Book for the Study of Personality and Politics* (Reading, MA: Addison-Wesley, 1976), 317.

30. Erich Fromm, *Escape from Freedom* (New York: Avon, 1969), xxi.

31. Ibid., 52–53.

32. Ibid., xiv–xv.

33. Ibid., xiv–xv, 52–53.

34. Herbert Marcuse, *One Dimensional Man* (Boston: Beacon Press, 1964).

35. Patricia Boling, "Why Public vs. Private Is Wrong," paper delivered at the Annual Meeting of the American Political Science Association, New Orleans, October–November 1985.

36. Hannah Arendt, *The Human Condition* (Chicago: University of Chicago Press, 1958).

37. Hannah Arendt, *The Origins of Totalitarianism*, 2d ed. (Cleveland: World, 1958), 338.

38. Ibid.

39. Ibid.

40. Raul Hilberg, *The Destruction of European Jews* (New York: Harper & Row, 1979).

41. Edward C. Banfield, *The Unheavenly City Revisited* (Boston: Little, Brown, 1974), 269–70.

42. I must admit that I have trouble with this premise, however, for I certainly think it is unlikely that this is any kind of "natural desire."

43. Marcuse, *One Dimensional Man*.

44. Carole Pateman, *Participation and Democratic Theory* (New York: Cambridge University Press, 1970).

45. Philippa Strum, *Louis D. Brandeis: Justice for the People* (Cambridge: Harvard University Press, 1984), 324 (quoting *Olmstead* v. *U.S.*, 227 U.S. 438 [1928], at 472).

46. "Lie(ing) Detectors Fail the Test of the Truth," *Machinist* (February 1986), 4–5 (this comprises a description of polygraph programs at Coors Brewing Company and other employers).

An earlier version of this chapter appeared in Stuart S. Nagel (ed.), *Research in Law and Policy Studies* (Greenwich, CT: JAI Press, 1988).

PART II

QUESTIONING THE CORPORATE-PROPERTY POWER ESTABLISHMENT

3 Questioning Corporations Law

THE CORPORATION HAS BEEN WITH US for a very long time. Its roots go back at least as far as the Roman Emperor Justinian. At the present time, the corporation is undergoing far-reaching and dramatic changes that will affect virtually the entire world. International competitive pressure and the assertion of territorial and market claims has made the large, American-based business corporation a major actor on the world stage. This is so much the case that it has become more accurate to refer to these large entities as multinationals rather than to characterize them as ''American'' corporations; and as multinationals, they have no particular loyalty to any nation, but instead often play off one nation against another in exploiting resources, dealing with workers, molesting and battering the environment, or finding consumer markets for the company's products. It goes without saying that they have no particular allegiance to the world community either.

Another basic and important set of changes now going on is structural in nature. Mergers, acquisitions, hostile takeovers, and other combinatory schemes are causing corporations to be brought into existence, to flourish (sometimes for a very brief moment in the sun), and then to be subsumed into some other entity or perhaps to die. Along with these games of shifting capital assets back and forth across the chessboard of corporate gamesmanship are the threatening corruptions that today's corporations seem so often to be immersed in—the savings and loan scandals, defense procurement irregularities, insurance fraud (and, it is said, the possible collapse of that industry), pension fund misuse, bankruptcy law misuse, insider trading, money-kiting schemes, antitrust violations, labor repression, consumer fraud, and bloated executive compensation levels.

With all of this dramatic and far-reaching activity taking place, it should be surprising that the law of corporations is not undergoing any similar dramatic or dynamic changes even though the call for reform is almost always in the air. The few changes that are proposed and are gaining currency, moreover, are likely to exacerbate the problems caused by an increasing concentration of resources and of political and economic power.[1]

Indeed, the history of corporations law is one of stubborn resistance to change of any kind, even though there are occasional accommodations made for discretion, for growth, for sweeping this or that mistake under the carpet, or for furthering monopolistic or oligopolistic business formations. There is also, of course, the even less occasional and often ineffectual gesture to the welfare of society and to the honored-in-the-breach social "good" of market competition. Such measures are best relegated to the category of misleading signals and representations. But of all the ironies of corporations law and history, by far the greatest is the continuance of outmoded legal doctrines alongside the realities of corporate growth and influence in both political and economic terms, the frequent corporate violations of the spirit or the letter of the laws or both, and the foregone conclusion of corporate political and economic dominance. These doctrines permit the creation of the corporate persona for various takeover, taxation, regulatory or other purposes, the skewing of social and economic policies because of the many abuses of the privilege of incorporation, the major role for the states (rather than the federal government) as the chartering agents for corporate citizenship, and a vast variety of other anomalies.

There are four purposes in mind as this chapter proceeds to question corporations law. The first purpose is to recall those doctrines and their premises that can be useful in assessing what the corporation is in the law, in American society, and in the world. In doing this, it is likely that some doctrines and premises of the law will be discovered—and dismissed—that no longer seem to have any good use. These may in fact obfuscate some of the purposes and meanings of the law of corporations and are therefore detrimental in their social and political effects. A second goal is to uncover such anomalies, to examine them in the light of historical experience and their late twentieth-century significance and their possible excision from the corpus of the law. A third objective is to trace briefly the history of the corporation through five fairly distinct periods of its modern existence; this will aid in the achievement of the first two goals and will promote recognition of the intense and unprecedented character of today's corrupt and socially irresponsible milieu of corporate activity (including the merger and takeover mania). The fourth goal is to array these activities against the dangers they present to the economy, society, and polity along with their sole redeeming feature, the aid they render to the cause of undermining and exploding a great deal of capitalist myth and propaganda.

This is a propitious time for such an examination. Corruption, merger mania, and misbegotten and undeserved privilege have overtaken the corporate world, the securities and finance industries, and the mentality of many business leaders. It is therefore not only the law but the canons of good sense that are violated. Questionable instruments of indebtedness have flooded into our markets, as well as those of foreign countries, to finance these activities, creating a speculative climate unrelated to the value of business firms or their shares and causing banking problems, tax revenue shortfalls, unemployment, and other economic disruptions. In addition, corporations are a major force in the arenas of international debt, the trade imbalance, consumer debt, agricultural debt, and government debt—all of which are at record or near-record levels—as well as within the mountain of indebtedness created directly by the companies themselves. All of these are major matters of concern at the moment. And all of these matters, and most especially the structural changes wrought by merger mania, require a redefinition of the business corporation and its place in late twentieth-century life. This redefinition and place, one can be quite sure, must rest upon something quite different than the dominant and noisy rhetoric we have had dinned into our ears through all of the 1980s and a part of the 1990s.

INCORPORATION: A PRIVILEGE, NOT A RIGHT

> In 1250 A.D., Pope Innocent IV forbade the practice of excommunicating a corporation convicted of a crime. He reasoned that because a corporation had no soul, it could not lose it.
>
> —Sheryl J. Wragg, *University of Detroit Law Review*[2]

> . . . corporations . . . are as . . . many lesser commonwealths in the bowels of a greater, like worms in the entrails of a natural man.
>
> —Thomas Hobbes, *Leviathan, Part II*[3]

> Probably the biggest thing happening in America these days is the reconstruction of the corporate economy.
>
> —Joseph Kraft[4]

A corporation is defined legally by its characteristics of limited liability, perpetual life, and persona, the fictive citizenship accorded it. It is ancient in its lineage, and the first charter recorded in the common law countries was granted in 1555.[5] Joint stock companies, as we all know, were important in promoting settlement of the American colonies and the exploration, commercial development, and exploitation of the East Indies and Asia. Corporations founded within the American colonies were generally organized for charitable, religious, educational, local government, and, less often, business purposes.[6] Partnerships remained the primary and most common business organization in America well into the nineteenth century.

A corporate charter has always been deemed a privilege in the law, not a right. The great concession is limited liability, being allowed to conduct business without risking the resources of investors beyond the total of their investments, and this privilege has historically been accorded with great reluctance and with a feeling that this is an extraordinary grant.[7] We may today regard this as a routine and accepted matter, but this has not been the case during most of the history of corporations.

Fear and suspicion have almost always accompanied the issuance of stock and the founding of corporations, and in most respects these feelings have been well-founded. (For a list of the world's largest companies that issue publicly held stock, see Table 3.1.) It has been amply recognized that corporations can be instruments of fraud and of political and economic power. Fraud is of course universally condemned and regarded as undesirable, but political and economic power are nearly always so regarded as well. The great Elizabethan jurist Sir Edward Coke, for example, never liked or trusted corporations. Neither did Andrew Jackson, Louis D. Brandeis, William O. Douglas, and hosts of others.

It can be seen at the outset, and with the briefest of introductions to the concept of the corporation, that a number of confusions can arise; and these confusions have often serviced the needs of those willing to use corporations for dubious purposes, whether legal or illegal. Straightfaced conservative proponents of corporate interests will often argue that corporations should have the same free speech rights, for example, as are applied to any other citizen; and that is fair enough. But they will also argue that because a corporation is not really a person, it should not be obliged to honor labor contracts after it has declared bankruptcy and continues to operate under Chapter Eleven rules. It has been argued that corporations should pay no taxes because they are merely an economic sieve, an entity that will merely raise prices in order to meet these revenue obligations. Very few of these advocates would seriously suggest that the rest of the citizenry, we noncorporate types, should also remain untaxed because it raises our cost of living. Nor would they be likely to favor the exemption of corporations from services such as fire protection, water, air pollution control, police, or the use of the facilities and benefits of public education. Because then we find that, lo and behold, corporations are persons once again.

These confusions do not end with such points of public debate. They are also found to exist, even among the participants in corporate affairs, in the tendency to regard some individuals and corporations as one and the same entity. This is the situation when a corporation seems to exist specifically to fulfill the wheeling and dealing whims of the person who controls it. Mesa Petroleum, often used as a vehicle in takeover fights, is the corporate machine of the famous raider T. Boone Pickens. The infamous Hunt brothers of Dallas, Texas, were for years Placid Oil, which they controlled lock, stock, and barrel and used for a variety of purposes. NVF Corporation and Sharon Steel are the useful tools of takeover artist and eminent wheeler-dealer Victor Posner, who, the business press tells us, profits well even when his companies do not.[8] This tendency to regard a real person and a corporate entity as the same being derives in fact from a major difference between them. The corporate entity can be founded, sold off, partly sold off, shaped, reorganized, redirected, subsidized, killed off, or placed in

TABLE 3.1 The World's Largest Companies That Issue Publicly Held Stock

RANK	COMPANY	RANK	COMPANY
1	NTT (*Japan*)	35	Chevron (*U.S.*)
2	IBM (*U.S.*)	36	BellSouth (*U.S.*)
3	Royal Dutch Shell (*Netherlands, U.K.*)	37	Tokai Bank (*Japan*)
4	General Electric (*U.S.*)	38	Daimler-Benz (*Germany*)
5	Industrial Bank of Japan	39	Unilever (*Netherlands, U.K.*)
6	Exxon (*U.S.*)	40	Eli Lilly (*U.S.*)
7	Toyota (*Japan*)	41	Toshiba (*Japan*)
8	Fuji Bank (*Japan*)	42	Johnson and Johnson (*U.S.*)
9	Sumitomo Bank (*Japan*)	43	Siemens (*Germany*)
10	Dai-Ichi Kangyo Bank (*Japan*)	44	Nestlé (*Switzerland*)
11	Mitsui Kaiyo Kobe Bank (*Japan*)	45	Mitsubishi Heavy (*Japan*)
12	Mitsubishi Bank (*Japan*)	46	Kansai Electric Power (*Japan*)
13	Philip Morris (*U.S.*)	47	Ford Motor (*U.S.*)
14	AT&T (*U.S.*)	48	Glaxo Holdings (*U.K.*)
15	Sanwa Bank (*Japan*)	49	GTE (*U.S.*)
16	Tokyo Electric Power (*Japan*)	50	PepsiCo (*U.S.*)
17	Wal-Mart (*U.S.*)	51	Boeing (*U.S.*)
18	Merck (*U.S.*)	52	NEC (*Japan*)
19	Bristol-Myers Squibb (*U.S.*)	53	Sony (*Japan*)
20	British Telecom (*U.K.*)	54	Hanson (*U.K.*)
21	Hitachi (*Japan*)	55	Japan Air Lines (*Japan*)
22	Coca-Cola (*U.S.*)	56	Deutsche Bank (*Germany*)
23	Long-Term Credit Bank (*Japan*)	57	Nintendo (*Japan*)
24	British Petroleum (*U.K.*)	58	Bell Atlantic (*U.S.*)
25	Matsushita Electric (*Japan*)	59	3M (*U.S.*)
26	Nomura Securities (*Japan*)	60	Waste Management (*U.S.*)
27	General Motors (*U.S.*)	61	Bank of Tokyo (*Japan*)
28	Procter & Gamble (*U.S.*)	62	Assicurazioni Generali (*Italy*)
29	Allianz (*Germany*)	63	Pacific Telesis (*U.S.*)
30	Du Pont (*U.S.*)	64	Nippon Credit Bank (*Japan*)
31	Amoco (*U.S.*)	65	Abbott Laboratories (*U.S.*)
32	Atlantic Richfield (*U.S.*)	66	Nissan Motor (*Japan*)
33	Nippon Steel (*Japan*)	67	Fiat (*Italy*)
34	Mobil (*U.S.*)	68	Fujitsu (*Japan*)

(*continued*)

TABLE 3.1 (*continued*)

RANK	COMPANY	RANK	COMPANY
69	Walt Disney (*U.S.*)	**85**	Seibu Railway (*Japan*)
70	B.A.T. Industries (*U.K.*)	**86**	NKK (*Japan*)
71	British Gas (*U.K.*)	**87**	Mitsubishi Electric (*Japan*)
72	American Home Products (*U.S.*)	**88**	Asahi Glass (*Japan*)
73	Ameritech (*U.S.*)	**89**	Imperial Chemical Industries (*U.K.*)
74	Nynex (*U.S.*)	**90**	Tokio Marine and Fire (*Japan*)
75	Southwestern Bell (*U.S.*)	**91**	Schlumberger (*U.S.*)
76	Mitsubishi Trust (*Japan*)	**92**	Yasuda Trust (*Japan*)
77	American International Group (*U.S.*)	**93**	Tokyo Gas (*Japan*)
78	Chubu Electric Power (*Japan*)	**94**	Elf Aquitaine (*France*)
79	Dow Chemical (*U.S.*)	**95**	US West (*U.S.*)
80	Mitsubishi Corp. (*Japan*)	**96**	Daiwa Bank (*Japan*)
81	Texaco (*U.S.*)	**97**	Fuji Photo Film (*Japan*)
82	All Nippon Airways (*Japan*)	**98**	Eastman Kodak (*U.S.*)
83	Roche (*Switzerland*)	**99**	Sharp (*Japan*)
84	Sumitomo Trust (*Japan*)	**100**	BTR (*U.K.*)

Source: "The World's 100 Largest Public Companies," *The Wall Street Journal*, Sept. 21, 1990. Reprinted by permission of *The Wall Street Journal*, © 1990 Dow Jones & Company, Inc. All Rights Reserved Worldwide.

various kinds of liaison with subsidiaries, holding companies, or financial institutions. A great variety of finance games, or just plain ego trips, is made possible, and often only possible, because of the existence of the corporation. There are laws that govern all these things, but they can hardly be said to be strictly enforced. Many of the problems with the law of corporations—or, for that matter, many other areas of the law—could simply be resolved if enforcement was a fact rather than a hypothetical formulation lying dormant on the statute books. The formulations advocated in this book might not be necessary, or at the least would be perceived quite differently, if law enforcement was an accepted norm in Washington and in the states. In any event, it is most certainly true that there are many gray areas in corporations law and corporate regulation in which purposes and actions are obscure, complex, and beyond the understanding of all but a few regulators, lawyers, and financial wheeler-dealers and their accountants. The corporation, in short, is an entity that permits tremendous flexibility in business and financial arrangements and, further, may be looked upon as the very engine of the capitalist system; but it also permits many mischiefs with many grievous results.

These are pointed up in those perennial questions that are asked about corporations: Can they commit crimes? If they can, can they be effectively punished? Can they commit torts? What standards of liability are to be used if they are committed? And, certainly, what is the extent of this liability—the total of the assets of the corporation? Can we look to the assets of individual officers or shareholders? These questions, which from time to time appear to be settled, seem to come to life again with every airliner that crashes, every mine that caves in, every BCCI-type banking scandal, or every Bhopal-type death. The only certain answer to any of these questions is that corporations, persons or not, cannot go to jail. They can pay fines and damages, but to what extent and under what conditions of liability?

These questions, anyone would acknowledge, hardly scratch the surface of the myriad of problems connected to the confusions of the corporate entity. At the same time, it may be objected, this is simply the wrong way to look at corporations. Much of the foregoing analysis has been informed by the concessionary theory, which bases its view of the corporation upon the premise that society has granted a major concession to corporate entrepreneurs, officers, and stockholders by awarding them the privilege of limited liability. Although this idea strikes me as sound and commonsensical, it is true that other theories govern the American view of the corporation as well. These include the one that says that the formation of a corporation is the creation of a contract between the shareholders, including the officers, and the state; this contract is in fact the charter granted to the corporation by the state. The contract theory took its most concrete form in the *Dartmouth College* case, which is of historical (though no longer legal) significance. Another view of the corporation widely held today is that we have long ago given up the concessionary idea with the more or less automatic chartering procedures now carried out in the names of administrative and economic efficiency.[9]

Finally, it should not be forgotten that corporations are treated differently in the various systems of law found in the world. There are even considerable variations in the family of common law systems. Because a major focus here is less upon what the law is than what it might become, we should keep in mind comparative legal models, as well as comparative models of just what this institution we call the corporation really is, as we critique and build upon the past. First, however, we should take a look at the past.

HISTORY OF THE PRIVILEGE

Corporations existed in ancient Rome, where the term itself originated. The state was regarded as a corporation, as were charities and hospitals and, after

Constantine, churches. Middle Ages canon law provided a framework for development of the corporate concept, and charters were granted to towns, churches, and charities. Business partnerships of the twelfth century gave rise to the idea, in the secular world, of a collective personality of members of the association, and this unmistakably is basic to the idea of the corporation.[10] The business corporation is, all the same, a latecomer to the Western historical experience; for even in the early nineteenth century, corporations were far exceeded in number by partnerships, the most common form of business organization. The first English corporate charter, granted in 1555, was hardly the precursor of any immediate rise of the business corporation as a commonplace entity, because corporations continued to be primarily municipalities, churches, and charities until the Industrial Revolution was well under way.[11]

Corporations, as many opinion polls will attest, have never been very popular. This may well be because they acquired an unrepentant seaminess early on; corporations had a bad name by the time of the outset of the Industrial Revolution. Lengthy treatises and chapters have been devoted to early notorious fiascoes, such as John Law's Mississippi Scheme, perpetrated in France, and the South Sea Bubble, which, most embarrassingly, won the financial participation of the British Parliament in 1711, aiding in the promotion of gullibility against victimized speculators. "Every fool aspired to be a knave."[12] Only a minority of people and Members of Parliament seemed to agree with Sir Robert Walpole that "stock-jobbing" was dangerous and would divert people from worthwhile trades and industries to their ruin in a hopeless quest for unearned riches.[13] The Mississippi and South Sea schemes were the best known of more than eighty that were floated, all with the same results, in the years before 1720. Among these were a scheme to make silver from lead, another to make lead from coal, and still another to metamorphose quicksilver into a fine and malleable metal.[14]

It should be noted in passing that stock-jobbing has an intriguing and sometimes amazingly consistent history from the period prior to 1720 down to the present day. The reputation of purveyors of stocks has changed to some extent from that time of fraud and duplicity to today's epics of Ivan Boesky, Michael Milken, and the now bankrupt "junk bond" firm Drexel Burnham Lambert—but it has not changed very much. The consistency and unity found in characters such as that time's John Law and today's Ivan Boesky are part of a common thread seldom found in other professions, trades, or walks of life.

The consequences of the frauds and schemes of the early eighteenth century caused Parliament to pass the Bubble Act of 1720, which not only forbade fraudulent practices but required a charter from the crown in order to set up a company. (Parliament itself could set up a corporation, but this was rarely done. The royal assent was therefore considered vital.) No private floating of shares was permitted. Some colonial corporations were chartered in England under this Act, but more important, the Act itself was exported to the colonies in 1741 so that even before independence, there was some corporate regulation in America. Some of the more wild-eyed free enterprise history buffs would probably like us to believe otherwise. Very little regulation was called for, however, because there were fewer than ten corporations in existence in the colonies prior to independence.[15] And the exporting of the Bubble Act did not prevent fraud and over-speculation in any event. The intense stock promotion of 1784–91, combined with the failure of the currency and the United States National Bank, resulted in the crash of 1792.[16]

The business corporation remained a relatively rare phenomenon until the 1830s and 1840s. Most corporations were municipal, church, charitable, educational, and other nonprofit bodies. And if a business corporation was established prior to this time, it was chartered in most cases for a limited and explicit purpose such as the construction and operation of a bridge, toll road, canal, or other public works project.[17] Limited liability and perpetuity were not invariably provided for, and the state governments, wary and fearful, required a separate legislative act for each charter.[18]

This should be noted with care. The quick and easy bureaucratic routines that are required as a commonplace today are a relatively recent approach within the total history of chartering. General procedures now call for the payment of a fee, the filing of by-laws, perhaps a statement of purposes that can be general and can change considerably over the life of a corporation, and the naming of those officers who can—and may—be the sole stockholders. Prior to the great economic expansion of the industrial age in both Britain and the United States, the granting of a charter was viewed as a special and serious matter for a legislative body. As one might expect, corruption accompanied this process; politicians of all times and ages appear to have this tendency. Nevertheless, the one feature of the law that remains a key to our understanding of the corporation has been, despite all, one that has been retained without change: the idea of privilege as the basis for chartering. The societal covenant that binds the corporation to this idea is one that was developed at a time when, it is safe to assume, it was highly doubtful that corporations were seen as the all-flexible instruments they were later to become: the holding company, the interlocking company, the foreign subsidiary, the shell used as the agent for a hostile takeover of another company, or the unit to be sold off by a conglomerate in need of raising cash for operation of other units totally unrelated to the business of such a unit.

The early days of the American republic saw a well-chronicled debate between business interests, perhaps best represented by Alexander Hamilton, and the planter interests who were anti-Federalist. Corporations were not really the focus of dispute, however, until the era of the Taney Court. Taney, the chief justice appointed by Andrew Jackson in 1836, brought to the Court a rural, Southern, and Jacksonian hostility to business and to privilege. Despite this, it was the Taney Court that applied contract law to corporations in the *Dartmouth College* case; and, just as important, this Court decided questions of state chartering procedures, first set up in the 1840s, and of access to the federal courts. It also had to make judgments on strict or loose interpretations of charters, which it viewed as contracts.

THE LEGACY OF STATE CHARTERING

The second major period of the history of corporations in the United States is one that is characterized by the routinization of chartering, which began in the 1830s and 1840s. (The first, which might be called "recognition of the privilege," includes the colonial period and the first fifty years of the nation's history.) This chartering, then as now, was in the hands of state governments. This fact will be explored further; for now, it suffices to show that legislatures did not easily let go of their chartering powers. They developed, in most states, five devices for the protection of the public's interests:

1. Narrow interpretation of charters
2. A reserve clause allowing legislatures to amend any charter at any time and for any reason
3. The creation of independent regulatory commissions
4. In some cases, a time duration for charters
5. In some cases, unlimited liability[19]

Most of these protections, and certainly their scrutinized administration, have long since gone by the boards. But these were popular measures in the period around 1845, because corporations were not held in high regard by the public and were often thought to be synonymous with monopoly.[20]

Britain achieved a like position in corporations law with the passage of the Joint Stock Companies Act of 1862. Because the British do not have a federal system, there was no anomalous or remarkable problem of state chartering. The routinization of corporate chartering was not entirely well received, however, and the Joint Stock Companies Act was mercilessly burlesqued later in the century in two Gilbert and Sullivan operettas, *The Gondoliers* and *Utopia Limited*. In the latter case, so the public would take note of this lampooning, the setting is in the South Seas, the locale of Britain's greatest stock swindle to that date.

The site of corporate chartering is legally (and therefore socially and politically) important in many respects. State chartering is tied to the principle, generally described as a majority or "mainstream" view, that an "internal affairs" doctrine must prevail. This doctrine holds that only one state, the site of incorporation, should be authorized to regulate a company and its relationships with officers, board members, and stockholders. This view runs up against the "outreach" doctrine with which some states claim the right to regulate corporations chartered elsewhere; in recent years, this argument has been mostly centered upon "unitary tax" laws, which are asserted against corporations on their worldwide net profits rather than merely those earned in the taxing state.[21]

This is one of the many confusions and dilemmas of corporations law in a federal system; for although corporations are chartered by one state, they carry out business in others and are therefore subject to the laws of these others. At the federal level, of course, there are hosts of laws and regulations of these state-chartered entities coming from the many and disparate agencies—the Securities and Exchange Commission; Federal Trade Commission; National Labor Relations Board; Environmental Protection Agency; Federal Communications Commission; and the Commerce, Justice, Defense, State, and many other departments and agencies.[22] It can be seen at a glance that federal, rather than state, chartering may have a great deal to commend it in terms of both logic and policy; but despite a campaign of considerable force on behalf of this cause around the turn of the century[23] and by the Ralph Nader public citizen groups in recent decades,[24] there has been virtually no movement in this direction. The issue for the foreseeable future is a dead letter.

A great impediment to such efforts has been the election of what are seen as hostile, probusiness administrations in Washington. And, at a broader level, we have been assured by acute writers and observers that "federalism means inequality,"[25] even though such a description or admonition about our system of government seems, to me at least, to argue against federalism.[26]

The privilege of incorporation, then, is largely in the hands of the states. This means that significant alterations of corporate structure, such as mergers, acquisitions, and hostile takeovers, often wind up in state courts. This was particularly the case in the days of gentle antitrust enforcement by the Bush administration. We are therefore often treated to the interesting and even remarkable spectacle of seeing the fate of a multinational corporation, possessed of billions of dollars of capital wealth, and with subsidiaries in fifty or more countries, being decided in a Delaware or other state court. Delaware, as most observers know, was the winner in the unseemly chartering competition resolved well before the turn of the century. This competition, denounced later by Louis D. Brandeis as an undesirable rush to the lowest common denominator, was fueled by business interests, the state governments, and—perhaps especially—the bar in the various states.[27] Delaware is today the home of more than 40 percent of America's corporations; and the reasons for the unqualified victory of this little state in this big competition are, undeniably, related to the relaxed view that it took at the time on corporations, chartering, and regulation. It is only fair to point out that Delaware corporations law today looks much more like the law of the other states, though some differences remain. Thirty-five states have adopted the Model Business Corporation Act, and a uniformity of corporations law has set in; the major competition between states today has shifted, in fact, to areas such as taxation, labor, and industrial development legislation.[28]

State statutes are nonetheless critically important in the law of corporations. They generally authorize broad discretion to officers and managers while they vary most in matters of stockholder-officer and manager relationships and in regulation of minority stockholders' options.[29] This broad discretion, combined with the "business judgment rule," which gives great leeway to corporate decision making, establishes a wide open arena for corporate actions of all kinds and, many would say, corporate dominance of the economy and political life (see box on page 50).

THE ARGUMENT AGAINST FEDERAL CHARTERING

The argument against federal chartering is one of the oft-repeated routines of the literature on corporations law. The following excerpts are taken from a typical treatment of the subject:

> The repeated refusal to federalize corporate law is based on sound policy reasons. First, having fifty jurisdictions participate in defining the contours of the modern corporate form fosters experimentation. The rapidly changing conditions of the business world continually place new demands on the corporate form. Each of the fifty jurisdictions can respond in its own way to such changes without the tremendous effect that would result if there were only one chartering source. Once successful responses are recognized, other states can adopt them.
>
> A second policy reason, which is closely related to the first, is the desire to create a market for corporate charters. If corporate law were completely federalized, shareholders would have no choice as to corporate form; they would have to accept the corporate form Congress offered. Shareholders, however, may have preferences for a variety of corporate forms. The existence of a pluralistic corporate law system results in competition among the States. If a state corporate statute does not maximize shareholder wealth, corporations can reincorporate [elsewhere]."
>
> *Source:* C. William Baxley, "The Constitutionality of the Delaware Anti-Takeover Statute," *Harvard Journal of Law and Public Policy* 13 (Winter 1990), 344–45

Let us briefly examine these typical arguments. The allusion to fifty states serving as a great variety of social and policy laboratories is one of the more overdone and naive arguments in existence in American politics. It ignores the point that states are undeniably the least responsive level of government to broad-based and progressive citizen concerns; at the same time, they are often manipulated by narrow lobbying groups, including corporations or certain influential industries, in the short legislative sessions, the relatively unknown administrative activities, the media-ignored atmospheres, and the relative isolation from the citizenry that characterizes most, if not all, state governments. The lack of political realism of this first argument is its greatest pitfall.

The second argument is even worse. It amounts to an endorsement of a fifty-member auction conducted mostly at the behest of corporations. Justice Brandeis used the forums of his day, including the Supreme Court bench, to denounce such an exercise as unseemly. It remains unseemly, but the argument made here endorses, all the same, the lowest common denominator pitch made by the states. And the naivete goes on: The writer talks about "shareholders" as though this group, the broad body of owners of a company, would take an active role in this exercise of shopping around for a good chartering or location deal. This would not be the case, of course.

It is the case, however, that a great deal of corporate regulation—in consumer affairs, in labor matters, in securities issuance and regulation, in environmental policy, and in many other areas—takes place at the federal level. There are many problems, to be sure, when regulation is centralized, but there is unquestionably a greater ray of sunshine showing us some of the corners in which the goings-on in Washington occur.

This leaves only room to characterize the type of argument that is being made. The answer: It is lawyerly.

Although a few states such as New York and California do have more restrictive chartering and other laws regulating companies (and it is significant that these are "outreach" states that attempt to regulate internal affairs of noncitizen corporations),[30] the fact remains that broad discretion and political and economic domination of the states and of the nation by corporate powers are the order of the day. This dominance has blurred and perhaps extinguished an understanding of the incorporation privilege. As Brandeis has lamented:

> The prevalence of the corporation in America has led men of this generation to act, at times, as if the privilege of doing business in corporate form were inherent in the citizen; and has led them to accept the evils attendant upon the free and unrestricted use of the corporate mechanism as if these evils were the inescapable price of civilized life.[31]

The giant multinationals of today are of course much larger and even more powerful than they were when Brandeis uttered these words more than fifty years ago. Half a century's efforts of reformers, rule makers, new rules, Naderites, and concerned citizens have been unable to stem the excesses of that age or the even greater excesses of this one.

CORPORATIONS, THE PRIVILEGE, AND THE LAW OF CONTRACT

The privilege of incorporation and the laws and policies one might reasonably expect to flow from recognition that this is a privilege have also been obscured by the history of contract law in this republic. Contract law and its relationship to the business corporation needs to be understood in two senses. The first of these is the recognition of the corporate charter as a contract and the history of this recognition in case law. The second is the broader recognition of a social contract in the Constitution that prevented most corporate regulation for several decades because of the "substantive due process" interpretations of this contract. Because many or most readers will be familiar with the law and these concepts, this section requires only a brief treatment.

Article I, Section 10, of the Constitution requires that "No State . . . pass any . . . ex post facto Law, or Law impairing the Obligation of Contracts." This Contract Clause had been given a narrow interpretation[32] until the Marshall Court decided to place it in a much different light, a generous construction that expanded the meaning of the term "contract" as well as the Founders' concept of "vested" property rights.[33] The signal decision uniting corporations and the Contract Clause was *Dartmouth College* v. *Woodward* (1819).[34] The *Dartmouth* case is often described as a matter of merely historical interest because today state-granted charters provide for changes in state law. But it is a landmark case because it held that a corporate charter is itself a contract founded upon mutuality, consideration, and trust. A legislature cannot therefore alter its terms. Some later decisions, however, do hold that the Contract Clause is no barrier to state regulation.[35]

As is well known, corporations and other defenders of private property grew in time to rely upon the "substantive due process" language of the Fourteenth Amendment much more than upon the Contract Clause. And they further relied, and quite effectively so, upon the Fifth Amendment and its proscription against the taking of any property without due process of law. These constitutional provisions were held out and supported by the Supreme Court on grounds of fairness, logic, and fidelity to a principle of certainty about property rights.[36] It is hardly surprising that this doctrine came crashing down in a case in which a major corporation was a litigant, *Jones and Laughlin* v. *NLRB* (1937).[37]

What is most remarkable, in a logical sense but also in terms of the cause of justice, is that even though the incorporation privilege has remained in place throughout the history of corporate and constitutional litigation, it has seldom been a part of economic rhetoric, and this is particularly the case over recent decades. This is true whatever the source of the rhetoric may be, and this includes the august opinions handed down by the courts themselves. It thus appears more than probable that a popular emphasis upon the virtues of free enterprise capital and the necessity of property rights—and, often in the case of organized conservative interests, just plain noise—have obscured this vital point of privilege.

The second important period of the history of corporations, which began in the 1830s and 1840s with routine corporate chartering and ended with new, or allegedly new, structural changes in the corporation in the 1920s, was one in which the doctrine of privilege of incorporation, though still legally and socially sound, was lost in the emphasis upon business interests, economic growth, and what were construed to be "private" property rights.

THE PRIVATE CORPORATION AND ITS PERSONA

Late nineteenth-century growth of the economy and of the giant corporation was accompanied by one judicial decision after another that broached the traditional stockholder-management relationship long recognized in corporations law.[38] The courts increasingly regarded stockholders as transient interests in a company, who always have available to them the option of selling and placing their investment money elsewhere. Because of this, stockholder use of mechanisms like the annual meeting or the fiduciary responsibility of the management became less possible. The courts validated management prerogatives through strong support of the concept of "piercing the corporate veil."

This doctrine allows, in situations of extremis, for shareholders or other interests to "go behind" the corporate veil—the corporate persona, if you will—in order to right some wrong, some inequity perpetrated by its management.

Fraud or other violations of fiduciary responsibility, the responsibility of trust that is inherent in corporate leadership, could cause this veil to be pierced. The late nineteenth- and early twentieth-century views of courts, however, were more adamantly than ever predisposed against piercing the veil; and with some exceptions today, this remains the case, for

> [i]n a literal sense, the corporate fiction is a basic assumption that underlies many commercial transactions; there must be compelling reasons before a court will ignore such a basic assumption.[39]

Broad latitude is therefore afforded corporate managements, and any corporate lawyer or free enterprise economist will be glad to tell you that this is the way economic life must be foreordained. This was not always the case, and that is for sure; but how can a modern management in a modern corporation otherwise respond to the continuous need to participate in markets with even a modicum of flexibility?

Such a question is not easily answered, especially in these days of calls for a new competitive will to be developed by American-based business and industry in order to stay afloat in the international arena. At the same time, it must be obvious to anyone in the business world that telling shareholders to vote with their feet, to sell their stock and go somewhere else, cannot be justified as an answer to dissatisfaction with management. Shareholders do not invest so that they can leave a company under duress. The Bush and Reagan administrations did come to the rescue. Knowing that shareholders can cause some discomfort at annual meetings and in other forums, the new rule on management compensation issues is that these are not a matter for the transient stockholder to be concerned with; this has therefore been put beyond the pale as an issue and is decided by a compensation committee that is composed of—what else?—in most cases, managers from other firms.

Around 1920, with variations depending upon the firm, corporate control in America passed largely from founder-inventor families to professional managements. This "managerial revolution," commented upon very extensively in the literature on corporations, gave an ostensibly new character to the corporate persona. We can in fact say that the 1920s marked the next era of corporate evolution.[40] Whether this change has had great social or political significance may in some ways be open to doubt, but there is a strong consensus that this marked an important turn of events for the many corporate cultures involved. Let us not be diverted by the installation of this more modern category of corporate leadership, however; for the questions we must ask from a political and social perspective remain the same.

Note that so far we have considered only the matter of shareholders. What about the general public? What kind of levers does it have against corporate mischief? This is an acute question in these days of breach of trust and rampant scandals, as amply reported in any issue of the business press or, for that matter, the general press. The general public surely cannot rely upon the cumbersome ways of antitrust enforcement, or the hopefulness—usually unrealized—of consumer law. They most certainly cannot rely upon the legal profession or the accounting profession and their corporate comings and goings. And what about company employees? These people and their union, if they are lucky enough to have a union, will be subject to all forms of chest beating and blackmail about the need for competitiveness, the threat to leave town, or the need for greater community or other subsidies. The employees are seldom in a position to question such assertions, even though these are usually made by an official whose bloated compensation level—five to six times that usually found in Germany, eight to ten or even eleven times that found in Japan, and a record seventy to eighty times that of the lowest-paid employee in the firm—is a major contributor to the lack of competitiveness.[41]

The short answer to these kinds of questions is that, in general, the American political tradition demands that all forms of power be legitimated by criteria of utility or responsibility.[42] But this is a lame answer to the question of gaining some measure of public control over corporations, because it ignores power realities and the slippery character of free enterprise rhetoric. Criteria of responsibility are hard to come by when one of the axioms of corporations law is that the robes of the corporate persona may be donned at one time and doffed at another.[43] And, again in general, it can be said with no compunction that the corporate persona seems to be an instrument that works well for the convenience of the corporation, but not necessarily for the convenience or fair treatment of anyone else.

THE PROBLEMS OF THE "PRIVATE" PERSONA

Samuel Bowles and Herbert Ginter point out that property rights are a given in American society and that these rights certainly obtain in the case of a private individual. But because we have draped the corporation with the robes of its persona and given it a "private" status, we tend to view corporate property rights in the same way that we look at individual property rights. The "chartered freedom" accorded to corporations provides for a structured association of a clearly discernible kind and nature with legally recognized privileges (again, not rights) and duties. As such, the corporation is no less a privileged political body than is a university, a trade union, a charitable organization, a cooperative, or any kind of nonprofit association. "Corporate property is therefore no more personal than is a university lecture hall or a trade union pension fund."[44]

Bowles and Ginter point out that the ascribing of property rights to a corporation amounts to a depersonalization of such rights. And this depersonalization of property rights, rights that we normally and historically have accorded the individual, is enmeshed in the myth of the corporate persona.[45]

The harm that stems from this is found in according a "private" status to this persona. The question has been asked by innumerable corporate critics, but never really answered: How can we regard a Delaware company, which has tens of thousands of employees, fifty or so international subsidiary branches, and billions of dollars worth of property, as a "private" entity? We know that this entity can make, break, and certainly shape the character of whole communities or sets of communities, that it can aid but can also disrupt our economic lives, and that in some circumstances it has even overthrown, or helped to overthrow, one government in preference for another—in Guatemala, in Chile, in Iran, in the Dominican Republic, and most certainly in the United States. (Anyone who doubts the latter example should review the activities of the corporate political action committee or, better still, look at the vast slush funds acquired by the Nixon regime—most of them illegally—from corporations.) Certainly, corporations affect the tax revenue picture, education, the nation's defense posture, the status of labor-management relations, and the environment. Yet we persist in regarding these agencies of government-like powers—or quasigovernmental powers, to use another form of understatement—as private entities. Their powers are vast, indeed monumental, but in the law they have a status similar to that of Uncle Ed's hamburger stand or Mom and Pop's incorporated corner grocery.

C. Wright Mills, Charles E. Lindblom, Mark Green, Ralph Nader, and a host of acute observers of the American society, economy, and polity have told us that it is more or less sheer folly to regard giant corporations as something that should be clothed in an archaic formulation of persona.[46] Mills in particular has derided anyone who desperately clings to that terribly blurred line that allegedly separates the "private" sphere from the governmental sphere when the subject is the large multinational corporation. To continue to regard the largest 500 American-based corporations as private only encumbers our social vision and our ability to understand our lives and our purposes.

Perhaps it could be argued that it is wrong to demand retention of the traditional idea of the privilege to incorporate while calling for recognition that the great multinational companies are private only in name. It is difficult to be bothered by such a charge. In the first place, one might cynically answer that this is in the grand tradition of corporations law and corporate politics, which recognize the persona fiction for some purposes but not for others; the admittedly true history of doing this shifting mainly in aid of corporations hardly presents a valid objection for doing this to benefit others. Much more seriously and importantly, it can be said with equanimity that recognizing and reviving the doctrine of the privilege of incorporation while also recognizing what corporations in fact have become in the world are complementary parts of the same thread of thought. Both of these claims, in fact, are a part of a strong and admirable American tradition that relies upon skepticism as the proper and realistic stance to take on any matter involving the business corporation.

Realistically, we are required for perhaps a long time into the future to deal with the doctrine of persona and the fact that, since the decision in *Santa Clara*

v. *Southern Pacific Railroad* in 1886,[47] persona is imbedded and intertwined with the Fourteenth Amendment protection the Supreme Court accorded the corporation in line with the Court's laissez-faire economic philosophy. It should be among our priorities, at the opportune time, to alter this terribly misleading characterization.

MANAGERIALISM

> For at least half a century, bureaucracy has been the logical alternative to the market as a principle for organizing human action. Both principles come together in the modern corporation, a bureaucracy operating in a market environment.
>
> —Dennis C. Mueller[48]

The great alteration of corporate character resulting in the managerial takeover of the 1920s brought about two important changes in the structure of the large business corporation. The first of these is self-financing of growth; the second, which is more to the point of the concerns of this study, is the split that occurred between ownership and management.

The self-financing of growth out of accumulated capital was not only a revolutionary development for corporations generally. It was, for a considerable time, a blow to the banks. Banks had relied upon corporate business in the financing of expansion throughout the history of the corporation in America, and this had particularly been in evidence during the exponential growth of the late nineteenth and early twentieth centuries. In certain respects, the banking industry never did make the necessary adjustments to this new direction until well after the Great Crash of 1929 took place.[49] There is a lesson here, because it is clearly the case today that the banking industry is again having to make any number of adjustments to the aftermath of the Reagan-Bush years of wholesale excess, and there are strong signs that they are not succeeding in this. The thrust of the Bush administration was to give banks even more leeway for the supposed purpose of increasing their competitiveness in financial markets by repealing important—and apparently prudent—reforms passed in the 1930s.[50]

The second great change, the separation of ownership and control, or ownership and management, is well-described in the classic work of Adolph Berle and Gardner Means.[51] The inventor-founders of the great companies had either passed on or witnessed the growth of the firm well beyond the size and structure they had controlled. More precisely, managerialism is defined as the idea that large corporations have become powerful, autonomous institutions largely independent of external influence or control. As large businesses, they are able to shape and control their environments rather than being controlled by them.[52]

Philip H. Burch, Jr., author of *The Managerial Revolution Reassessed,* a 1972 study, found the Berle-Means thesis flawed. He demonstrated that a great deal of the relevant data simply were not available at the time they did their research. He also questioned their sample size and their classificatory scheme.[53] Whatever the case, it is manifestly true that any number of large corporations still bear the personal stamp of their founder or founders, and these persons may still hold a significant share of the stock. When this is not the case, a company's culture may carry on for years or even decades in an atmosphere created by the founder. Newer firms obviously reflect the values and outlook of the founder. The Mars family has retained its candy empire and the Fords were important to the automobile firm until very recently. The distinctive culture of Apple Computer, though it is certainly changing now, for a long time was clearly under the influence of its aggressive and imaginative founders.

One important and dominant feature of corporate life of course remains the same even in the case of companies that have moved from family to management control—the ego of powerful controllers of corporate destiny. There is no question that this played a role in the absurd payment of $700 million to Ross Perot to quit the board of directors of the financially strapped General Motors Corporation in 1986.[54] And corporate egos have a curious way of coming full circle in the whirligig of mergers, acquisitions, and hostile takeovers: Some Esmark executives, who had cheerfully fired executives of subunits their company had taken over, found themselves unemployed when Beatrice Foods took over Esmark; but these Beatrice executives were in turn fired by some former Esmark people who were in an investment group that took over the firm and made it a privately held corporation.[55]

DUTIES AND OBLIGATIONS OF MANAGERS AND DIRECTORS

The basic change wrought by the managerial revolution, the separation of ownership and control, sets up new kinds of antagonisms that persist to this day.[56] Unless one is myopic enough to believe that the interests of stockholders and management are virtually the same—and one can easily demonstrate the contrary—it can be assumed that freedom of management from effective discipline by stockholders will enable and encourage the pursuit of its interests. Maximization of the value of the firm, hence, the wealth of the stockholders and probably the long-run interests of the employees (often the most forgotten people in corporate machinations), is quite often a secondary goal of managers as they pursue their own interests. The problem is supposedly met, according to some apologists, by making managers and directors, as well as the controlling shareholders, into fiduciaries who owe certain legally enforceable duties to the corporation and its stockholders, though not the employees or, say, the community in which a headquarters or plant is located. These obligations are the duty of care and the duty of loyalty. The duty of care deals with the amount of time and effort and the level of skill and judgment that the top officers and directors are supposed to bring to the operation of the firm. The duty of loyalty deals with conflict-of-interest problems and the obligation of officers and directors to put the interests of the stockholders—rather than themselves or, most certainly, society at large—ahead of personal gain or any other consideration. Both the duty of care and the duty of loyalty are court-enforceable by the bringing of "derivative" suits by stockholders in the name of the firm against any breach committed by officers or directors.[57]

Remedies based upon the right to sue, however, are less usable and reliable in these days of clogged dockets, tremendous legal expense, and the vagaries and uncertainties of litigation. It is difficult to find successful suits against leveraged buyouts (LBOs) by the management of a firm, for example, even though these almost always bring conflict-of-interest considerations into play. LBOs are discussed in more detail below.

Another remedy, the use of "outside" directors on boards who will presumably look at corporate matters more objectively, has been quite exhaustively studied and found wanting.[58] There is a strong tendency to recruit like-minded people with similar "insider" characteristics and biases, leading to groupthink and other undesirable results. Fiduciary responsibility and loyalty to the firm tend to pale in a milieu of like-minded people. Just as important, management often holds a monopoly on necessary information, and board members are dependent upon management, or its lawyers and accountants, for this information. Because information is power in the corporate world, this situation can hardly breed independent thinking.[59]

Further evidence of the decided difference in interests that exists between shareholders and management can be found in the truism that this is a very common and strongly held perception of the shareholders; and, even more to the point, it is a perception that they act upon. This is why there is a Fund for Stockowners Rights and why many annual meetings, brief and undemocratic as they are, see managements peppered with questions about their policies and, very often, their salaries, bonuses, pensions, and private jet planes.[60]

GROWTH AND COMPETITION STRATEGIES OF THE MULTINATIONAL CORPORATION

At the same time, there can be little doubt that the period in which managerialism was held to be the *major* defining characteristic of the large corporation is past. It continues to exist and it surely is important. By 1960 at the latest, however, the large business corporation had taken on another and equally important characteristic—it had become an interconnected entity, locked into relationships with other corporations in an arrangement that usually looks more like that of a syndicate than anything else.[61] In addition, the large business corporation had become international, or more precisely, multinational, locating its subsidiaries in many countries without owing any particular allegiance to any of them.

Before leaving the managerialist period, however, it is appropriate to mention some of the work of the business historian Alfred D. Chandler, Jr. His findings, familiar to most students of business literature, have much to do with the evolution of the business corporation in America and bear particularly upon the managerialist period. His studies of large business enterprises confirm that they grow in and dominate some industries, but not others. Steel, for example, would fit the first case and clothing the second. These basic industrial structures of the 1880–1920 period developed a remarkable stability, according to Chandler, so that large oil companies, machinery companies, rubber tire firms, and others held their positions within their respective industries over this entire period. These companies had immense advantages accrue to them as a result of being among the first in their respective fields. They enjoyed economies of scale, they had a solid capitalization, and they rationalized production to fit lower unit costs. They therefore maintained their dominant positions in these industries not only through the period until 1920 but through the managerialist and even later periods. It was in the managerialist period, of course, that the great advantage of self-capitalization was most realized.[62]

Chandler also found that manufacturing firms within the same industry tended strongly to formulate the same growth and competitive strategies. The advantages in these arenas, all the same, lay with those "center" firms (his term) that had the advantages of earlier formation and deeper capitalization resources. Most profoundly, Chandler discovered that the patterns he had devised as characteristic of the structures of American industry could also be found in business organizations in other countries. This suggested that universal economic and business principles had been applied in the early phases of the Industrial Revolution and that these were still being applied. This raises a question, a momentarily uncomfortable question, about those whose opposition to big corporations—populist types, Socialists, or others—seems to rely upon a feeling that they are "unnatural" developments.[63]

The case against large corporations made by these people hardly needs to rely upon such an argument in any event, but the findings of Chandler are suggestive in a way that may be analogous to public policy as it has developed in the matter of utilities. Public utilities are regarded as natural monopolies; that is, they are located in industries in which the public interest is said to be served by the presence of perhaps only one firm. Before the Carter-Reagan era of deregulation, it was generally believed that one telephone company or one power company could best serve the public in such industries; in exchange for the privilege of operating a monopoly enterprise, the business submits to regulation of its rates, the prices it charges the public for its services. Because trusts can be seen to develop out of the industrial patterns discovered by Chandler, it could plausibly be argued that these natural patterns call for a strong dose of regulation just as the monopoly conditions enjoyed by a public utility require it. Today, one would be likely to hear the argument that trustlike conditions do not obtain because trusts, after all, are illegal; that foreign competition strongly tends to make regulation unnecessary; and that promoting competitiveness of American-based and traditional industries should in any event be our major emphasis. Although there is some trendiness in these arguments, they still miss the point that antitrust violations continue to occur and these are not in the public interest.

The managerialism epoch did not last long, historically speaking, but it must be remembered that it is still with us; the difference is that since 1960 or so, corporations have accumulated the multinational characteristic as well. Today the corporation is multinational, managerial in terms of control, and based upon the incorporation privilege, even though this seems to be often ignored or forgotten and is routinely brought into existence with simple chartering procedures.

All of these characteristics—multinationalism, managerialism, routinized chartering, and the forgetfulness surrounding the privilege—represent major flaws in the concept and structure of today's corporation; not surprisingly, each of these developments coincides with expansions of corporate power.

FURTHER EXPANSIONS OF CORPORATE POLITICAL AND ECONOMIC POWER

The past two epochs of corporate history have left us with entities that are both interlocked (see Table 3.2) and multinational. They are newly involved, however, in a furious rush of merger, buyout, and takeover activity that is quickly altering their shape and character anew; even though we have always had corporate mergers, even though the pace of mergers is greater in some economies than those of the United States, and even though this pace has slowed a bit in the early 1990s, it is clear that this country has never seen a period of activity that can compare with the scale of 1980 to the present.[64]

But this is getting slightly ahead of our story. It is first necessary to pause and take a look at some of the economic forces and, more pertinently, changes in the law that have accompanied the developments of the later interlock and multinational period and the present merger mania period. There are of course more of these than can be profitably recounted within the confines of a single study, but there are four major concerns—the rise and dominance of corporate PACs, or political action committees, in the political process; the founding of free speech (including commercial free speech) rights for corporate persona;[65] the use of bankruptcy law in the furtherance of corporate aims other than mere relief from creditors; and, not least, the great variety of administrative mandates or, more often, laxities that have been a hallmark of the Bush and Reagan administrations and that may be perceived to be in the corporate interest but are certainly not in the public interest. All of these expansions of corporate power, most of which are exercised at the expense of the rest of us, are further aided and abetted by low levels of corporate taxation at the federal (and often the state and local) level and by law breaking and involvements in what we may call the "underground economy" on what is estimated to be a fairly grand scale.[66]

TABLE 3.2 Interlocking Directorates of Thirteen Major U.S. Corporations

	AT&T	BankAmerica	Citicorp	Chase Manhattan	Prudential	Metropolitan Life	Exxon	Manufacturers Hanover	J. P. Morgan	General Motors	Mobil	Texaco	Ford
AT&T	—	4	21	22	11	17	10	19	18	15	13	2	9
BankAmerica	4	—	3	2	2	4	—	2	2	—	—	—	3
Citicorp	21	3	—	18	14	23	7	26	30	12	9	2	3
Chase Manhattan	22	2	18	—	10	18	3	27	17	8	7	1	5
Prudential	11	2	14	10	—	6	1	8	5	8	6	1	3
Metropolitan Life	17	4	23	18	6	—	9	12	20	24	6	1	6
Exxon	10	—	7	3	1	9	—	3	6	15	6	2	4
Manufacturers Hanover	19	2	26	27	8	12	3	—	25	16	7	3	1
J. P. Morgan	18	2	30	17	5	20	6	25	—	11	2	1	6
General Motors	15	—	12	8	8	24	15	16	11	—	5	3	6
Mobil	13	—	9	7	6	6	6	7	2	5	—	4	6
Texaco	2	—	2	1	1	1	2	3	1	3	4	—	1
Ford	9	3	3	5	3	6	4	1	6	6	6	1	—

Source: U.S. Senate Document 95–107, 95th Congress, 2nd Session, 1978, p. 29.

POLITICAL ACTION COMMITTEES

The story of corporate PACs and their influence has been well-chronicled elsewhere. The details of their operations would put us well beyond the aims of the present work. This is an issue that is greatly bedeviled by First Amendment free expression considerations, so that the crafting of any reforms or regulations in this area would have to be done with special care. Corporations do have freedom of expression, and this freedom must be observed. But what has generally occurred in recent years is the legalization of the buying of candidates, offices, and elections, a process that had been kept better hidden in the pre-Watergate days when such practices were illegal. Those were the days when a myriad of companies were handing over great gobs of cash in paper sacks—literally, in paper sacks—to the Nixon administration to be stored in Chief of Staff H. R. Haldeman's safe. The reforms that established PACs, which were partly the work of liberal lobbying efforts, do have the merit of more honestly portraying the brokerage arrangements that exist between public officeholders and big corporations. But this more open exercise of corporate political power and the relationships fostered by it are still hardly characterized by even scant attention to the public's interests, and it may even be the case that corporate power is marginally enhanced by the more open exertions of influence now permitted.[67] Recent journalistic reports have shown, for example, that candidates and office-holders now seek out PACs on a year-round basis, and these excesses of self-degradation seem to know no bounds.[68] Within corporate structures, it is certain that the presence of PACs can add one more dimension of coerciveness to the lives of employees, for what career-minded hopeful will refuse a request to contribute to the firm's political fund? Even if she/he personally opposes the policy goals and/or candidates to be supported?

CORPORATE FREE SPEECH

The recognition of corporate free speech and corporate commercial speech as rights has occurred as a result of recent Supreme Court decisions.[69] This right heretofore had not been accorded to corporations as part of the whole rationale of the limited liability company, its perpetuity, and especially its persona. It is fair to say that, for the most part, the assertion of a corporation's views has never been a real problem throughout the history of this country. We and all libertarians can nevertheless now be comforted because this new construction of free speech has been officially ensconced within the constitutional framework. This formalization of what had already been going on is significant because this is a nation that places great store in legalities and constitutionalism. If push should ever come to shove, a dislodging of this freedom would be a much more formidable task in the absence of the Supreme Court's landmark rulings of the early 1980s.[70]

Looking at the broad landscape of corporate and constitutional history in the United States, it must be asserted that these decisions nevertheless represent a reneging on the original deal. The original deal was that corporations acquired persona, perpetuity, limited liability for its owners and the privilege—not the right—of doing business and, for that matter, of existing in exchange for a number of considerations; among the latter can surely be found the assumption that a corporation is not accorded the rights in the Constitution that are accorded an individual. This may sound harsh at first, but you as an individual certainly do not enjoy the special privileges, such as limited liability, that we have placed at the door of the corporate world. Fair is fair, as they say, and this has now become a lopsided arrangement if we are to admit that democracy requires some sense of balance.

It is a pity, and in light of this development a greater pity, that corporations do not see fit to grant this right to others at all times. Freedom of expression on the job can be assumed to be a largely unrealized right on the corporate scene. Corporate powers are also loathe to accord free speech rights to other economic entities. The "captive audience" rule remains in effect in the field of labor-management relations, permitting the corporate management's voice to be heard on the subject of union organizing of the employees, but not allowing equal access to the union's arguments. At one time this was permitted by a National Labor Relations Board rule. Likewise, the surveillance of workers, an increasing practice and therefore an increasing problem, inhibits and restricts speech, whether this is done by company informers or done electronically. And leafletting in those privately owned but necessarily public places, the shopping malls, has been fought hard and for the most part successfully. The Supreme Court has also told us that it is okay for a public utility to send out its propaganda with its billings and charge us for it, but naturally, it is verboten for a public utilities consumer group to have equal access to this forum.[71] In sum, the corporate world appears to favor free speech, but mostly, or perhaps solely, for itself.

MISUSE OF BANKRUPTCY LAW

The use of bankruptcy law to serve a variety of corporate purposes is not an unusual practice today or historically, but recent years have seen this carried to new heights—or is it new depths? The various attempts to thwart torts claims, in the asbestos as well as other industries, have received a tremendous amount of publicity in the past few years.[72] Somewhat less attention, it appears, has been given to the destruction of labor contracts and therefore of labor unions through the misuse of the bankruptcy mechanism. Continental Airlines is the firm that helped to set this new practice in place. Once again, the Supreme Court has been benign in its view of these activities, so that even so sacrosanct a capitalist institution as contract law can be compromised in new and clever ways.[73]

THE REGULATORY ATMOSPHERE IN THE BUSH, REAGAN, AND CARTER YEARS

The position of corporations in the economy and in society is profoundly shaped by what government bureaucrats do. The corporate world has had what can only be called an historically favorable atmosphere in which to work in recent years because those who administer the relevant laws, supposedly in the public interest, have often been loathe to do anything. They certainly have been given a wide berth by the Bush and Reagan administrations. This is a widely held public and press perception; but this was also true, by and large, of the Carter administration and probably several administrations before that. Deregulation has been one of the shibboleths of the Bush, Reagan, and Carter years; and the public has borne the brunt of a whirlwind of rewards to anticompetitiveness, which seems to be the long-run result in industries ranging from high-tech to airlines, in reduced standards of meat inspection and job safety, and, replete with scandals and payoffs as well as plain old maladministration, in failing to enforce environmental statutes. There have been very occasional meritorious departures from this mind set, as in the Food and Drug Administration's sometime insistence upon more honest labeling of products or in the Securities and Exchange Commission's cases against Ivan Boesky, Daniel Levine, Michael Milken, Neil Bush, Drexel Burnham Lambert, and other criminals and fraud artists. Such rare events are overshadowed, however, by those gross EPA scandals under Reagan, the dropping of two decades of litigation against the monopolistic IBM Corporation, the wrist slapping Attorney-General Edwin Meese III ordered for E. F. Hutton for its check-kiting scheme, the HUD contract fixers, the Pentagon procurement scandals, the condoning of antilabor violence, and other deviations from the norms of decency. Sometimes the goal of an administration well-endowed with PAC money shows up in the ways it chooses not only to enforce the laws, which often lends a high degree of discretion to officials, but in the guidelines and manner in which a program is administered. The overly generous "HHI Index" formulation for antitrust cases (see below) makes it unlikely that many will ever see the light of day and the decision to place antitrust enforcement largely in the hands of economists, rather than lawyers, are good examples of this.[74]

CORPORATE TAXATION: A SAD TALE

Taxation is one place, of course, where artificial persons could prove that the privilege of incorporation means a great deal to them. Revenue is sorely needed by the federal government: It has a national debt of well over $4 trillion and is looking at annual deficits, in the early 1990s, that will well exceed $300 billion. Unfortunately, and for many years now, as part of the philosophy that what is wrong with the initiative of the wealthy is that they do not have enough money and that what is wrong with the poor is that they have too much money, it has been asserted almost as a truism that American-based corporations do not pursue investment, expansion, and job creation as well as they could because the taxation system is against them.

This has never been true because corporations' tax bills, generally speaking, are not onerous and corporate contributions to the national treasury, if we look at the trend, have been declining as a percentage of sources. The economy-damaging, debt-producing, and income-redistributing (for the wealthy) tax revisions of 1981—it would be wrong to call them a "cut," because for most people they were hardly this—allowed a company, for example, to purchase a tax loss from another firm if it should need one. (This particular piece of nonsense has since gone by the boards.) A recently produced study of corporate taxation—or, mostly, the lack of it—has even concluded that the tendency to invest, innovate, and create jobs is *inversely* related to corporate tax liabilities.[75] (Are low profit margins the best kind of incentive?) More to the point, the discussion of corporate structure, governance, and law that follows, along with the arguments and data on the matters of mergers, acquisitions, and hostile takeovers, will strongly demonstrate no particular need to continue to worry about whether corporations can find the wherewithal with which to amuse themselves as they play financial games of moving assets around and then move them around again. The worry should be directed toward helping corporations to learn the full joys of their privilege and their citizenship by paying fairly for them.

It is ostensibly the case that corporation taxes were increased by the Tax Reform Act of 1986 and again in 1990. I believe in waiting to see what kind of work imaginative accountants and lawyers can produce before concluding that companies will actually see a rise in their obligations to government. But even if we assume that the 34 percent rate now on the books is fully applied without benefit of loopholes or concessions, it is lower than that found in most countries for which data are available (see Table 3.3), and this certainly includes nations that are perceived to be competing well with, or simply outstripping, the efforts of corporations in the United States.

When state and local taxation are examined, the picture most often painted—and most accurate—is one of generous governments falling over one another to provide tax breaks, free use of city services and/or public utilities for a given number of years, sometimes free factories or free land or both, and, perhaps most often, a nearly ironclad guarantee that the work force will be undemanding, docile, and most certainly nonunion.[76] Even these entitlements are often not enough, however, and in a relatively short time, the firm moves to another state, to Mexico, or to a distant Third World nation.

It is therefore a waste of time to worry about corporations losing their incentive to invest because of taxation levels. Their eagerness to hurry along to other locations argues instead for taking advantage of their presence to help finance social programs, education, or capital works. If they are not getting a free ride, they are nonetheless enjoying a level of taxation, hence, a level of social obligation, that is far below their socially possible and even desirable level.[77] What is politically possible is of course another matter. It is difficult to imagine our PAC money-soaked officeholders doing anything meaningful or fair about corporate taxation. Corporations seem more interested, in any event, in taking over one another or merging with one another than they appear to be intrigued by the kinds of investment opportunities we have learned in our business courses that they care about—the hard slog of imaginatively using capital to develop markets, product innovation, or job creation. One perhaps reasonable hope is that exposure to the truths of corporations' tax levels will help to undermine the great mythology we have built over the years about investment and job creation. It has always been a more complex process than this, and it has invariably involved all of us who help to make national prosperity a possibility.

TABLE 3.3 Corporate Tax Rates: Selected Countries

Germany	56% on retained profits, 36% on distributed profits
Denmark	50%
Ireland	Sliding scale from 40% to 50%
Greece	49% with several exceptions
France	45%
Japan	31% to 43.3% on retained earnings, 25% to 33.3% on distributed earnings
Belgium	Sliding scale from 31% to 43%
Mexico	42%
Netherlands	42%
Portugal	Sliding scale from 30% to 40%
Italy	36%
Brazil	35% plus 10% surcharge
Spain	35%
United States	34%
United Kingdom	29% for small companies and 35% for large companies
South Korea	20% for small companies and 33% for large companies, if listed on the stock exchange; 20% and 30% if unlisted
Taiwan	15.25%

Source: "Comparative Corporate Tax Rates in the World," *The Wall Street Journal*, Aug. 22, 1986. Reprinted by permission of *The Wall Street Journal*,

Corporations have contributed more than their share to the activities of what we call the "underground economy," and particularly to the tax evasion arena of this great morass. In this way, it can be clearly seen, corporations have aided in undermining respect for law and for the standards of conduct one might reasonably expect from the privileged position accorded by their charters.[78]

RESTRAINTS ON CORPORATIONS

It cannot be claimed that corporations are without restraints. These obviously exist. The five listed by Ira Milstein and Salem Katsch are federal and state laws on corporate organization, structure, and management; economic leverage brought on one hand by market competition and on the other by antitrust laws; the federal taxation system; direct regulation such as that posed by OSHA, the EEOC, or the NLRB; and social values and public opinion.[79] These restraints, none of which is currently strong and some of which have never been strong, have been notably weakened over the past two decades or longer. None of these restraints, considered by themselves or considered in combination, provides any serious obstacles today to multinational corporate power. They certainly do not amount to countervailing forces of significance.

SOCIAL USEFULNESS OF THE CORPORATION

> The large private corporation fits oddly into democratic theory and vision. Indeed, it does not fit.
>
> —Charles E. Lindblom
> concluding sentence in *Politics and Markets*[80]

Lindblom uses these interesting sentences to close out his renowned examination of the world's politico-economic systems. Despite the clarity of his work, he is often asked just precisely what he meant when he wrote these words. The following is his reply to my query on this point:

> If the Western European and North American nations are democracies, then corporations, which flourish in them, fit into democracy very well. But that is not my argument. My argument is that they do not fit into democratic theory, vision, or aspiration.
>
> By that I mean to point to several features of corporations. They exercise political power or influence disproportionate to the power and influence of ordinary citizens to a degree that I have never seen justified or made place for in any theory of democracy or version of democratic aspiration or vision. The sources of the disproportion are outlined in my chapters on business and include what I call the privileged position of business, . . . also the assignment to corporations as organizations some of the rights and privileges that democratic theory assigns only to persons, also corporate access to funds that can be made powerful in politics, also business' ability to use the corporation as an already existing and ready organization that can be given political assignments, also corporate programs, better financed than those of other groups, for influencing, "educating," or indoctrinating public opinion. Democratic theory sometimes acknowledges these features of contemporary politics as departures from democracy; it does not fit them into democratic theory.
>
> Hence democratic theory continues to be concerned with a factored out set of political processes called democracy rather than incorporating those mentioned above.[81]

Lindblom is hardly alone. The peculiar exceptions made for corporations in democratic theory have been noted by a wide and diverse set of thinkers, including G. D. H. Cole, John K. Galbraith, C. Wright Mills, Thomas K. McCraw, Robert B. Reich, and not least, Robert A. Dahl, a colleague and close collaborator with Lindblom.[82] Some of these writers and thinkers might not agree with

Lindblom's characterization of Western Europe and North America as areas governed by democratic states, but that is not a major concern here.

The point is that the business corporation, as Lindblom states, is not consonant with democratic theory; and it is not a long reach to state that the corporation also fails to fit the spirit of democratic aspiration very well. It follows that if this is so, it is conceivable to think and to say that the business corporation as we now know it is outmoded and no longer needed. Alternative structures, which are possible as well as practical and even efficient within the broad meaning of that term, can and should be developed. Such structures should be democratic in nature and essence and would also be aimed at socially desirable goals beyond the mere acquisition of power and capital.[83]

For those who might say that alternatives will not work, it is necessary to point out that the present corporate structure works neither socially, politically, nor in some respects economically. Until this present era of excess comes to an end—and when it does, it will surely be in part because of the excesses—it is not really rational to argue that the business corporations presently constituted and operative are socially useful, except perhaps to a few narrow interests.

It is necessary, however, to build as we scrap. Social and political institutions cannot be willed out of thin air. This means that four frames of reference must be borne in mind if this building is to occur:

1. *An international frame of reference.* One can only deal with a multinational corporation in a multinational legal framework. The United Nations has at long last started down this road, but it is apparently going to be a long time before any meaningful regulation of companies will occur at the international level. As long as there are Switzerlands or Cayman Islands around that ''understand'' the problems of corporations, whether these be finance, labor relations, or consumer or environmental responsiveness matters, the problems of regulation will continue to be enormous and even intractable. Moral suasion, though limited as a force, can count for something; this was the pressure, for example, that worked to cause some major multinationals to divest themselves of at least the appearance (if not the reality) of doing business in South Africa in recent years. The UN has good potential as a regulatory body because a majority of the membership is made up of Third World nations; and even though these are now lending a more ''understanding'' ear to corporations, they must answer to constituencies that are oppressed by the multinationals. In addition, it is in Third World countries where not only economic pressures but also environmental pressures are most acute—the forests are chopped away with reckless abandon and solid and toxic wastes are dumped there by the industrialized countries—and population and food supply strains. It is also the Third World that best realizes that the world economy, as opposed to the economy of some nations, is in serious decline in such matters as total production.[84]

2. *Continuance, into the foreseeable future, of the corporation as a form of business organization.* Because this is the reality, two arenas—government and the corporation itself—will continue to be terribly important. In the first, this will mean using democratic processes where possible to influence parties, candidates, and officeholders as well as bureaucrats. In those many places in the United States where democracy is seen as a sham involving no meaningful choices or possibilities, political education must be focused for now on this fact in the hope that the potential for democratic aspirations can emerge. In the corporate arena, the governance structures offer little hope of change; nevertheless, it is possible to point out in letters to the editor, points of order at annual meetings, and other forums that taxation levels are unfair and too low, executive compensation levels are too high, the corporation is carrying out reactionary political programs and schemes, boycotts may be necessary, and so forth. The corporate world is diverse enough that examples can be held up to show what is possible. Ben and Jerry's Ice Cream, a Vermont firm, for example, supports a great number of social conscience causes and holds executive salaries down. Just one example, like Ben and Jerry's, can loosen the insistence upon doing things the long-held corporate way in the name of a pseudo "efficiency" or a vaunted matter of executive discretion.
3. *Reestablishment of national-level regulation.* Regulation of corporations can be effective at the margins. It is clear that the people of the United States believe we should have a just society in which health, safety, education, housing, and the general welfare are givens. Such a society is only possible when there are adequate consumer protections, workable antitrust laws and enforcement, an unfettered right to organize labor unions and engage in bargaining with employers, environmental safeguards, regulation of financial institutions, and a sense of social responsibility developed in the business and corporate world.
4. *The development of alternative institutions.* These are already in abundant existence—nonprofit organizations, cooperatives (both for producers and consumers), a great variety of publicly owned or semipublic institutions, and, perhaps most important, the workers' control of industry model, which has been the object of considerable experimentation in Britain and other countries.[85] The development of alternatives is an approach with decided advantages. If the institutions that are founded are indeed superior to the outmoded model, they will develop their own appeal and will in effect make the argument for themselves. If they are not well-grounded in reality, they will surely fail. It will be important to give such institutions a chance to work, and it will be necessary to ensure that they are treated fairly within whatever milieu they find themselves. This is a critical matter, because many kinds of institutions can be said to have never had a fair chance in America—a social democratic party, a national health insurance system, or real employment security programs, for example.

The historically important model of the corporation in America has really failed even on its own terms, but the terms were really never that attractive in the first place. The business corporation, undemocratic in its nature and essence, is an anomaly in any society that has democratic aspirations for its people.

TOWARD THE FUTURE

While we attend to this set of considerations, it will be necessary to emphasize and reemphasize that the business corporation rests first and last upon the generally misused privilege we the public have accorded to it. It will be necessary to ensure that at some point corporations begin to become real members of their communities, to pay their fair share of taxes, and to end our indulgence in their games of blackmail built around the threat of relocation. And it will be important to develop strict and well-enforced guidelines for the treatment of the environment, the community, the consumer, and the company's work force, and to see that these protections do not fall victim to perverse politicians or bureaucrats.

At the moment, we are far away from even these minimal hopes, but insistence upon democratic and humane norms for a democratic and humane society should not be a strange or unacceptable set of goals.

NOTES

1. In late 1991, these included the Bush administration proposal to repeal the Glass-Steagall Banking Act of 1933's protection against bank use of deposits for stock market plays, a variety of federal and state proposals to set limits on damage awards, and the Bush proposal for an unprecedented free trade agreement between a developed nation and a Third World country—the North American Freed Trade Agreement, for which Congress has passed a "fast track" negotiation stance. Many other proposals were developed for such matters as further deregulation and even more regressive tax legislation than we are now experiencing. It is likely that we will be surfeited with even more rightist policy proposals, given the plethora of conservative think tanks planned and already in existence; on the rise of state-level right-wing think tanks, see a Scripps-Howard dispatch by Peter A. Brown dated June 3, 1991.

2. Sheryl J. Wragg, "Corporate Homicide: Will Michigan Follow Suit?" *University of Detroit Law Review* 62 (Fall 1984), 67.

3. Thomas Hobbes, *Leviathan*, Part II, Library of Liberal Arts Edition (orig. pub. 1651) (Indianapolis: Bobbs-Merrill, 1958), 261.

4. *Los Angeles Times*, December 25, 1985.

5. W. R. Scott, *The Constitution and Finance of English, Scottish and Irish Joint Stock Companies to 1720* (Cambridge: Cambridge University Press, 1910–12), ii, 37.

6. Joseph S. Davis, *Essays in the Earlier History of American Corporations*, 2 vols. (Cambridge: Cambridge University Press, 1917), 4–5.

7. Ibid., 6–12; Lawrence M. Friedman, *American Law: An Introduction* (New York: W. W. Norton, 1984), 151; G. R. Elton, *England under the Tudors*, 2d ed. (London: Methuen, 1974), 241–42, 246–51.

8. Allen Sloan and Harold Seneker, "How Posner Profited Even When His Companies Didn't," *Forbes*, April 8, 1985, 42.

9. *Trustees of Dartmouth College* v. *Woodard*, 4 Wheat. 518 (1819); for a brief review of the various theories of the corporation utilized in the law, see Robert W. Hamilton, *The Law of Corporations in a Nutshell* (St. Paul: West, 1980), Chap. 1; also see the excellent collection in Warren J. Samuels and Arthur S. Miller (eds.), *Corporations and Society: Power and Responsibility* (Westport, CT: Greenwood Press, 1987).

10. Harold J. Berman, *Law and Revolution: The Formation of the Western Legal Tradition* (Cambridge: Harvard University Press, 1983), 354.

11. Ibid., 215–21.

12. Charles Mackay, *Extraordinary Popular Delusions and the Madness of Crowds* (London, 1841 and 1842; rptd. New York: L. C. Page, 1932), 52. Chaps. 1 and 2 describe these schemes in detail.

13. Ibid., 50.

14. Ibid., 54–60.

15. Davis, *Essays*, 6–12, 26. The founding of the first commercial corporation in America, the New York Fishing Company, took place in 1675, and the first price-fixing conviction of a manufacturer occurred in 1679; George Kurian, *What's What in American Business* (Chicago: Probus, 1986), 1.

16. Ronald E. Seavoy, *The Origins of the American Business Corporation, 1784–1855* (Westport, CT: Greenwood Press, 1982), xii and Chaps. 1 and 2.

17. Ibid.

18. Ibid., 237. Public utilities commissions came much more into vogue, of course, after the 1877 U.S. Supreme Court decision in *Munn* v. *Illinois*, 94 U.S. 113.

19. Ibid., 238.

20. Deborah DeMott, "Perspectives on Choice of Law for Corporate Internal Affairs," *Law and Contemporary Problems* 48 (Summer 1985), 161–62.

21. The *Michigan Law Review* 82 (April/May 1984) is devoted entirely to the problems of federalism and corporations law and considers a large number of important issues.

22. DeMott, "Perspectives on Choice of Law." Any standard text or casebook in constitutional law will set out the history of parallel regulation, or its lack, in America.

23. Horace L. Wilgus, *Should There Be a Federal Incorporation Law for Commercial Corporations?* (Ann Arbor, MI: Wahn, 1905).

24. Ralph Nader, Mark Green, and Joel Seligman, *Taming the Giant Corporation* (New York: Grossman, 1973).

25. Aaron Wildavsky, "Federalism Means Inequality," *Society* 22 (March/April 1985), 42.

26. Gerald L. Houseman, *State and Local Government: The New Battleground* (Englewood Cliffs, NJ: Prentice Hall, 1986), Chap. 3.

27. Philippa Strum, *Louis D. Brandeis: Justice for the People* (Cambridge: Harvard University Press, 1984), 341 (quoting dissent in *Liggett* v. *Lee*, 288 U.S. at 533 [1933]).

28. James W. Hurst, *The Legitimacy of the Business Corporation in the Law of the United States, 1789–1970* (Charlottesville: University Press of Virginia, 1970), 146. For a discussion of the interstate competition for business and industry, see Houseman, *State and Local Government*, Chap. 14.

29. Ira M. Milstein and Salem M. Katsch, *The Limits of Corporate Power: Existing Restraints on the Exercise of Corporate Discretion* (New York: Macmillan, 1981), 3–4.

30. DeMott, "Perspectives on Choice of Law," 161–198; also see W. E. Kirk III, "A Case Study in Legislative Opportunism: How Delaware Used the Federal-State System to Attain Corporate Pre-eminence," *Journal of Corporations Law* 10 (Fall 1984), 233–60.

31. Strum, *Louis D. Brandeis*, 340 (quoting in *Liggett* v. *Lee*, 288 U.S. at 533 [1933]).

32. *Calder* v. *Bull*, 3 U.S. (3 Dall.) 386, 1 L.Ed. 648 (1798).

33. *Sturgis* v. *Crowninshield*, 17 U.S. (4 Wheat.) 122, 4 L.Ed. 529 (1819); *Fletcher* v. *Peck*, 10 U.S. (6 Cranch) 87, 3 L.Ed. 162 (1810).

34. 17 U.S. (4 Wheat.) 518, 4 L.Ed. 629 (1819).

35. *Charles River Bridge Co.* v. *Warren Bridge Co.*, 36 U.S. (11 Peters) 420, 9 L.Ed. 773 (1837); *Slaughterhouse Cases*, 83 U.S. (16 Wall.) 36, 21 L.Ed. 394 (1873); *Munn* v. *Illinois*, 94 U.S. 113, 24 L.Ed. 77 (1877); *Stone* v. *Mississippi*, 101 U.S. 814, 25 L.Ed. 1079 (1880).

36. *Lochner* v. *New York*, 198 U.S. 45, 49 L.Ed. 937 (1905); *Coppage* v. *Kansas*, 236 U.S. 1, 55 S.Ct. 240 (1915); *Adkins* v. *Childrens Hospital*, 261 U.S. 525, 43 S.Ct. 394 (1923).

37. 301 U.S. 1, 57 S.Ct. 615, 81 L.Ed. 893 (1937).

38. Hamilton, *The Law of Corporations*, 67.

39. Hurst, *The Legitimacy of the Business Corporation*, 58.

40. Hamilton, *The Law of Corporations*, Chap. 6.

41. *Wall Street Journal*, June 4, 1991; *UAW Washington Report*, June 9, 1991.

42. Samuel Bowles and Herbert Ginter, *Democracy and Capitalism: Property, Community and the Contradictions of Modern Social Thought* (New York: Basic Books, 1986), 170.

43. Two of the essays in Samuels and Miller (eds.), *Corporations and Society*, are pertinent here: Chap. 5, "The Idea of the Corporation as a Person: On the Normative Significance of Judicial Language," by Warren J. Samuels, and Chap. 6, "The Jurisprudence of Corporate Personhood: Misuse of a Legal Concept," by John J. Flynn.

44. Bowles and Ginter, *Democracy and Capitalism*, 170.

45. Ibid. 170–73.

46. C. Wright Mills, *The Power Elite* (New York: Oxford University Press, 1956); Charles E. Lindblom, *Politics and Markets: The World's Political-Economic Systems* (New York: Basic Books, 1977); also see Bertram Gross, *Friendly Fascism: The New Face of Power in America* (New York: M. Evans, 1980).

47. 118 U.S. 394 (1886).

48. Dennis C. Mueller, *The Modern Corporation: Profits, Power, Growth, and Performance* (Lincoln: University of Nebraska Press, 1986), 1.

49. Robert Sobel, *The Age of Giant Corporations: A Microeconomic History of American Business, 1914–1984*, 2d ed. (Westport, CT: Greenwood Press, 1984), 76–78.

50. See n. 1.

51. Adolph A. Berle and Gardner Means, *The Modern Corporation and Private Property* (1932; rptd. New York: Harcourt, Brace, 1968).

52. Mark S. Mizruchi, *The American Corporate Network, 1904–1974* (Beverly Hills: Sage, 1982), 15.

53. Philip H. Burch, Jr., *The Managerial Revolution Reassessed: Family Control in America's Large Corporations* (Lexington, MA: Lexington Books, 1972).

54. *Wall Street Journal*, December 1, 1986.

55. Robert B. Reich, "Enterprise and Double Cross," *Washington Monthly* 18 (January 1987), 17–18.

56. Kenneth E. Scott, *Corporation Law, the American Law Institute and the New International Economics* (Stanford: Stanford Law School, 1983), esp. 1–2.

57. Ibid., 1–2.

58. James D. Cox and Harry L. Munsinger, "Bias in the Boardroom: Psychological Foundations and Legal Implications of Corporate Cohesion," *Law and Contemporary Problems* 48 (Summer 1985), 83–135.

59. Mueller, *The Modern Corporation*, 2.

60. See the letter to the editor by Carl Olson, Chairman, the Fund for Stockowners Rights, *Wall Street Journal*, November 26, 1986.

61. Mizruchi, *The American Corporate Network*, 177, says that "to understand corporate control, corporations must be viewed as elements of an interorganizational system." Also see the following, all of which, in their individual ways, support or strongly allude to the idea of networks (or syndicates) of corporate organization and control in America; they believe, in short, that corporate power and organization must be seen as a nexus as much as, or more than, a single unit: Ronald S. Burt, *Corporate Profits and Cooptation* (New York: Academic Press, 1983); David M. Kotz, *Bank Control of Large Corporations in the United States* (Berkeley: University of California Press, 1978); Beth Mintz and Michael Schwartz, *The Power Structure of American Business* (Chicago: University of Chicago Press, 1985); Mark V. Nadel, *Corporations and Public Accountability* (Lexington, MA: D. C. Heath, 1976) ; Michael Useem, *The Inner Circle: Large Corporations and the Rise of Business Political Activity in the U.S. and U.K.* (New York: Oxford University Press, 1984); Thomas R. Dye, "Strategic Ownership Positions in U.S. Industry and Banking," *American Journal of Economics and Sociology* 44 (January 1985), 9–22; Thomas R. Dye, "Who Owns America: Strategic Ownership Positions in Industrial Corporations," *Social Science Quarterly* 64 (December 1983), 862–70; Harold R. Kerbo and L. Richard Della Fave, "Corporate Linkage and Control of the Corporate Economy: New Evidence and a Reinterpretation," *Sociological Quarterly* 24 (Spring 1983), 201–18 (and the debate that follows in subsequent issues).

62. Alfred D. Chandler, Jr., *The Visible Hand: The Managerial Revolution in American Business* (Cambridge: Harvard University Press, 1977).

63. Ibid.

64. This classificatory scheme is influenced by Chandler and by the categories found in standard business texts and other treatments of American business history. Merger activity, obviously, has periods of greater and lesser waves through this history.

65. These two are the most important increases in corporate political and economic power in recent times, according to Edwin T. Haefele, "Does the Corporation 'Fit' in a Democracy? Fictive Persons and Preference Functions," paper delivered to the Annual Meeting of the American Political Science Association, New Orleans, August 1985.

66. Lester C. Thurow, "Off the Books: The Underground Economy," *New York Review of Books* 32 (November 21, 1985), 34–37. Another activity, reported less frequently than in years past but still apparently significant, is bribery of foreign officials; the fact that this is now clearly illegal may have put a damper on some of it.

67. Larry J. Sabato, *PAC Power: Inside the World of Political Action Committees* (New York: W. W. Norton, 1985).

68. Amy Dockser, "Nice PAC You've Got Here . . . A Pity if Anything Should Happen to It," *Washington Monthly* 18 (January 1987), 21–24.

69. *Metromedia* v. *San Diego*, 453 U.S. 490 (1981); *First National Bank of Boston* v. *Bellotti*, 435 U.S. 765 (1968); *Central Hudson Gas* v. *Public Service Commission of New York*, 447 U.S. 537 (1980); *Consolidated Edison* v. *Public Service Commission of New York*, 447 U.S. 530 (1980); Daryl G. Hatano, "Should Corporations Exercise Their Freedom of Speech Right?" *American Business Law Journal* 22 (Summer 1984), 165–87.

70. Walfred H. Peterson, "The Burger Court and Freedom of Commercial Speech," paper delivered to the Annual Meeting of the Western Political Science Association, Las Vegas, April 1985.

71. This decision was handed down in February 1986; the most notable of the shopping center free speech cases is *PruneYard Center* v. *Robins*, 447 U.S. 74 (1980).

72. Mary Kuntz, "On the Docket: Everybody Out of the Pool," *Forbes* 136 (December 16, 1985), 83–86, introduces the torts crisis. Recent research demonstrates that the great liability crisis that is upon us has largely come about because of corporations suing each other; see the *Wall Street Journal*, December 31, 1990. On misuse of bankruptcy laws, see "Chapter 11—A New Way to Break Labor Contracts or to Sidestep Liability Suits," *Business Week*, January 20, 1986, 58–61.

73. Ibid.

74. On the HHI Index, see the next chapter; on economists replacing lawyers in antitrust enforcement, see "Is Anti-Trust a Matter of Economics or Law?" *Washington Post* (national weekly edition), December 28, 1986, 16.

75. Citizens for Tax Justice study as reported in the San Francisco *Examiner*, February 12, 1986.

76. Houseman, *State and Local Government*, Chap. 12.

77. "Big Firms That Pay No Income Taxes," San Francisco *Chronicle*, July 18, 1986.

78. Thurow, "Off the Books."

79. Milstein and Katsch, *The Limits of Corporate Power*.

80. Charles E. Lindblom, *Politics and Markets* (New York: Basic Books, 1977), 356.

81. Letter to the author dated June 25, 1991.

82. Gerald L. Houseman, *G. D. H. Cole* (Boston: G. K. Hall, 1979); John K. Galbraith, *The New Industrial State* (Boston: Houghton Mifflin, 1971); C. Wright Mills, *The Power Elite*; Thomas K. McCraw, *Prophets of Regulation* (Cambridge: Belknap Harvard Press, 1984); Robert B. Reich, *The Next American Frontier* (New York: Times Books, 1983) and *Tales of a New America* (New York: Random House, 1987); Robert A. Dahl and Charles E. Lindblom, *Politics, Economics, and Welfare* (New York: Harper & Brothers, 1953).

83. E. F. Schumacher, *Small Is Beautiful: Economics as if People Mattered* (New York: Harper & Row, 1973).

84. Joyce Kolko, *Restructuring the World Economy* (New York: Pantheon, 1988).

85. Robert A. Dahl, "Power to the Workers?" *New York Review of Books* 15 (November 19, 1970), 20–24; also see Dahl, "Workers' Control of Industry and the British Labour Party," *American Political Science Review* 41 (1947), 875–900.

4 Questioning Merger Mania and Corporate Regulation

A summer of shame and scandal in financial markets around the world is raising questions about the ability of regulators to protect investors from fraud, favoritism and price-fixing.

—*Wall Street Journal*, August 28, 1991

Regulation is a lagging indicator.

—Richard Breeden, Chair,
Securities and Exchange Commission[1]

THINGS HAD SUNK SO LOW in the financial world by the late summer of 1991 that an enterprising baseball card manufacturer started producing cards featuring Charles Keating, Ivan Boesky, Michael Milken, and other figures associated with the various insider trading, check-kiting, savings and loan failure, T-bill auction-fixing, and other scandals that rocked Wall Street and other financial centers.[2] This overarching greed truly reached international proportions, with scandals shaking (for example) the Tokyo Stock Exchange and much of the international banking fraternity that had associated itself in one way or another with the Pakistan-based Bank of Credit and Commerce International (BCCI); the magazine *Asiaweek* reported that the financial world from Tokyo to London was reeling.[3]

It is far from certain, all the same, that many of those absorbing their information from the *Wall Street Journal*, *Business Week*, *Forbes*, *Barrons*, *Fortune*, or similar sources were concluding that the problem might be systemic. More often than not, a shoulder-shrugging, people-will-always-be-that-way, business-as-usual response prevailed.

In a way this is strange, because articles or stories depicting labor union foibles or corruption will often bring the analysis from such readers, and certainly from these publications, that the problem is indeed systemic.[4] Whatever the case may be, it is certainly true that many or most of us are conditioned to accept existing structures and arrangements, including corporations and their malregulation, as some kind of ultimate rationality. And this is the case in business or economics or political science or any field because that which exists is the "given" and anyone who questions existing arrangements may well be seen as beyond the pale.

CORPORATE STRUCTURE AND RATIONALITY

Some of these people undoubtedly hold to something resembling the Edmund Burkean stance that those who question tradition should reexamine themselves; tradition, after all, is the accumulated and culminated wisdom of the ages. As has been shown before, however, corporate traditions are not very old in the present-day schemes of business, legal, governmental, or cultural affairs. The corporation only became the dominant form of business organization in the third and fourth decades of the nineteenth century in the United States, and there is some evidence that it may have already served out most of its days of usefulness. It may have to give way to other forms of commercial or social arrangements sooner than most of us think. It has had to make great changes to date in order to survive—from small to large, from family owned to managerial, and from national and/or local to multinational. Whether it has the flexibility and vision needed to continue remains to be seen.

It might be stated, in the wake of the enormous changes going on in eastern Europe and what is less and less referred to as the USSR, that the corporation is going to come into its own more than ever. We do not know, however, what is going to happen in that part of the world. We do know that the opinion polls taken in those areas show a preference not for a U.S.-style capitalist model of an economy, but instead for a Swedish-style social democracy in which corporations surely play an important role. This role is nonetheless tempered by a commitment to a social reality that entails safety nets and floors of various kinds in order to make inhumane circumstances of life less likely to occur, at least in an economic sense.

A NEW CORPORATE EPOCH

Now the corporation is embarked upon a new epoch of basic structural change and of social response to this change. From the days of easy chartering to managerialism and even multinationalism, we have never seen anything quite like it. This new change, begun around 1980, transforms it from a producer and seller of goods to a banklike buyer and seller of securities and, most notably, of other companies. This newest and most dynamic change of course may be signifying death throes, but no one can be sure. Corporate defenders would merely say that it demonstrates flexibility and an awareness of subtle changes occurring on a day-to-day basis in the worlds of finance and commerce. Some of the gurus of business studies, such as Peter Drucker, have in fact looked at the corporate future and have deemed it to be bright indeed. Whatever is signified, it can be shown that the public interest is seldom a measure, concern, or "given" in these acts of massive movement of assets across the chessboard of corporate relationships; and, I would argue, it is an irrational state of affairs that lies at the basis of all of this activity.

If rationality is to be a criterion, moreover, it must be pointed out early and often that in other climes and places, the corporate model as most Americans know and appreciate it has been rejected, reformed, or even slated for future oblivion. In Sweden, for example, where low unemployment and inflation rates have predominated for much of the time since 1945, a stock purchase system has been established that is centered upon the nation's trade unions; therefore, in a couple of decades, the unions might well own the companies. No one really knows how this will work out because it has not been done before, and there are some wide loopholes in the law. The point is that Sweden has turned its back on the profit-making corporation as the key to its economic and social future.[5] This shows, incidentally, that the Soviet model so often held out as the alternative to the American system is hardly the kind of scheme to which we must resort; the alternatives are as limitless as the imagination of humankind, and these unquestionably include cooperatives, worker-controlled firms, perhaps union ownership, and an array of other possible experiments.

Corporate defenders may well concede that things could be made better, that these institutions are undemocratic, or that they control too much of our political and economic lives. There is a trade-off, all the same, that they will point to, namely, that corporations are the best profit-making machines yet devised and that they are vital to economic growth. Even the most casual observer must concede that the business corporation is often a great earnings mechanism, and it certainly does contribute to economic growth. It is decidedly not the case, however, that mergers, acquisitions, and takeovers improve corporate growth and performance. Often as not, the furious and ego-driven games played with corporate assets yield uncommonly baleful human miseries and community disasters. In addition, the cause of growth requires examination in light of a considerable number of problems that, if done in detail, will move us well beyond the goals of this study. We do know, however, that heedless growth can hurt the environment, produce social and political tensions, and even undermine the traditional goals of the business corporation. We further realize that an emphasis upon short-term profit and growth goals, which are all too often the operations base of American managements, may not even be in the best interests of the firm. Finally, a "small is beautiful" economics has emerged over the past two decades that calls for sensitivity to human-scale needs as well as to the needs of the environment, and this viewpoint eschews growth as the "ideology of the cancer cell."[6]

RATIONALITY AND ORGANIZATION

The quest for rationality in the organizational forms found in society invariably leads to the examination of organizational behavior. It is plain that organizational behavior, including that of business corporations, cannot solely be understood in rational terms, just as it cannot be solely understood in economic terms. We have benefited from years of exposure to the work of Luther Gulick, Everett Maslow, Francis E. Rourke, Dwight Waldo, and others who have pointed out that large organizations reflect, to an overwhelming degree, the interests—and the irrationalities—of the people who run them. Many decades have passed since Thorstein Veblen set out the psychological importance and psychic values attached to status. The modern classics of organizational behavior invariably allude to, and often analyze, the irrational aspects of the corporate world and even corporate structure.[7] John Kenneth Galbraith has penetrated the nature and purposes of the corporation and concluded, with ample impressiveness, that these organizations exist for purposes that often have little to do with making a profit. At times and in any number of circumstances, the behavior patterns of large corporations differ little from those of large government bureaucracies.[8] In light of this, it is not surprising that deep and informative thinkers such as Hannah Arendt have questioned the setting up of "public" and "private" spheres of activity. The methodological, analytic, and philosophical problems with such assumptions are daunting and go well beyond the shallow suppositions and superstitions of the business world.[9]

THE CORPORATE POWER ELITE

It has already been pointed out that there is a thoughtful literature of the social sciences that denies that many differences lie between the goals, administrations, and leaderships of large government departments and large corporations. The "power elite" framework best identified with the late C. Wright Mills argues that a small elite governs the nation and that this often shifts leadership positions between the governmental and private sectors. Mills held that the elite institutions, all of which are repressive, are political, military, and corporate.[10] They are led and controlled by members of an elite that is neither responsive to popular will nor committed to principles of democratic governance. Without going further into Mills' viewpoint or into the work of the hundreds or more social scientists who have extended and refined his great contribution, it can be seen that the characteristics as well as the personnel of these institutions—if Mills was right—can be expected to take on more similarities than differences. They are, after all, a cohesive group.[11] It goes without saying that those who do not support a Millsian "power elite" view may cling quite rigidly to the line that supposedly separates the public and private spheres. Certainly, this seems the case, for example, with Presidents Bush and Reagan and the members of their staffs.

It is also the case, however, that close analysts of the business corporation who work within the business and economics disciplines have come to recognize that the classic view of rational economic actors, those shadowy characters who people the worlds of the supply and demand charts, is largely inapplicable and almost useless when it is applied to the business firm.[12] I do not understand why, but economists—and, for that matter, political scientists and public administration specialists—seldom concern themselves with the mistakes of the corporate world. Business faculties do, of course.[13] But an amazing amount of ignorance continues to reign as facile observations are made about corporate behavior, about the motivations of executives and boards, and about the alleged chasm between large organizations that are supposedly private as opposed to public. A great deal of free market myth and just plain wishful thinking is built upon these particular sinking sands.

It is critical, as we look at the great (and great amount of) activity surrounding mergers, acquisitions, and hostile takeovers, to bear in mind that we are dealing with what is often an ego game. A major merger broker has described ego as a very important factor in the process, and the literature on this subject has made this amply clear.[14] It follows that on a great many occasions, this ego problem may be collective; that is, the activity undertaken may be satisfying many more elite people than just the chief takeover artist. The merger brokers, the bankers, the defending and promerger lawyers, sometimes the accountants, the "white knight" company officials, and any number of other participants may feel that this is a game of satisfying aggressions and related instincts, fighting a nonviolent war of thrust, counterthrust, and nerves. They do tend to verify Veblen.

WHY MERGERS, ACQUISITIONS, AND HOSTILE TAKEOVERS? AN EXAMINATION OF PROCESS AND RATIONALE

> Takeovers are destructive.
>
> —A prominent merger attorney[15]

> You've got perhaps ten men guiding the future of corporate America.
>
> —Ivan Boesky, well-known arbitrageur, merger investment specialist, and convicted inside trader[16]

Mergers, acquisitions, and hostile takeovers are still hot stuff. The past two or three years have seen a slackening of this activity, but 1,500 to 3,000 of these deals took place in individual years in the 1980s.[17] The dollars involved were less than $20 billion a year in 1974, more than $40 billion in 1980, approximately $180 billion in 1985, and well over $200 billion in 1986. These combinatory activities have remained above an annual level of $100 billion.[18] The fourfold and greater increase that occurred in the years 1980 through 1986 shows that a major restructuring of corporate America has taken place and is still going on. The end, in fact, is nowhere in sight. This major surge of restructuring has compelled the establishment of a new period in the history of corporations based in America. The results of this tremendous and far-reaching activity are as revolutionary as the ownership-management split or the development of multinationalism. We have the shifting of capital, jobs, headquarters and plants, ownerships, debt burdens, and instruments of finance on a massive, indeed on a record, scale in a relatively short period of time, and no one seems able to gauge all of the effects that can be expected from all of these activities (see Tables 4.1 and 4.2).

It should be asked, if this analysis is going to be consistent, whether this merger, acquisitions, and takeover activity makes any difference in the way we should think about corporations. After all, it has been seen that a great many writers and observers believe that the largest multinationals are now networked and combined into nearly omnipotent political and economic forces.[19] What difference does it make, in light of this characterization, that General Electric and RCA become a single organization? Or that IBM buys MCI Communications? Or that this giant oil company is taken over by that giant oil company?

TABLE 4.1 The Fifteen Largest Takeovers to Date

ACQUIRER	TARGET	VALUE ($ bil)	DATE
Kohlberg Kravis Roberts	RJR Nabisco	$24.72	4/89
Chevron Corporation	Gulf Corporation	13.30	6/84
Philip Morris	Kraft	12.64	12/88
Time Warner	Warner Communications	12.64	1/90
Bristol-Myers Company	Squibb Corporation	12.53	10/89
Texaco	Getty Oil Company	10.13	2/84
Beecham Group PLC	SmithKline Beckman	8.28	7/89
British Petroleum Co. PLC	Standard Oil Ohio*	7.56	6/87
Dow Chemical	Marion Laboratories**	7.08	12/89
E. I. Du Pont de Nemours	Conoco Inc.	6.92	9/81
Campeau Corporation	Federated Department Stores	6.51	7/88
Kohlberg Kravis Roberts	Beatrice Cos. Inc.	6.25	4/86
United States Steel	Marathon Oil	6.15	3/82
General Electric	RCA Corporation	6.14	6/86
Grand Metropolitan PLC	Pillsbury Company	5.76	1/89

*Bought remaining 45% of company
**Bought 67% of company

Source: Mergers and Acquisitions 25 (Philadelphia: MLR, September/October 1990), p. 88.

The truth must be admitted that mergers, acquisitions, and takeovers, even at the new highly accelerated level, do not do much to basically alter or affect such a characterization except to give it a little more verification and justification. The more naive writers and observers seem to regard it as conglomeration gone amok. This is the kind of activity that excites many of those on the sidelines—business writers and the financial press, for example, as well as droves of popular-level "how to" writers who are interested in telling the public how to make a fast buck so that they can make a fast buck. And it emphatically involves those who are concerned with business and corporate efficiency, profit purposes, and rationality. It should also concern those of us interested in the public questions raised, for it is obvious that the great spate of mergers, acquisitions, and takeovers is aimed at (1) concentration that can further centralize and strengthen the elite forces in our society or (2) the use of corporate assets or the stripping of such assets through capital transfers from one subunit to another or through selling a subunit. We also know there can be deleterious effects upon consumers, workers, communities, and the environment. It is possible that research and development can be hurt or can become misguided. There are taxation questions that are surely affected by such activity, including the main one of these: Why do we have a taxation system that rewards the indebtedness that is almost always a major element of these efforts? There are international implications for trade, competitiveness, and such concerns as Third World development and international debt. Some Canadian critics of U.S.-based corporations have stated that the declining international trade position of the United States and the corporations situated within it is a major reason for the feverish merger, acquisition, and takeover mania of recent years.[20] And speaking of debt burdens, those that are established as a result of takeover activity, whether in the form of bonds issued by the attacker or of the increased debt taken on by a firm as a result of a successful or unsuccessful takeover fight, could have disastrous economic results. There is little question that ethical, legal, and policy problems are raised by all this activity and that much of it informs us about the character, expectations, and policy results that are endemic in a capitalist system.

MANAGEMENT AND REGULATION

Merger mania also raises more mundane management questions, but some of these have far-reaching social results. The manic tendency is now part and parcel of the system, says Richard Phalon:

> The short-term incentives that make management run are part of the equation. . . . If the size of an executive's paycheck is keyed to such indicators of annual "performance" as pre-tax profits, return on equity, or the market price of a company's stock, there is at least a subliminal bias in the direction of instant gratification. Takeovers are one way to

> make the numbers and make them now, whereas the returns on long-term plowback of capital into new fields usually take a long time to realize.[21]

A great deal of business literature of recent years has told us that American managements are too short-term in their perspectives and in their expectations of association with a firm. Japan is held out as an example to emulate in this arena, even though such comparisons are often too facile or even invalid. But it must be conceded that the point we are mainly concerned with here, that incentives in executive compensation schemes and perks may lead to merger or takeover activity, is a possibility or even a commonplace event. It is also the case that many compensation schemes reward executives regardless of performance. No clear compensation pattern exists; and the stockholder has been relieved of the right to establish or even question compensation levels through the enactment of recent Securities and Exchange Commission rules. Such rules seem out of line, not only for reasons that support democratic theory, but because compensation levels in the United States are now the highest in history—eight to ten times the level of Japan, five or six times the level of Germany, and 72 to 80 times the compensation level of the lowest paid employee.[22]

Another obvious cause of merger, acquisition, and takeover activity is the easy-going regulatory atmosphere found in Washington in recent years. This unfortunate state of affairs exists across the board—the SEC, the Commodity Futures Trading Commission, labor regulation in agencies such as the NLRB and OSHA, consumer protection agencies, and antitrust enforcement. Although the classic Republican argument made by Presidents Bush and Reagan condemns centralization in government as wrong, centralization in the corporate world is apparently right and good. The blindness is complete on every front: Secretary of Commerce Robert Mossbacher used donated corporate jets to travel around the country; his predecessor, Malcolm Baldrige, even denied that such a thing as ''merger mania'' exists, ignoring the government's own statistics.[23]

TABLE 4.2 Major Industries Involved in Mergers, Acquisitions, and Hostile Takeovers Since 1983

advertising	electric appliances	oil
aerospace	electric batteries	paper
airlines	electronics	railroads
banking	food processing	real estate
brokerage	food retailing	soft drinks
cellular radio	genetic research	telecommunications
computers	liquor	transportation
cosmetics	mass media (of all kinds)	
department stores	mining	

One last point before we take up the merger, acquisitions, and hostile takeover process in greater detail: All corporate changes of this kind are burdened with transaction costs; that is, a host of costs comes into play when this kind of activity, ultimately successful or not, is undertaken. Not the least of these are the heavy fees paid out to merger brokerage firms, accountants, and other professionals who provide services. One prominent New York law firm involved in these processes no longer even bothers to bill by the hour, but sends out flat fee statements of several million dollars. The transaction costs also include relatively small things such as changing the company logo and name and even the stationery. Those who defend these activities, then, must defend the taking on of these expensive burdens, which for any company amounts to a substantial financial commitment.

BEGINNING STEPS OF THE PROCESS

The combination process begins with a lie. This is because the Williams Act of 1968 requires disclosure of ownership of significant blocks of securities; and if a takeover artist such as T. Boone Pickens, Carl Icahn, or Victor Posner acquires, with the use of a shell corporation, as much as a 5 percent interest in a company, this must be disclosed. (This may sound fair enough as a requirement, but President Ronald Reagan urged its abolition.[24]) When this information is provided to the Securities and Exchange Commission, it will be accompanied with an explanation.[25] This explanation, which will appear in the financial press, is invariably a statement that the acquirer has bought into the company for solely investment purposes. No one, of course, believes this, especially if the investor is a well-known attacker or takeover artist. It is assumed that this is a lie, and in the vast majority of cases, it is.[26] Before such an item even appears in the financial press, however, informed investors will have bought into the stock; for despite the SEC rules against insider trading or disclosure, the tips will be out on Wall Street. The trading activity of a merger or takeover target invariably shows that this is the case.[27] When the stock really begins to take off as a result of the buyout expectations, these insiders will of course profit. The biggest insider of all, obviously, is the investor who has reported his or her 5 percent or greater interest, and this person can be expected to profit merely from buying into the company and staking out an interest. Because the stock will go up on this information in most circumstances, the acquirer can to a major extent determine his or her own profit in a way that is analogous to the proverbial shooting of fish in a barrel. At the very outset of the takeover process, then, we have three ethical and legal policy problems to grapple with: the lie itself, the insider money-making caused by the announcement and the tips prior to the announcement of this lie, and the self-directed insider advantage of raising the price of securities merely by stating an interest in them.

ANTITRUST NONENFORCEMENT

A second set of problems presented almost immediately by buyout activity is found in antitrust considerations and enforcement. This is particularly the case in the proposals for mergers or takeovers that are horizontal, that is, those that involve the combining of former competitors. (It is the opinion of a set of writers on corporations law, including the present one, that vertical mergers can be just as bad for the economy, the political system, and the general public as horizontal ones.) At the moment, it would be difficult to characterize antitrust enforcement as anything other than lax. Mark Green and John Berry quote a writer who has said that the current kinds of administration with which we have been blessed operate ''on the theory that the bigger government gets the more wasteful it gets, while the bigger business gets the more efficient it gets.''[28] Neither the Bush nor the Reagan administrations demonstrated anything other than a considerable sympathy for the combination process. Neither of them offered any programs or plans for dealing with the catastrophe of merger mania. In fact, both administrations maintained what critics call a ''fix-it'' policy by which the government often counsels merger and buyout candidates. The merger or other combination can thus proceed as the company or companies fix potential antitrust problems by selling overlapping divisions or by making other suggested adjustments. Congress, after all, might get interested in any terribly overt shenanigans, though this is quite unlikely. The ''fix-it'' process has the undeniable effect of making the Justice Department a regulator rather than a prosecutor, and it is in fact an understanding partner in the combination process.[29] In addition, the Reagan administration devised an ''HHI Index,'' which the Bush administration carried on, which was developed to determine whether monopolistic or oligopolistic conditions are threatened by a proposed merger or takeover (see box). This index, named after Herfindahl and Hirschman, has the virtue of relying upon a simple formula, but it has the defect of being a much more lax and watered-down guide to measuring monopoly or oligopoly than has been used in the past.[30]

Unfortunately, even this formula is often jettisoned because, apparently, the government is not particularly concerned about antitrust problems. The Robert Bork view holds sway. Bork, an influential legal scholar, former federal judge, and unsuccessful Supreme Court nominee, has written a treatise, well-accepted by the faithful, that argues that antitrust law is hopelessly outdated, unworkable, and ultimately unenforceable.[31] It is true that we still have a Justice Department with an Anti-Trust Division and a Federal Trade Commission; but the philosophy of the administrations in power since 1981 and perhaps before, and the liberal guidelines of the HHI Index, if they are observed at all, cut their work loads tremendously. So we have this second and crucial set of problems also raised at the outset of the process, and the interests of the public will and the public good are hardly being heeded.

THE HHI (HERFINDAHL-HIRSCHMAN) INDEX AND HOW IT WORKS

The HHI Index, devised by the Reagan administration and used in the Bush administration, is a much more generous measure than has been used in the past. It sets a figure that determines the competitiveness of a given industry. With this Index, 10,000 equals a perfect monopoly and 0 is a totally atomistic market. A merger, buyout, or takeover that increases the Index by 1,000 or more will result in antitrust action; and a smaller increase will result in no action. These are said to be rough estimates of a given situation, but neither the Reagan nor the Bush administration ever deviated from this guideline.

For an example of how the HHI works, let us assume that the be-bop industry is made up of five firms:

Firm A has 35% of the market
Firm B has 25%
Firm C has 25%
Firm D has 8%
Firm E has 7%

The HHI for this industry is 2,588, a figure achieved by squaring each percentage of the market held by one of the firms. The computation is

$$35^2 + 25^2 + 25^2 + 8^2 + 7^2 = 2{,}588$$

A combination of Firm A with Firm B would obviously call for action because the HHI would be raised by 1,750 points to 4,338, and a merger of A and E would call for no action, bringing the HHI only to 3,078. In addition to supplying a generous formula, the government signals in advance whether antitrust action is likely in a given situation.

Receipt of the offer of purchase causes no conniptions in the target company if this offer is friendly, that is, if the offer carries no apparent threat to the future of the firm's viability, employees, or, most especially, its top management. (Employees often lose out even if the merger is a friendly one.) In these rather chummy circumstances, the offer is usually anticipated at a certain point in time. Unfriendly offers, however, are often unanticipated and can cause a great deal of consternation. Will the firm continue to exist in some recognizable form or another? In the case of the profitable and well-run Carborundum Corporation, the answer was clearly negative; and because the takeover interests had no attention-span requisite for taking care of the conventional operations of Carborundum, they bled the assets of the company and then allowed it to die.[32]

On other occasions, the word goes out to stand and fight. Lucky Stores, faced with a buyout threat recently, fought to the last employee for its right to remain unsullied and independent. The company purchased large amounts of its own stock to fend off a proxy fight, not an atypical response to a hostile takeover bid. It then closed its profitable Gemco outlets, firing 14,000 people, whose only fault was picking Gemco as their employer. This suggests another question: Will the firm be able to maintain its labor policies or, in some cases, its labor contracts?[33] Employee rights, it seems reasonable to assume, should be a paramount concern.[34]

THE FATE OF MANAGEMENT—AND THE COMPANY

The question usually treated with greatest concern and reverence, both at the level of action and in the business press, is what kind of treatment is going to be accorded the management and top executives of the target company. Will they be called upon to provide their expertise and leadership, or will they be shunted aside? In the case of the Carborundum Corporation, the unwise decision to throw out the management was made early. In all such cases, of course, undertakings are given by the takeover company to the effect that everyone's best interests will be taken into account; all the same, managements find that even after the most soothing of words are uttered about their future, they are abruptly or gradually replaced. Book company executives have found to their dismay, in one instance at least, that they were replaced by broadcasting industry people when the latter took over a publishing firm; it was explained that, after all, broadcast personnel, like book people, are in communications. Generally, experience shows that the very top-level people in a firm have nothing more to fear than a ''golden parachute'' arrangement of pay and other considerations of severance that will make them rich even if they are no longer powerful. In taking Beatrice Companies private, which admittedly was one of the best of such deals, $30 million of corporate assets were allocated for six top officials and another $30 million was divided among 54 senior vice-presidents and other lesser officials.[35] Such a draining of corporate assets, even in a big firm like Beatrice, seems hardly justified for the purposes of a leveraged buyout. Certainly no social end can be seen in such an arrangement. The SEC and Justice Department have recently been looking at such arrangements a little more carefully (which is not saying much), and in the case of some firms, stockholders have registered strong protests or even filed suits.

Within the very narrow and restricted terms of the capitalist and corporate worlds, an agreement to a tender offer, or a proposal for a buyout, may be justified or unjustified.[36] There may be some economic or profit sense in not resisting a tender offer, and this may well be in the best interests of the stockholders. It may also be the case that resistance is the best course to follow in the interests of the future of the firm, its managers and top officers, and perhaps the stockholders. These arguments must be looked at from a wider perspective, however, because the decision to resist, for example, can have social, political, and economic effects that go well beyond the narrow confines of a single company. Before doing this, however, it is necessary to take a harder look at what a leveraged buyout really is and to examine the rewards and the depredations of "greenmail," the moneys paid to takeover attackers who fail in their quest to win control of companies.

WINNING BY LOSING: GREENMAIL

It is necessary to point out, before proceeding with any further description or analysis of the merger and buyout process, that many tender offers are made with no thought of actually taking over a company. The objective in this case is to lose the takeover battle by being bought off with greenmail. Greenmail is the premium over market value paid by a company to a takeover artist for its own stock in order to obtain this person's withdrawal from a proxy fight, the fight for control of the firm. Let us assume a market value of $40 per share. It goes perhaps to $52 on the news of a takeover attempt. Again, the reader is reminded that here is already a great short-term appreciation on an investment that has occurred merely because the takeover artist decided to make it happen. Let us further assume that after considerable legal and proxy-fight maneuvering, the takeover investor is prevailed upon to sell her or his interest in the company and to give up the thought of taking it over. When this occurs, there is a contract drawn up that guarantees that the takeover artist will not try to do this again for a set number of years. In exchange for this agreement, the stock held by the attacker is bought by the company for a price of perhaps $62. These terms would not be considered unusual in a takeover fight. It should also be remembered that the takeover investor accumulated this stock while lying about it to the SEC, as one invariably does, and saying that the accumulation was only for investment purposes.

Most takeover attempts result in greenmail, not in the acquisition of control. In other words, most takeover attempts are unsuccessful and, it is often alleged, are meant to be. The takeover investor would have to actually run a company if he or she won, and that is not usually the object of this game. Greenmail amounts can be substantial. Some recent examples are $100 million paid to Sir James Goldsmith by St. Regis Paper, $163.6 million paid to Carl Icahn by Chesebrough-Ponds, $180 million given to Rupert Murdoch by Warner Communications, $325 million paid to Saul Steinberg by Walt Disney Productions, $471.7 million awarded to the famous (or infamous) T. Boone Pickens by Phillips Petroleum, and $1.28 billion paid to the Bass brothers by Texaco.[37]

Greenmail payments can substantially weaken a corporation; in the Disney case, for example, the floating of a large amount of debt was necessary to pay off the takeover artist and the company's debt-to-equity ratio was for a time severely affected. This ratio is presently at near-record levels for all of corporate America, and much of the reason lies in these kinds of activities. Some companies sell off assets and others turn to high-interest instruments known as junk bonds. Whatever financial strategy is decided upon, the corporation can only come off badly from a takeover battle.

Losing the fight is obviously not so bad for the takeover specialist. No management chores have to be undertaken, after all; the agreement to give up future attempts to take over a firm is hardly a major sacrifice. There are thousands of listed companies to which one may turn in order to begin the process all over again. In the case of well-known takeover investors, such as Icahn, Pickens, the Belzberg brothers of Vancouver, Canada, or Victor Posner, one usually expects little else. Research is carried out to find ripe candidates that have the features of a strong cash position, little or no debt, by-laws that are amenable to a takeover effort, and, ironically, sound management. In a well-publicized endeavor, one takeover artist offered a prize of $100,000 to the member of his class—he was a part-time instructor—finding the best takeover candidate for him.[38]

Considering the tremendous harm and possible economic ripple effects caused by greenmail, the business press and even some law journal treatments of the subject show an amazing indifference, an attitude that might charitably be called a benign overview.[39] One might expect defenders of capitalism to look askance at processes that may have the tendency to undermine their beliefs, their propaganda, and the system itself; but Wall Street and the world of corporate finance have never shone as centers of deep thinking about broad effects of their transactions upon society.

One should also bear in mind that the mechanism used to effect the takeover threat, maneuvers, and eventual withdrawal is a holding company, that is, a corporation. It is a dummy, to be sure, and not a corporation in the ordinary sense of an entity connected in the public mind with production, services, long-term growth, research and development, or even very many employees. It is just a takeover machine, a place to park assets or provide a legal name for one's efforts, and a greenmail extractor. It has nothing at all in common with the corporation envisaged by the founders and forebears in the law who gave us the doctrine of the incorporation privilege. Above all, perhaps, it exemplifies the fears that guided the reluctance to charter the private, profit-making company.

LEVERAGED BUYOUTS

> . . . the hostile take-over offer is a misuse of a basically sound business concept.
>
> —Stephen C. Diamond[40]

The mergers, acquisitions, and takeovers that are subjects of this study are leveraged buyouts if they succeed. A leveraged buyout is any acquisition of a company that leaves the acquired operating entity with a greater than traditional debt-to-equity ratio.[41] There are varieties of leveraged buyouts, as one might imagine. They can be aimed at assets acquisition or stock acquisition or both. They can be aimed at a division or part of a company such as those found in a conglomerate. And they can be fostered by arrangements involving secured or unsecured financing. In many respects, leveraged buyouts are more dazzling to behold than cash buyouts or greenmail deals, for they involve the massive shuffling of legal, corporate, structural, and personnel details and arrangements in ways that can enrich well-placed individuals who have actually put little or no cash or collateral into the deal.

The history of leveraged buyouts has changed markedly since the 1960s. Then, it was usually a secured transaction (i.e., one financed by the accounts receivable, fixed assets, and inventories of the target company). Usually, this was a matter of a large entity swallowing up a smaller one. This was an age of formation of great conglomerates like LTV, Gulf and Western (now Paramount Communications), ITT, and Litton Industries. Great abuses took place; the milking of small ''cash cows'' was a common event.

The process is typically quite different today. The transaction is often (perhaps even ordinarily) unsecured. The acquirer can often be smaller than the target company. The pattern is generally one in which debt is layered upon debt. A lender, helped into this process by a broker specializing in buyouts such as the criminally convicted and now bankrupt firm of Drexel Burnham Lambert, takes an equity kicker and subordinates its debt instead of insisting upon collateral. This combination of equity and subordinated debt then entices another group of unsecured lenders to lay on a level of senior debt, because the company's cash flow is seen to have the ability to service the debt. The emphasis in this kind of deal is in fact cash flow rather than collateral. The downside risk is fairly great, but the rewards of leveraged financing can and may exceed the profits one might ordinarily make in other investments. Inflation, as one would expect, has from time to time helped this process along. It has also been helped by the acquisitions of skills for this kind of deal put together by Drexel and other brokers. (Until its recent demise, Drexel was far and away the most important firm in the business of hostile takeovers[42]). Perhaps the most important key to such deals, however, has been the matter of contacts and influence; in other words, the corporate politics of who knows who.

A high rate of return was demanded by the various insurance companies and thrift institutions (savings and loans) so that such investments were indeed attractive. Both kinds of institutions, but especially the thrifts, are now suffering in part because of this. Everyone appeared to gain from this great leveraging game (except, of course, the general public)—the borrowers who got a high rate of return, the lenders who also earned this, the brokers, the lawyers, the specialist ''fixers'' like the convicted Michael Milken. The basic belief was, and continues to be, that all will be well as long as the cash flow stays up.[43] Again, as in so many parts of today's debt markets, junk bonds are expected to do their magic.

One particular form of leveraged buyout deserves comment. This is the one, much in vogue in recent years though a little less so now, in which a relatively small number of investors, bankers, and others take a company out of the stock market altogether. The company "goes private." This occurred in the case of Beatrice (now coming back on the market), R. H. Macy, and other companies, some of them extremely large, billion-dollar-asset firms. The primary actors in such a deal are the managements of a company. These individuals may start out with a relatively small stake in the company and never bother to acquire much more during their tenure as officers and managers of the listed firm. They acquire all of a company, however, after this form of leveraged buyout takes place, along with their fellow officers and managers and a few select outside investors. The buyout is managed with a huge amount of debt, much of it in the form of junk bonds. Some of these "gone private" deals result in the company having a debt-to-assets ratio as high as 80 percent. The important point from the standpoint of this study is that a conflict of interest invariably is set up within the management as it serves its own interests at the expense of the stockholders and at the expense of its fiduciary responsibilities. There is no escape from such a conclusion, and the "love it or leave it" argument—that a discontented shareholder can always sell his or her shares—begs the question and simply will not wash.[44] Once again, we are far away from the rationale of fiduciary responsibility that emerged in economic literature and in the law in order to justify the corporation in the era of the stockholder-management split.[45] It is little wonder that this kind of leveraged buyout is referred to as "the ultimate lockup" of assets by management in a discussion by a merger lawyer on the subject.[46]

JUNK BONDS

> Junk bonds . . . are like a tinderbox.
>
> —Carl L. Reisner, lawyer and merger specialist[47]

Through much of this discussion, junk bonds have been an important reference point. This is because these admittedly shaky debt instruments have been overwhelmingly important engines of the merger, acquisition, and takeover activity so characteristic of the American, and for that matter international, corporate scene today. The industry of mergers and takeovers, particularly the brokerage houses, prefer the term "high-yield" bonds. Despite such objections, junk bonds remain not only the most common usage, they are the most descriptive of what these debt instruments are really like.[48]

These kinds of bonds have always been around, at least in this century, but they have had no great importance in securities markets until the arrival of the freewheeling 1980s. They are indeed high-yield, which reflects their stature in the world of securities and debt instruments. A further reflection is their rating: Neither Moody's nor Standard and Poor's, the two bond-rating services, gives them any rating at all. They are not AAA, AA, A, B, C, or anything. They get no rating because they deserve none. The purchaser of a junk bond is taking a chance, and a greater chance than is taken with most investments.

It is true that investing in junk bonds *may* yield more to the investor than safer alternatives, and a number of business and financial publications have recently and eagerly set out slightly better marginal gains for junk bond investors for certain periods that exceed the yields on Treasury bills. What does this prove? Nothing. The T-bill purchaser with the smaller return, and it was in no case very much smaller, may have slept better. Perhaps more amusing as a defense of junk bonds is a series of advertisements issued in 1987 by Drexel Burnham Lambert that tell stories of how businesses succeeded and jobs were created because of junk bonds. Experience since that heady time suggests that businesses have also failed and thousands of jobs have been lost because of junk bonds.

The reason junk bonds have always been around is because some corporations invariably have financial troubles. The classic use of junk bonds has been to get a company "over the hump," to give it perhaps one last chance to become profitable again by allowing it to borrow at very high rates of interest. The investors who purchase such instruments realize that this is risky.

No threat to the economy was posed by junk bonds as long as they represented something like 3 or 4 percent of the debt instruments in the market. Today, these have moved within range of 20 percent of the debt instruments floating around, and the reason for this is simple enough. They are the preferred vehicles for mergers, acquisitions, hostile takeovers, leveraged buyouts, fighting off takeover threats, and other uses, including, of course, their original use. Their value, which is basically nothing, is premised upon the future sale of assets of the target firm. In other words, junk bonds are nothing in most instances except a promise to liquidate some of the assets of a company once a takeover attempt has succeeded.[49]

This point needs to be underlined. Except in the case of mostly cash friendly mergers and acquisitions, most of the activity discussed in this chapter is directed at *asset liquidation*. Hostile takeovers and leveraged buyouts have the selling off of company assets in mind as the way out of the intensely leveraged debt situation they create. Ted Turner, for example, once intended to float vast amounts of junk bonds, as many as he could print, in order to take over CBS. His intention, never unclear, was to sell off such company assets as rich local outlets of this or that division. His effort did not succeed for a variety of reasons, including prudent defenses established by the network. But a smaller CBS would have been the result of these machinations if they had been successful. Many takeover attempts are successful, of course, and these always result in the sale of assets.

It can be seen that unhealthy social, political, and economic effects can flow from the overuse of junk bonds, but there is a critical factor in this that may be overlooked by some analysts. In the past, junk bonds were almost all held by banks. With all of their faults, banks remain the best institutions to invest in these instruments because they are in a position to be understanding about new troubles or hurdles by a bond-floating firm. Because junk bonds have historically been held by banks, it has been possible to alleviate some of their potential negative economic effects. Junk bonds are now found, however, in every nook and cranny of investment markets. Not only banks, thrift institutions (which buy many of them), insurance companies, investment funds, pension funds, and brokerage houses are among the purchasers, but also many individual investors who are attracted to the high-interest yields. This array of institutions and individuals cannot provide the same debt management and help that banks can; they can hardly be understanding about new problems or unanticipated developments faced by the debtor firm. The junk bond holders of today, then, are brittle rather than flexible, rigid rather than liquid. If a junk bond–floating company runs into trouble, there is a good chance that it will not be able to deal with it.[50]

The implications of all this can be broad indeed. The next crash could be a junk bond crash, and this is recognized even by many of the brokers who write such instruments into being.[51] We may have gone back, in a slightly different way, to the pre–Bubble Act days; the results could be cataclysmic.

Unquestionably, these concerns were behind the 1986 proposal by then Federal Reserve Board Chairman Paul Volcker to establish margin requirements on the floating of junk bonds. It had been possible until then to issue junk bonds with a margin of only 10 percent of their capital value. Volcker proposed that all junk bonds be issued with a requirement of 50 percent.[52] The Reagan administration and a chorus of ideological think tanks strongly objected, although the reasons for the objection were never very clear and, for the most part, were befogged in the usual theological platitudes about free enterprise. During the period of one month in which the Board took opinions on the proposed rule, a compromise was worked out. As a result, the rule today is that a 50 percent margin is required only in the event of a hostile takeover attempt. It is not necessary, however, in order to float these dubious instruments for the sake of friendly mergers or acquisitions or for leveraged buyouts of most kinds.[53]

This kind of sugarcoating of the problem will not have much effect, because hostile takeovers are only a small minority of the combinatory processes. The great bulk of corporate restructuring therefore can continue to be placed at the mercy of junk bonds.[54] The cataclysm, which we must hope will be stayed by any number of economic variables and events, still looms in the background, adding one more shaky dimension to an already unsteady economic structure.

DEFENSES

Offense requires defense. In the corporate world, boards of directors and top managements do not sit idly by while their fiefdoms and perks are threatened. They undertake, usually at great cost,[55] those measures that will ensure their success and, with it, the failure of the takeover forces. These defenses are as follows:

1. *Buying up your own stock.* One of the best ways to inhibit a proxy challenge is to simply make less of the company's stock available. This can be done by a standing offer to buy back a certain number of shares at a certain price. Wall Street has seen hundreds of such offers made in recent years, and investors have made some money on these because the price offered is at least modestly generous on most occasions. Buying up your own company's stock, needless to say, does not fit with the mold of the capitalist legend that says that companies in a free enterprise system will expand, innovate, develop new markets, and make jobs available. This is hardly likely to occur if the firm, worried about the tender offer, enters the market to buy back the stock that represents a part of its capitalization. What we have here is a distortion produced by mergers, acquisitions, and hostile takeover activity.[56]
2. *Use a leveraged buyout scheme to take the company "private."* This effectively removes any takeover threat, but it also sets up an invariable conflict-of-interest problem for management that can redound to the disadvantage of shareholders. So this is not necessarily a good idea.
3. *Establish an extraordinary majority requirement for approval of a tender offer.* This is a common by-laws change being made nowadays, for there is almost no corporation that does not have some fear of being taken over. In some cases, 80 percent approval of a tender offer that has been turned down by the board of directors is required. It can be argued, no doubt, that extraordinary majorities fit with patterns of democracy; after all, most constitutions require extraordinary majorities for their amendment or abolition. But the tenor of such a provision as this is still undemocratic. Corporations are not democratic in the first place, and that is part of the problem with them; it follows that this kind of provision buttresses this undemocratic state of affairs.
4. *Avoidance of cumulative voting.* Some states, such as California, permit minority shareholders to elect board members with a tactic of cumulative voting. Delaware does not permit this, and in fact, most corporations do not allow this in their by-laws. Charters have been switched to Delaware in order to prevent cumulative voting, displaying once again the nuances and inconsistencies established by a state system of chartering. The results of such avoidance, then, are undemocratic and this, it is fair to say, is the intention.
5. *Staggering terms on the board of directors.* This may be the most common device extant for producing results unfavorable to takeover forces. Its mechanics are obvious and require little in the way of comment.
6. *Fair price provision.* This merely requires approval of a "fair price" for the stock and/or assets of the firm in order for a merger, acquisition, or

takeover to take place. Who determines the fair price question? The board, of course, which may be prone to find a fair price only on the rarest of occasions. Needless to say, this is a popular by-law.[57]

7. *Restrictions on the calling of special meetings by stockholders*. Again, this is a provision that requires little comment. Its undemocratic features seem obvious enough.
8. *Employee stock-option plans (ESOPs)*. The presence of an ESOP plan in a company over a period of years, which normally facilitates stock purchases by the workers by offering discounts or, at the very least, the convenience of an automatic payroll deduction, will naturally tend to build a large and important constituency of stockholders whose loyalties are likely to be with the incumbent board and management. At the same time, ESOPs can provide firms with a lot of money to play around with, so they are popular even if a takeover threat is not taken into account.[58] It is probable that ESOPs are the best obstacle to throw into the path of those making a tender offer. Most observers of ESOPs see little to criticize about this institution, but some of their effects are likely to be counterprogressive. They may, for example, socialize employees to believe that they are truly sharing in the governance of the company, which is never true, or that they have a big and important stake in capitalist economics, also a highly dubious proposition.
9. *Creating different classes of common shareholders*. This ploy has been used by the Potlatch Corporation in the hope of fending off a takeover. A by-laws change was made that stated that stockholders of record by a certain date in the past would have voting rights at the annual meeting, whereas those who acquired stock past the date in question would have no such rights. Such a provision is obviously aimed at new acquirers of shares who may have a takeover in mind. One of the difficulties of this approach for Potlatch was that this placed the company in technical violation of the rules of the New York Stock Exchange (NYSE), though there was nothing unlawful about this. The NYSE, according to its own rules, should have delisted Potlatch but declined to do this; the truth is that the company would simply have listed itself on the American or over-the-counter (OTC) exchanges.[59] It can be seen that there are both regulatory and moral problems with this approach. Certainly any argument in favor of granting voting rights to one set of common shareholders and not to another is fraught with some logical, moral, and consistency problems.
10. *Taking the "poison pill."* This is one of the most severe distortions created by the mergers-acquisitions-hostile takeovers area, and in truth it is an approach that invariably will not work. A corporation that is convinced that it looks good to potential takeover forces decides to change its indebtedness balance sheet by borrowing large sums or, more likely, by acquiring a company and incurring a great deal of indebtedness in

order to do this. The "poison pill" examples are those instances in which this is done in the face of good business sense, that is, the acquisition is made or the indebtedness is incurred simply to change the overall indebtedness structure. "Cash cows," after all, are the most likely takeover targets. Those firms with little or no debt but a good cash flow and overall health are the ones deemed most desirable. The "poison pill" drastically changes the desirability of a firm, but this also means that the company has undertaken a dubious venture just to make itself less attractive. This scheme fails to fit into any of the conventional arguments or propaganda for the free enterprise system, but more important, it does severe damage to stockholders, employees, and friends of the firm whose welfare is tied to it.

11. *The "white knight."* When all else fails, the board and top management can call in a friendly suitor to try to effect a merger that will save the positions of the corporate officialdom. As much as possible, the board and management will seek to obtain assurances that this friendly takeover will not result in their disassociation from the company, but this may happen anyway. The "white knight" scheme is therefore often considered to be the last resort.

These defenses, quite naturally, may be combined, or there may be variants of them established from time to time. As the brief analysis of each of them reveals, their effects on the corporation seeking to defend itself can certainly distort their purposes as these are understood in free enterprise apologias and propaganda. What must be emphasized here, however, is that the adoption of these defenses can hurt stockholders, employees, creditors, and such interests as promotion hopes and pension rights.[60]

REASONS FOR MERGERS, ACQUISITIONS, AND TAKEOVERS

> A little greenmail and some junk bonds, and you're in business.
>
> —James M. Needham[61]

Recently, a list was compiled of the twenty-five worst business decisions in American history. On the list, as one might expect, were Ford Motor Company's decision to produce the Edsel and Transamerica/UA's decision to produce the very expensive, commercially disastrous film *Heaven's Gate*. Much more interesting, however, is the fact that ten of the decisions were mergers and/or acquisitions, including such recent notables as Du Pont–Conoco, U.S. Steel–Marathon Oil, Pan American–National Airlines, Exxon–Reliance Oil, and

Atlantic Richfield–Anaconda.[62] Many others would have been good candidates for the list. ITT acquired all kinds of incompatible companies in the 1960s. General Electric lost $3 billion or so on Utah International before severing that connection. And Mobil, famous for its ads exhorting us to understand the oil industry's need for favorable tax treatment so that more drilling can be done, bought that famous lemon Montgomery Ward. Not only was there no oil to be found in hardware, sleepware, and appliance departments, there was no profit in the old catalogue and department store business either. Even more bizarre, perhaps, was Gulf Oil's takeover of the Ringling Brothers Circus, although this was more profitable.

The central question that must be asked in this newest epoch of corporate history is: Why should companies engage in the business of mergers, acquisitions, and takeovers? What justifies this activity? We know there are social and economic costs not only for the corporations involved but for many people, business firms, communities, and governments of this nation. So what are the benefits?

Usually, one of the first responses is that people make money out of this activity—brokers, lawyers, banks, takeover artists, insiders who know about the deals in advance, stockholders who go along for the ride, certainly a great many corporate directors and managements, and even the golden parachutists. And making money is good, isn't it? It is hardly the case, despite such a transparently thin claim, that making money for certain groups of people can by itself justify activities that have the potential of so much harm—junk bonds floating around and ready to melt away to nearly nothing; unemployment; a variety of economic dislocations caused by plant and headquarters movements; the failure to invest in new plant, equipment, or research and development; some tax rip-offs (though certainly legal) associated with interest deductions; the milking and neglect of companies that are taken over; the creation of monopolistic or oligopolistic entities; the abuses of SEC and stock exchange regulations; the subordination of shareholders' rights and interests; the breaking of labor contracts; the deleterious effects upon pension plans; and a host of other evils of broad impact.

It is often urged that mergers, acquisitions, and takeovers are attempts to develop a greater efficiency through such means as rationalization of an industry or the development of economies of scale. There is no evidence that, in overall terms, this in fact occurs, but there is a fairly large body of evidence to the contrary. This may occur to any of us as an impression if the past few years are surveyed, for these have seen the sizing down of conglomerates and fairly frequent sales of previously acquired firms. Mobil, ITT, LTV (which is now bankrupt), General Electric, Paramount Communications (formerly Gulf and Western), Transamerica, and many other companies have divested themselves of what they once described as "synergy." The employees of Avis Rent-a-Car, sick of being shunted around for the purpose of these games, bought out the company and took it private after six sales and as many restructurings.

There are any number of studies that state or explicitly demonstrate that the efficiency argument is beyond redemption. Peter Earl, for one, shreds this argument with mounds of logic and data.[63] Likewise, three well-known studies cited by Green and Berry give the efficiency argument a strong coating of dubiety.[64] A listed summary of findings in the *California Management Review* shows that empirical evidence for the efficiency argument is lacking and that mergers and acquisitions are likely to achieve a contrary result.[65] And a detailed cross-national study of mergers and acquisitions literature of seven countries—the United States, the UK, Belgium, France, Germany, Sweden, and the Netherlands—again indicates that the strong balance of hard evidence runs heavily against the proponents of combination.[66]

It is occasionally argued that mergers, acquisitions, and especially hostile takeovers are useful in establishing something more like the "true" value of the stock price of a firm's securities. This of course redounds to the benefit of the shareholders and, because a hostile takeover threat looms, will tend to put the management and directors on their toes. Hostile takeovers not only boost stock prices; they also remove complacency from company leaderships. T. Boone Pickens tries to make these arguments in order to put an aura of social responsibility around his activities. These are bald assertions. There is a problem with developing hard evidence about the true value of stock prices and whether and how the market evaluates these. It is certainly not the case that managers and directors can be judged by the price the market has set upon the firm's shares. And for all we know, the incumbent managers and directors are more efficient, stable, savvy, and reliable people than are Pickens or other takeover artists; there are good reasons for thinking, quite to the contrary, that people like Pickens are not really interested in running a company at all.[67]

A further argument for combinations points out that it is simply easier sometimes to take over a company and its assets—capital position, accounts receivable, good will, and especially its reserves of natural resources if it has any—than it is to drill for oil or plant trees, or find distribution networks, or invent catchy new brand names. There is much truth in this, especially if the argument is confined to the context of the balance sheet. It still begs a host of questions about antitrust considerations, market competitiveness, social and political influence and results, and, most certainly, the typical propagandistic stance taken by individual companies and their interest group spokespersons in the U.S. Chamber of Commerce, the American Petroleum Institute, the National Association of Manufacturers, and (with some exceptions here) the Business Roundtable. What may be best at the management level, however, may not be the best alternative for society, and, as we have seen above, for the economy.

A further justification states that although there are no tangible benefits that are obvious at the moment, these will appear in time. The tremendous amount of corporate restructuring that is taking place in the frenzy over mergers, acquisitions, and takeovers must be seen, we are assured, as a free market response to a new set of conditions. The "invisible hand" of capitalist wisdom is working its will, and patience will reward us if we can only wait to see the results of all this activity.[68] It is certainly true that we do not know what the future may bring, but this trivial truism amounts to the only content of this argument. For the moment, we can see this argument for what it is: a facile and weak bag of promises. We should endure all of the dislocations and heartache wrought by this activity because in the future, we shall reap rich rewards! This argument is in the same category as the one that justifies combinations on the basis that some people make money from their formation, and it carries us just about the same distance.

A corollary to these arguments and concerns surrounds the question, what happens to merged firms? What is the history of companies that have undergone these processes of combination? The evidence developed by a variety of sources shows rather conclusively that merged firms usually perform less well than companies as a whole do.[69] Very often, of course, they are characterized by crippling debt structures that were brought on by the shuffling of finances and assets so common to the combinations process.

The arguments that seek to justify mergers, acquisitions, and hostile takeovers are, in sum, mostly weak and cannot be sustained. It should be observed in light of this that, undaunted, the propaganda goes on; and in the face of overwhelming evidence to the contrary, the shibboleths of efficiency, the great future ahead of us all, and so forth are straightfacedly presented to business groups, citizens' forums, congressional hearings, and other arenas of concern and action.[70]

CAPITALIST MYTH AND MERGERS, ACQUISITIONS, AND TAKEOVERS

Apologists for the free enterprise myths that pervade capitalist societies are caught in any number of dilemmas because of the manic drive behind mergers, acquisitions, and takeovers in recent years. You must believe in the enterprise system or you must not. And if you do, it is hard to condone—as, for example, Adam Smith surely would not—the combinatory actions and assumptions of recent years. If you do condone these, then you must do extensive backing and filling with your arguments to show how new conditions, or the anomalies of corporate structure, or the record of government intervention (almost always blamed), or some other factor has altered our classic understanding of market competition. Needless to say, this can be done and is done constantly. But the results, no matter how clever the sophistry, are at the least inconsistent and at the worst amount to persiflage. And seldom are these arguments arrayed against the irrationalities of the misuse of the incorporation privilege or the Delaware-led cause of state chartering.

The crux of the matter, from the standpoint of free enterprise and capitalist propaganda, is that the long-heralded benefits of the system—the response to markets, rational decision making, achievements of product innovation and research, consumer satisfaction, efficiency—must be recast in propaganda efforts such as the Drexel Burnham Lambert series on the benefits of mergers, acquisitions, and takeovers. It can hardly be claimed, for example, that one of the great strengths of companies today is their commitment to the community in which a plant or headquarters is located; and this was a staple in the 1950s, for example, in the propaganda of the paternalistic corporation. And it is difficult indeed to show how a company and its employees are benefited by being shunted through a series of restructurings in a relatively short period of time—as in the Avis example of six buyouts or, to be more mundane, in a corporate identity that proceeds from Planters Peanuts to Standard Brands to Nabisco to RJR Nabisco (see Table 4.3).

POLICY OPTIONS AND THE FUTURE

All kinds of policy prescriptions suggest themselves as recent corporate history is surveyed. Simply removing the tax incentives, such as deductions for interest on debt, for merger-acquisition-takeover activity would be a good start. Volcker's original margin requirement for junk bonds—50 percent for all of them, not just those used for hostile takeovers—is a worthwhile proposal. Better disclosure rules in corporate governance and especially in merger-acquisition-takeover activity would help to alert the public, stockholders, and various affected parties. The use of junk bonds should probably be restricted in a variety of ways and we should try to return to using them for reasons related to their original purpose. Greenmail should be against the law, and both civil and criminal sanctions should be enacted; a bill has been offered on this matter by Senator Howard Metzenbaum of Ohio. A better-scrutinized review of what the intentions of combinatory processes really are can also be made possible through various enactments and administrative regulations. The exchanges should at least police listed firms enough so that violations of the Potlatch kind do not occur; if they do, delisting is in order.

A great deal can be accomplished without enacting any new laws or regulations. The reestablishment of regulation, the renewal of antitrust enforcement with more rigorous guidelines, and a vigorous policy of requiring adherence to the law could do a great deal to bring about a measure of social (if not political) responsibility to the corporate world. The tools are there on the books: the Celler-Kefauver amendments to the Clayton Act, the Federal Trade Commission Act, the Hart-Scott-Rodino Act, the often-violated Williams Act, and so forth.[71] This is not to say that enforcement, or even the laws themselves, was adequate prior to the gross laxity of recent years, but it would be healthy for the American polity to return to the rule of law in matters of corporate organization and restructuring.

TABLE 4.3 The Identity Problem: A Partial Listing of RJR Nabisco Company Products (Enhanced by Recent Acquisitions)

A product list of this one conglomerate helps to illustrate how remote the firm is from product names familiar to the consumer and, thus, the imposition of one more obstacle to the designation of corporate responsibility and activity. This company's list of products was chosen because many of the brands are household names though consumers may not be aware that they are marketed by RJR Nabisco. They represent acquisitions not only of Reynolds but of firms acquired by firms acquired by Reynolds; for example, Standard Brands was acquired by Nabisco before Nabisco was acquired by Reynolds.

TOBACCO PRODUCTS

Bright
Camel
Carter Hall
Century
Doral
George Washington
Madeira Gold
More
Now
Prince Albert
Royal Comfort
Salem
Sterling
Vantage
Winston

FOOD, LIQUOR, RESTAURANTS, AND OTHER PRODUCTS

A-1 Steak Sauce
Almost Home
Arrow cordials
Babycham Perry
Baby Ruth
Barrelhead Root Beer
Beaulieu (BV) wines
Black Forest Girl
Black Velvet
Blue Bonnet
Boggs cranberry liqueur
Bouchard Pere and Fils
Breath Savers
Brer Rabbit molasses
Bubble Yum
Butterfinger
Canada Dry
Care-Free gum
Chips Ahoy
Chung King
Club Cocktails
College Inn broths
Cream of Wheat
Cuervo Tequila
Davis baking powder
Don Q Rum
Dos Equis
Dromedary
Egg Beaters
Fleischmann's liquor
Fleischmann's margarine
Grey Poupon
Harry and David Fruit-of-the-Month Club
Harvey's Bristol Cream
Hawaiian Punch
Heublein cocktails
Inglenook wines
Irish Mist liqueur
Jacare wines
Jackson and Perkins roses and plants
Kiku Masumune sake
Lancers
Life Savers
Malcolm Hereford's Cows
Matador tequila
McMaster's whiskeys
Milk-Bone
Milk-Mate syrup
Milshire gin
Mr. Salty
Monsanto Chianti
Moosehead
Morton frozen foods
My-T-Fine puddings
Nabisco Fig Newtons
Nabisco Mystic Mint
Nabisco Shredded Wheat
Nabisco Social Tea Biscuits
Nabs
Oreos
Ortega
Patio frozen foods
Planters nuts
Planters oil
Popov vodka
Relska vodka
Ritz crackers
Royal puddings
Smirnoff vodka
Snap-E-Tom
Sunkist soft drinks
T. J. Swann
Tahitian Treat
Tokaji Aszu wines
Triscuits
Valbon French wines
Waverly crackers
Wheat Thins
Wink
Wright's Liquid Smoke
Yukon Jack
Zantigo Mexican restaurants

The regulatory context and agenda were abruptly changed in 1981, and the results have been sad indeed. Presidential executive orders 12291 of February 17, 1981, and the follow-up 12498 of January 4, 1985, established a Presidential Task Force on "Regulatory Relief" and what was later called President Reagan's Task Force of Regulatory Review; the latter was metamorphosed into the "President's Council on Competitiveness," chaired by Vice President Dan Quayle. The idea of these task forces and agencies is to reduce the regulatory burdens faced by American-based industries—savings and loan associations, defense contractors, brokerage houses, and so forth—so that we can more zealously work toward a true free enterprise system, whatever that may be. The great discretionary powers given to the White House by itself have resulted in many giveaways to corporations and other vested interests, the net effect of which has been a weakening of the economy and greater inequalities in social and political life.[72] It appears obvious that these commissions should be abolished at the earliest opportunity.

Realistically, however, there are no policy options of even the quite modest sort listed in these paragraphs that could be called currently available. There is only the headlong thrust away from even the most modest social control of multinational corporate giants, which are now interlocked, networked, and syndicated into an almost unassailable nexus of power.[73]

A current demand, which is becoming ever more shrill, calls for the abolition of antitrust laws on the ground that competitors, most especially the *keiretsu* combines that characterize much or most of Japanese industry, are not subject to antitrust laws. The reasons for losses of competitive advantage are much more complex than this, however, for they include the machinations of product innovation, the excessive salaries and benefits of American executives when viewed in a competitive and just light, relative savings and investment factors, overt governmental industrial policies (and, it should be pointed out, the United States has none of these), comparative treatments of labor (which is more job secure in Japan), and a variety of economic policies. In addition, there is good evidence that the Japanese trade deficit will become less serious in the years to come, though deficits with other nations, particularly in Asia, are likely to rise. None of these factors, any more than the arguments refuted before, are compelling reasons for doing away with antitrust law.

Corporate structures and characteristics said to be the trends of the 1990s and beyond require a brief comment. Some of the recent literature in this area contends that the new corporation will be "leaner and meaner" and far more difficult to become a part of; employment opportunities of a full-time or permanent nature are mostly vanishing. One new model often mentioned and given a variety of names is what I call the "center and rings" model. In this sleek and competitive dynamo of an organization, the "inner ring" will be made up of those fortunate few who will be full-time and permanent employees. These privileged people will have better incomes, more security, and, most assuredly, better benefits (including health benefits) than the rest of us. The "second ring,'' which may involve the greatest number of people, will be made up of temporary employees. These will float in and out of the organization as they are needed. They may have a somewhat dubious benefit of lots of free time, but they are also going to experience lower wage levels, a great deal of job insecurity, and—you guessed it—no benefits. The third, or ''outer,'' ring will consist of consultants who are technically not a part of the firm at all but who are seen as dynamic forces who will keep this new model of enterprise hummingly competitive. Their advice will presumably be good or they will not be consultants for long, and they may or may not enjoy employee benefits of one kind or another with their consulting firm.

It is more or less expected that corporate recruitment of permanent employees will often, but not invariably, come from the ranks of the temps. This will surely be the hope of most of the temps, of course.

Instead of being delighted with such a ''lean and mean'' model those of us who have broader concerns about civic virtue, the economy, and society must assume a quite critical—if not cynical—stance. Such a ''circle and rings'' model, if brought into existence on a large scale (and there are already strong portents of it in employee policies of companies like Sears), will mean that few of us will become acquainted with economic security; and social, political, and economic equality will be even more unlikely to be achievable. The advantage of looking at such a model critically is that it may force us to rethink a large batch of issues—from national health insurance to the position of temporary employment firms in our society—and to try to achieve a progressive consensus on them.

In the meantime, corporate interlocks and combinatory processes march on to ever-higher planes of power and authority over the body politic.

THE CORPORATE STATE

How long it will take before these interlocks achieve total control of the economic and political processes of the United States is of course a matter of conjecture, but the hour is late. The best evidence is that this is occurring at a rapid enough pace so that it can be achieved at some time in the near and foreseeable future. If total control is achieved—and there is an argument that it already has—the result will be something like the corporate state. In a corporate state, the organization of both the government and the economy is tied closely and formally together. The purest model of such a system in recent times may be Fascist Italy under Mussolini, though there have certainly been strong imitators in Argentina, Spain, and other countries. Individual freedom and opportunity under such a system are snuffed out by this great agglomeration of wealth and power. And under this system, there is a syndicate for each major industry jointly run by business interests and the state.

American politicians do not advocate the corporate state, but they often advocate assistance in various forms to the corporate world in the name of the national defense or keeping domestic industries competitive or, most certainly, in the hope that they will locate here rather than there. In a world of multinational corporations, such policies are ultimately futile if not venal.

The dangers are obvious. The corporate state would probably not appear to us in exactly the same form that it came to the Italians in the 1920s; the variables of politics seldom work in this way. Time, multinationalism, and a great many structural changes have occurred since then in any event, so that a quite different design or shape should be anticipated. The danger is there, all the same, requiring us to fix our focus and our efforts upon the principles of fairness, equality, opportunity, liberty, and law; none of these values, as Charles E. Lindblom points out, appears to fit with those of the profit-making business corporation.[74]

NOTES

1. *Wall Street Journal*, August 28, 1991.
2. *Wall Street Journal*, September 4, 1991.
3. *Asiaweek*, July 26, 1991, 20–21.
4. See Chapter 5.
5. Kristina Ahlen, "Sweden Introduces Employee Ownership," *Political Quarterly* 56 (April/June 1985), 186–93.
6. Richard Phalon, *The Take-Over Barons of Wall Street: Inside the Billion-Dollar Merger Game* (New York: G. P. Putnam, 1981), 241; E. F. Schumacher, *Small Is Beautiful: Economics as if People Mattered* (New York: Harper & Row, 1973).
7. Herbert Simon, *Models of Man* (New York: John Wiley, 1957); James G. March and Herbert Simon, *Organizations* (New York: John Wiley, 1958); Alvin W. Gouldner, *Patterns of Industrial Democracy* (New York: Free Press, 1954); H. Igor Ansoff, *Corporate Strategy* (Harmondsworth: Penguin, 1965); C. Wright Mills, *White Collar: The American Middle Classes* (New York: Oxford University Press, 1951). Some of this sensitivity to organizational behavior is found even in Alfred Marshall's *Principles of Economics* (London: Macmillan, 1980).
8. John Kenneth Galbraith, *The New Industrial State* (Boston: Houghton Mifflin, 1971).
9. Hannah Arendt, *The Human Condition* (Chicago: University of Chicago Press, 1958); also see Patricia Boling, "Why Public vs. Private Is Wrong," paper delivered at the Annual Meeting of the American Political Science Association, New Orleans, August–September 1985.
10. C. Wright Mills, *The Power Elite* (New York: Oxford University Press, 1956).
11. Ibid.
12. Peter Earl, *The Corporate Imagination: How Big Companies Make Mistakes* (Armonk, NY: M. E. Sharpe, 1984).
13. Mark Green and John F. Berry, *The Challenge of Hidden Profits: Reducing Corporate Bureaucracy and Waste* (New York: William Morrow, 1985), 199–200.
14. Ibid., 189.
15. Quoted in *Time*, May 14, 1984, 46.

16. "M & A Momentum Sustained," *Mergers and Acquisitions* 19 (the 1985 Almanac and Index), no. 5, 7; *Time*, December 23, 1985, 42.

17. *New York Times*, May 19, 1985; San Francisco *Chronicle*, March 12, 1986; *Fortune*, January 20, 1986, 26.

18. See the three sources listed in n. 17.

19. Walter Adams and James W. Brock, *Dangerous Pursuits: Mergers and Acquisitions in the Age of Wall Street* (New York: Pantheon, 1989); Maurice Zeitlin, *The Large Corporation and Contemporary Classes* (New Brunswick, NJ: Rutgers University Press, 1989).

20. Mel Watkins, "Ten Reasons to Oppose Free Trade," *This Magazine* 20 (April 1, 1986), 13–16; Fred Gudmundson, "Free Trade: The Real Agenda," *Canadian Dimension* 20 (September/October 1986), inserted pp. 1–15.

21. Phalon, *The Take-Over Barons*, 241.

22. *Wall Street Journal*, June 4, 1991.

23. San Francisco *Chronicle*, March 12, 1986.

24. Robert Heilbroner, "Realities and Appearances in Capitalism," Robert B. Dickie and Leroy S. Rouner (eds.), *Corporations and the Common Good* (Notre Dame, IN: University of Notre Dame Press, 1986), 33.

25. Ira M. Milstein and Salem M. Katsch, *The Limits of Corporate Power* (New York: Macmillan, 1981), 67–73.

26. There are rare circumstances in which this may be the truth, but this is never the case when a well-known takeover artist is involved unless, of course, he/she later loses interest in the company for some reason. Friendly mergers may not yield quite the same results as hostile takeovers, but the price appreciation of a stock is the normal result and expectation in any buyout activity.

27. The financial press can provide many examples of this, but a good example is set out in *Time*, May 14, 1984, 47.

28. This writer was "T. R. B." of the *New Republic*; Green and Berry, *The Challenge of Hidden Profits*, 196.

29. Fort Wayne *Journal-Gazette*, September 22, 1986.

30. See the discussion in Donald I. Baker and William Blumenthal, "De-mystifying the Herfindahl-Hirschman Index," *Mergers and Acquisitions* 19 (Summer 1984), 44.

31. Robert H. Bork, *The Anti-Trust Paradox: A Policy at War with Itself* (New York: Basic Books, 1978).

32. Green and Berry, *The Challenge of Hidden Profits*, 191–93.

33. Barbara J. Leukart, "Dealing with Labor When a Company Is Sold," *Mergers and Acquisitions* 19 (Spring 1984), 40–44.

34. An early review of this book by an anonymous business faculty member included the comment that concern about employee rights in a corporation is "communistic."

35. San Francisco *Chronicle*, November 20, 1985.

36. A tender offer is a public bid for any or all of a corporation's shares. Payment can be made in securities or cash. A tender becomes "hostile" when the target resists and the bidder persists. The terms "merger" and "acquisition," though technically different, have come to be used often interchangeably and synonymously to describe the merging of two firms; Green and Berry, *The Challenge of Hidden Profits*, 190.

37. Charles L. Marinaccio, "Forcing Corporate Raiders to Walk the Plank," *Business and Society Review* 53 (Spring 1985), 28.

38. *Wall Street Journal*, February 4, 1987.

39. Jonathan R. Macey and Fred S. McChesney, "A Theoretical Analysis of Corporate Greenmail," *Yale Law Journal* 95 (November 1985), 13–61.

40. From the introduction in Stephen C. Diamond (ed.), *Leveraged Buyouts* (Homewood, IL: Dow Jones-Irwin, 1985), 9. This book has a great deal to commend it as a guide to the intricacies of the subject.

41. *Wall Street Journal*, December 13, 1985.

42. Introduction by Diamond, *Leveraged Buyouts*, 3–8.

43. Ibid.

44. Ibid.

45. Ibid.

46. Carl L. Reisner in "Roundtable: Key Legal Issues in Acquisitions and Defenses," *Mergers and Acquisitions* 20 (Summer 1985), 32.

47. Ibid., 30.

48. *Wall Street Journal*, December 13, 1985.

49. Ibid.; *New York Times*, May 19, 1985; San Francisco *Chronicle*, December 24 and 31, 1985; also see Diamond, *Leveraged Buyouts*.

50. San Francisco *Chronicle*, December 24 and 31, 1985; also see Federal Reserve Board press releases and letters to members of Congress made available to the public and dated December 6, 1985.

51. San Francisco *Chronicle*, December 24 and 31, 1985.

52. Federal Reserve Board press release, December 6, 1985.

53. San Francisco *Chronicle*, January 2, 1986; *Wall Street Journal*, January 8, 1986.

54. San Francisco *Chronicle*, January 2, 1986.

55. Green and Berry, *The Challenge of Hidden Profits*, 207–11.

56. Buying up its own stock is one of the worst things a corporation can do according to Robert Heller, *The Naked Executive: Games Executives Play* (New York: E. P. Dutton, 1985), xvi–xvii.

57. "Takeover Defenses: Trigger Devices Gain Favor," *Mergers and Acquisitions* 19 (Winter 1985), 892.

58. Diamond, *Leveraged Buyouts*, 5.

59. San Francisco Sunday *Examiner and Chronicle*, January 3, 1985.

60. For a simulation of a board of directors faced with a hostile takeover attempt, see "The Board under Siege," *Mergers and Acquisitions* 19 (Fall 1984), 56–63.

61. "Roundtable: The M&A Market in 1985," *Mergers and Acquisitions* 19 (1985 Almanac and Index), 11.

62. George Kurian, *What's What in American Business* (Chicago: Probus, 1985), 177.

63. Earl, *The Corporate Imagination*, Chap. 10.

64. The Lowenstein, Birch, and Wharton studies are described in Green and Berry's *The Challenge of Hidden Profits*, 201–2.

65. Allen Michel and Israel Shaked, "Evaluating Merger Performance," *California Management Review* 27 (Spring 1985), 109–18.

66. Dennis C. Mueller (ed.), *The Determinants and Effects of Mergers: An International Comparison* (Cambridge: Oelgeschlager, Gunn, and Hain, 1980), Chap. 10.

67. Robert J. Allio and Robert M. Randall, "T. Boone Pickens Wildcats on Wall Street" (interview), *Planning Review* 13 (July 1985), 6–11, 44–45; T. Boone Pickens, "Free Enterprise without the Entrepreneur?" *Vital Speeches of the Day* 51 (July 1, 1985), 565–67.

68. "How the New Merger Boom Will Benefit the Economy," *Business Week*, February 6, 1984, 42–50.

69. Earl, *The Corporate Imagination*, Chap. 10; *The Determinants and Effects of Mergers*, Chap. 10; Michel and Shaked, "Evaluating Merger Performance"; Green and Berry, *The Challenge of Hidden Profits*, 201–2; Kenneth M. Davidson, *Mega-Mergers: Corporate America's Billion-Dollar Take-Overs* (Cambridge: Ballinger, 1985), 117–316.

70. Edward L. Hennessey, Jr., "Mergers: Good and Bad," *Vital Speeches of the Day* 51 (June 15, 1985), 535–38.

71. For a lighter and more entertaining review of many of these laws, see Thomas K. McCraw, *Prophets of Regulation* (Cambridge: Belknap Press, 1984).

72. Susan J. Tolchin and Martin Tolchin, *Dismantling America: The Rush to Deregulate* (New York: Oxford University Press, 1983); Susan Rose-Ackerman, "Deregulation and Re-regulation: Rhetoric and Reality," *Journal of Law and Politics* 6 (Winter 1990), 287–310.

73. See n. 19.

74. Charles E. Lindblom, *Politics and Markets: The World's Political-Economic Systems* (New York: Basic Books, 1977); for a review of regulation of combinatory behavior in Europe, see Horst Satzky, "The Merger Control Regulation of the European Economic Community," *Journal of Comparative Law* 38 (Fall 1990), 923–48.

5 Questioning Labor Law

A former lawyer for the . . . National Labor Relations Board (NLRB) suggests in a . . . book that companies violate the law in order to remain non-union. Robert Pearlman, who now advises management on union-busting, says in *Winning Union Campaigns* that the consequences of illegal labor practices "must be kept in perspective—they must be subordinated to the prime objective, which is remaining union free."

"If you rigidly adhere to the guidelines" of the law, "the odds are that you will end up with a union," Pearlman says. . . . Even if the NLRB finds your violations of the law so severe that it orders you to bargain with the union, "the board won't issue [such an order] until two to four years" later and the order's effect will be minimal, he states.

—*UAW Washington Report*[1]

LABOR LAW SHOULD BE INCLUDED in any work that seeks change and reform of the political system in any meaningful terms. For at least four decades, it has been administered and adjudicated in manifestly unfair ways.

At the level of custom and tradition, for example, a person with a labor background has never been appointed to the National Labor Relations Board, the most important rule-making agency in the field. People with corporate backgrounds, including blatant promanagement types, have had such appointments, however, along with those "neutral" rational-professional types who became less numerous and noticeable in the Nixon-Ford, Reagan, and Bush years.

Most important, the law provides ready-made union-busting mechanisms for any employer with the least amount of determination to carry them out. Strikers can be legally fired and replaced by new employees who will then be the only voters permitted in an election to decertify the union. The manifest unfairness of this is opposed by the American people in public opinion polls even though neither support for labor unions nor civil libertarian sensibility often show up in such polls.[2] And if this and many other weapons in the law fail to work, delay can be the employer's potent ally. Workers have been waiting for ten years or more, in some cases, for NLRB and court appeals to play themselves out after they have voted for a union and a contract. Finally, the employer can turn to illegal tactics of coercion, intimidation, and dismissal—often, according to many reports and articles in the business press, on advice of their lawyers, knowing that the chances of being caught are slim to none. There should be little surprise, then, that foreign scholars and observers (as I have had the chance to witness), when exposed to this panoply of repression, tend to regard labor law in America as a crude and cruel hoax.

Experts in the field, all the same, point out that the present is a particularly auspicious time to review labor law proposals. "Labor-law theory is enjoying a kind of intellectual rebirth"[3] in economics and the law, though to date it seems to be missing in my own discipline of political science. New analyses of unions, the workplace, and the rights of workers and managements have appeared, and these challenge old assumptions and seek to define more precisely, logically, and empirically the objective conditions of current employer-employee relationships and their governance. Usually, such studies are accompanied by policy proposals, as in the works of James B. Atleson, Richard B. Freeman and James L. Medoff, Charles Fried, Robert E. Smith, and Paul Weiler.[4]

Significantly, Congress has produced a study, the first in many years, that surveys the Labor-Management Relations Act (LMRA) and its enforcement. It is titled "The Failure of Labor Law—A Betrayal of American Workers."[5] Just as interestingly, however, are the kinds of "analyses" we have heard in recent political campaigns and ad campaigns in which the labor movement, with its 20 million members, has been characterized as a "special interest." This is interesting indeed, because other more narrowly based groups—the National Association of Manufacturers, for example—seem to escape this label.

THE POLITICAL IMPORTANCE OF UNIONS

The majority of scholarly analyses of labor law emanate from the disciplines of economics and law. Correlative contributions are provided by history, sociology, industrial relations, and the increasingly important field of labor studies. A relatively small number of political scientists have devoted much of their time to the study of labor unions, although the subject crops up often within the domain of interest-group studies.[6]

One of the difficulties caused by this state of affairs is that labor unions are often not appreciated in scholarly writings for their political impact and contributions. They typically are subjected to economic analysis (especially, it seems, in law review treatises), and too often they are scrutinized within a vacuum. It is hardly fair, to say nothing about the intellectual worth of such projects, to look at unions from such a one-dimensional perspective.

Unions must be weighed in terms of the need for political, organizational, and industrial justice. Such needs may be regarded as inefficient, uneconomic, or violative of the spirit of free enterprise, though the literature of economics, taken together, hardly makes such a case.[7] Pluralist political theorists, such as

Robert A. Dahl and Charles E. Lindblom, are likely to see labor organizations as balancing forces in the political system, providing a necessary countervailing influence against corporate and business interests.[8] This view might also be appreciated, for example, by some Democratic Party leaders, officials, and officeholders; by allied groups such as civil rights organizations; or by labor union members themselves.

In 1984, the argument was frequently made (or, perhaps more accurately, alluded to in the television commercials of candidates like John Glenn, Gary Hart, and Ronald Reagan) that labor unions are a "special interest" with too much political and economic power. In 1991, Secretary of Labor Lynn Martin opposed the bill banning striker replacements with the lame claim that its passage would give unions too much power. The National Right-to-Work Committee, amply funded by corporate and right-wing sources, spends all of its time trying to cripple unions at the national or state legislative (or court) level; its belief is that unions have too much power. Why the power and influence of labor unions is a terrible thing, compared to the strength of business corporations, the largest of which are multinational, or of farm groups, environmentalists, or whatever, is never entirely made clear. Just what it is about unions that comprises such a horrific menace is not spelled out. Certainly, there has been excess and corruption in labor organizations, although those instances of corruption surely pale in comparison to the banking, savings and loan, Pentagon, and other scandals of recent years. In any event, the corruption that appears most serious and most evident, as well as most highly publicized, is that which is associated with unions such as the Teamsters or the International Longshoremens Association, unions that, ironically, supported George Bush, Ronald Reagan, and Richard Nixon, and that typically support Republican candidates for the presidency and other offices.

In 1988, labor law was a nearly invisible issue in the presidential campaign, a fact that could be interpreted as a sign of the increasing impotence of the labor movement. Issues in which labor has much more than a marginal interest—Social Security, medical care, day care, and taxes, for example—did play some role. But the atmosphere of the campaign, not to mention the result, was hardly beneficial to labor. The hysteria generated on such matters as crime, gun control, and the American Civil Liberties Union membership of candidate Michael Dukakis shows that a more prominent labor presence in the campaign might simply have added to the hysteria-mongering and red-baiting.

Certainly unions, as organizations made up of human beings, are likely to be characterized by human foibles here and there from time to time. Typically, union leaders and officials are required to pay smaller bonding fees than corporate officials because they steal less and less frequently. But corruption and excess are hardly indices of great power in any event. For those who worry about the bogey of "labor power," however, recent research should be reassuring and should put such fears to rest. Unions now have a measurably lessened presence in Washington than they have had in the past, whereas business groups, presumably a countervailing force, have a greater presence than in the past and far greater strength than the combined resources of labor organizations.[9]

A great body of casual evidence suggests that the power and influence of the labor movement is at its lowest point since at least the 1920s. Membership is declining in both real and absolute terms. Contracts negotiated over recent years have involved fewer, if any, gains and are often settled on retrograde terms: lower wages, reduced benefits, and worsened working conditions. Headquarters and organizing staffs of the unions have been cut. And labor's candidates for the presidency, the supposed beneficiaries of all this great power, have generally considered themselves lucky if they win more than half a dozen states and the District of Columbia (see Chapter 6).

My concern with the role of unions in the political life of America, then, rests upon two considerations. First, the necessary balance unions supply against business, corporate, and other conservative interests, if they are in a state of reasonable health, can help to provide a good measure of democracy as well as working-class sentiments in the political arena. One does not need to subscribe to a pluralist or "polyarchy" model as descriptive of American politics, society, or government to hold this concern. One can merely be animated by the desire to see a need for power and influence for groups and organizations *other than* the multinational business corporations, their lobbyists, and their powerful elected and nonelected friends in government. Labor unions have always proved in this century to be central to countervailing coalitions of any importance.

Second, unions must be cared for and protected in order to ensure the welfare of their members, as well as their nonmembers, in industry and the professions who benefit indirectly from wage, fringe benefit, working conditions, and legislative gains. There is great social desirability in having a just, humane, and decent set of conditions prevailing in the workplace. A concern for unions is by definition a concern for justice as the basis for our existence during that forty-hour, five-day period most Americans regard as the workweek. Current statistics on living standards, health care, safety on the job, and other matters indicate that labor is hardly fulfilling its traditional role; even in the few industries that are doing fairly well, employers are demanding—and getting—"givebacks" on wages and conditions that required years of struggle to win in the first place.

These two reasons for being concerned about the welfare of unions can be viewed in another way. The concerns are based upon what unions do for the broader social and political system as well as what they do for the more narrowly banded pursuit of self-interest, that is, the welfare of their members (though in no respect can the latter really be interpreted to be narrow).

To a great degree, it can be shown that the law, as it is legislated, executed, and enforced, is the most decisive factor affecting the fate of unions. This is suggested in a myriad of sources, including Jonathan G. Axelrod; Charles Fried; Richard A. Posner; Paul Weiler; and Archibald Cox, Derek C. Bok, and Robert A. Gorman.[10] Because the terms of the law and its enforcement and administration are so vital to labor-management relations and because unions are weak, battered, and threatened in unprecedented ways today, it is more than likely that the law and/or its enforcement and administration have operated unfairly with regard to the treatment of labor organizations. This is hardly based upon surmise. There is a great body of evidence, developed both in broad and general terms and in specifically anecdotal terms, that suggests that this is the case.[11]

LEGAL CHOICES AND PARAMETERS

Inferences about the policy choices available under existing labor law can be made from the previous overview of industrial relations; from trends in policy making, especially as outlined in the significant 1984 congressional report; and, most assuredly, from the measures of political strength of labor unions.[12] They can be made on a comparative basis as well, for it can be shown that the strength of unions varies from country to country, just as the conditions and terms of labor law and its enforcement and administration, that great and important variable, are different and unique from country to country.

Although labor union membership and political strength are in apparent decline in the United States, for example, the Canadian labor movement has enjoyed a considerable expansion over recent years under what appears, at all odds, to be a more favorable set of legal parameters. Canadian, Scandinavian, and continental European and other experiences suggest that, assuming that we can predict within some acceptable range of error the likely results of labor legislation and rule making, we can virtually "parcel out" power to labor or to management (or, perhaps in the case of compulsory arbitration, to government).

The ability to do this is well within the grasp of governments because in most cases legislation and administration have yielded the intended results. The Wagner Act was passed in 1935, not only to legalize and protect the right to organize unions but also, as its preamble states, to encourage union growth and development. This remains the stated purpose of government in the preamble, even though the act was substantially amended in 1947. And although other factors, such as labor scarcity in the World War II years, were surely important, the Wagner Act years correlate with a healthy and growing labor movement.

The amendments, known as the Taft-Hartley Act, have never been well received or well regarded by the unions in this country; and it is certainly true that the Taft-Hartley years, particularly since 1954, coincide with a long-term decline of the labor union movement climaxed by the current era of weak bargaining contracts, rare organizing victories, and a new low of union membership, well under 20 percent of the nation's work force. These have also been years of more restrictive and hostile (as far as unions are concerned) labor legislation as well as much more restrictive and hostile enforcement. There is less than passing concern for the words incorporated into the preamble.

It is sometimes objected that the decline of unions has as much to do with the kinds of firms and industries in which they have traditionally held their greatest strength as much as it does with hostile legislation and enforcement. These firms and industries, after all, are in decline; but figures show that the unions are in decline even *within* the framework of these traditional areas of strength.[13]

It is true, commonsensically, that variables other than the law can affect the fortunes of labor-management relations. The literature of the industrial relations discipline brims with debate and varieties of analysis of this issue.[14] It remains the case, nevertheless, that labor law as written and enforced cannot help but greatly control and direct the course of labor-management relations and, thus, he fate of labor unions.

It is fair to conclude in all events, then, that labor unions and managements are strongly, if not totally and decisively, affected by labor law and its administration and enforcement. For a long period of time, moreover, these have worked largely to the detriment of organized labor, and the pace of this anti-unionism has greatly accelerated in recent years.

THE STANDARDS OF LAW

It is wise to remind ourselves of the standards we have reasonably come to expect of law. What does law purport to be in America or, for that matter, in any of the "common law" countries? A concise listing is probably as good for our purposes as any that has recently been published:

(1) The law on a particular issue is pre-existing, clear, predictable, and available to anyone with reasonable legal skill;
(2) The facts relevant to disposition of a case are ascertained by objective hearing and evidentiary rules that reasonably ensure that the truth will emerge;
(3) The result in a particular case is determined by a rather routine application of the law to the facts;
(4) Except for the occasional bad judge, any reasonably competent and fair judge can reach the "correct" decision.[15]

Admittedly, this is an idealized model. Because the law is hardly close to being perfect, we cannot expect such standards to be invariable. What we have a right to expect, however, is a proximate relationship between these principles—for they are, after all, what the law purports to be—and the everyday practices found in labor law enforcement and administration.

TESTING THE STANDARDS

First, is the law on any particular labor-management question preexisting, clear, predictable, and available to anyone with rational legal skill? Any number of major principles of labor law have been around for a long time: the doctrine of exclusive bargaining agent, the obligation to bargain in good faith, the "right-to-work" option of the states, the procedures for petitioning for a union representation election. But it would hardly be sound to call American labor law pre-existing, clear, or predictable.

The National Labor Relations Board, which is empowered to administer and enforce the National Labor Relations Act (NLRA), has given us an elephantine and confusing maze of rulings of greater or lesser clarity. NLRB rulings have been on both sides of the "captive audience" rule,[16] the question of bargaining in good faith, and certification and decertification procedures, to cite some examples.[17] These instances exemplify many other issues. Such confusions are not limited to NLRB rulings; they also apply to the courts, where labor law is more subjectively and inconsistently handled than most branches of the law. More to the point, administrative and court rulings seem to follow the fortunes of partisan politics, the general political climate, and the philosophies and affiliations of board members. Today, these forces work mostly against labor.[18]

The second point, that the facts relevant to the disposition of a case are ascertained by an objective hearing and evidentiary rules that reasonably ensure that the truth will emerge, is not readily applicable to labor law in America. Coercion carried out by bosses against workers in these matters can be subtle or overt, but it will succeed in many or most cases. The fact of coercion is therefore seldom ascertained. The employer has so many tricks up his or her sleeve that it is impossible for the law to catch up with them. A reformed union-buster now confessing to his many but personally profitable misdeeds has stated that a common phone call to the home of a very active organizing worker might say:

> You think your old man is at the union meeting. He ain't never been at the union meetings. He's been out with Barbara Jean every night.[19]

The cruelty, unconscionability, and coerciveness of the work of the hired union-buster is so bad, according to this apostate, that one cannot be a decent person and carry out this work. And he adds that he has "no doubt that there is not a unionbuster in this country that can be successful if he or she does not routinely, and daily, break the law."[20]

A MULTIFLAWED SYSTEM

At least one worker in twenty who exercises her/his right to vote for a union in a collective-bargaining representation election is now fired for taking this stance, and this does not count unlawfully fired employees who do not pursue the legal remedies supposedly available to them through the NLRB or grievance procedures.[21] Chances are no better today than one in two that a union that has won an election will ever be able to negotiate a contract with the employer, because of the wide variety of legal and illegal weapons available to the latter.[22] A long-delayed election or unfair labor practice hearing therefore tends strongly to secure an antiunion result.

There are structural flaws in American labor law that make this situation inevitable. Each of these could be the subject of a study, but they can only be briefly reviewed here. First, the delay built into the system, which works to the advantage of the employer, can thwart a just claim made by the most militant and unified of labor organizations. This delay can proceed through three levels of NLRB proceedings and then in some cases through a possible three levels of federal court proceedings, with possibilities of rehearings along the way. Years; costs; and the machinations of employers, their lawyers, consultants, and, quite often, NLRB officials and judges stand between workers and justice.

Second, this great tradition of delay, along with many of the tenets and traditions in the structure of the law itself, leads to the almost totally pervasive disease of illegality that is extant in this field. The pace of the coercion and intimidation has picked up to the point of being rampant. The unregulated profession of labor relations consulting has clearly been involved in this encouragement of employer illegality, but this is also true of the legal profession. The canons of the legal profession in no way justify this, but the canons are largely ignored in the face of the opportunism presented by this legal swamp.[23] The law is thus regarded as something that is functional for the comparatively elite interests and purposes of employers; when it is not, it is to be ignored or thwarted. The result for labor unions is that, although they are dependent upon the law and its machinations, they are not protected by the law; needless to say, labor law commands little respect among workers or union leaders who understand how it works—or, more precisely, fails to work.

"FIRE AT WILL"

Lastly, the United States continues to abide by the archaic "terminate-at-will" doctrine, an anachronistic plague upon the employer-employee relationship that sanctions firings for any reason other than matters protected by a contract, procedures established for government employees, or the various antidiscrimination laws. A boss, for example, may fire a worker simply because the political views of the latter are found distasteful.[24]

William B. Gould of Stanford Law School has aptly described this situation:

> We live in an age and in a country where the concept of employment rights, rights which relate to the ability to provide for oneself and one's family and to the basic human dignity of workers, have lagged far behind the evolution of rights afforded individuals in such areas as access to and protection of property.[25]

It can be seen that the entire environment of labor-management relations could be markedly changed with the elimination of any one of the previously listed flaws, and we will return to some of their implications.

APPLYING LAW TO THE FACTS

Next, we examine an issue that has already been partly addressed, whether the result in a particular case is determined by a rather routine application of the law to the facts. Labor law changes with the fitfulness and fortunes of NLRB board membership and probably, to a lesser extent, with changes in the NLRB bureaucracy. Labor law changes according to the political climate, which today is conservative. There is no obvious reason, for example, why the board should no longer insist in certain cases, despite the clear mandates of the NLRA, that employers bargain in good faith.[26] There is no obvious reason for interminable delays when unions petition for an election (or, at other times, for the remarkable speed at which decertification elections become authorized). The strictures of labor law in the United States, rather than conforming to routine, appear to conform as much to the value preferences of the decision makers who control it.[27]

The evidence cited above clearly shows that it is not true that ''except for the occasional bad judge, any reasonably competent and fair judge (or, in the case of labor law, administrative or public official) will reach the ''correct decision.'' The ''correct'' decision may rely upon precedents, but it is almost as likely to come from the predilections, philosophy, and partisan attachments of the field examiner, board member, or judge.

IMPACT OF PERSONNEL

The important point of personnel selection for the administration of labor law must be addressed. Some of the informal rules involved have blatant characteristics of absurd toleration of bias. Perhaps the most damning of these is the general understanding that persons with apparently balanced views of labor and management rights and interests can be named to the National Labor Relations Board, along with persons who have established records of strong management ties and a clear bias for the perspectives of management. It is never possible, however, no matter what the general climate may be or whether we have a Republican or Democratic president, to appoint a person with a labor-affiliated background to the board.[28]

With only neutrals and management types on the board, prudence will cause us to expect that the balance will most often be one of favoring management interests. The situation is even more absurd than this, however, for some of the management types are people who are opposed to the letter and spirit of the NLRA as well as to its enforcement when the direction is against management interests. "Law and order" again go out the window at the behest of conservative and elite interests.

The best—or worst—example of these forces at work is Donald L. Dotson, a Reagan appointee who left his NLRB chairmanship when his term expired in 1987. Dotson claimed that unions destroy "individual freedom" and stated, as recently as 1980 in an *American Bar Association Journal* article, that "collective bargaining means the destruction of the marketplace as the mechanism for determining the price of labor."[29] It can be said that Dotson and the many people like him who have served on the board represent more than the case of the "occasional bad judge." This is the old fox guarding the chicken coop situation, unless we can somehow uphold the absurdity that it is alright to give the major position in labor law enforcement to an appointee whose stance is dead set against the preamble, the statement of purposes, of the NLRB.

ASSESSMENT

In varying degrees, but in all important particulars, labor law presently fails the tests of the traditional definitions of law in American society. It is neither clear, predictable, nor routinized. Its administration must be faulted, for its strongly biased decision makers seem only to be motivated by a desire to "gut" the law. Its processes for obtaining evidence and its basis for decisions include avoidance or ignorance of evidence, achieving their purpose through delay, and a recognition that multiple acts of coercion and intimidation are unlikely to have costs or punishments in most instances. Labor law is too often—or altogether—a victim of political and value orientations that are particularly objectionable because they result in standing the law on its head. Labor law, as can be seen, suffers from the paradox of being authoritative without necessarily fulfilling the conditions, needs, or even definitions of law.

These realities place labor law in America in a context similar to that of taxation law, which is not respected because it is not believed to be fair, or, perhaps, a drinking law that is honored in the breach at least as often as it is observed. It has been pointed out over and over again that unions are fighting to maintain their Wagner Act rights even as managements seek to subvert these by mostly illegal means. In other words, the current strong drive against unions, even in those offices and plants where they currently hold jurisdiction as bargaining agents, is creating a situation in which Wagner Act rights of organizing and of free association continue to exist only in those ever-decreasing kinds of situations in which they are fought for all over again and won again.[30] The absence of respect for labor law is now moving against its authority as well. "What we have is the law of the jungle," a management attorney has told me candidly, and union leaders and members are increasingly describing labor law in this way.[31]

Economic pressures on unions also continue to be turned up, and this exacerbates the situation because employers are thereby further encouraged to be recalcitrant and law-breaking. The Bush administration's proposed U.S.-Mexico Free Trade Agreement, which has no hard data in support of it and may be offered for a variety of purposes, nonetheless carries with it a strong threat against American workers; and it is unlikely that the White House or the conservative think tanks that offer it advice have not thought of this. In a powerful way, this agreement will carry on a tradition of promoting declining wages and working conditions in North America. The U.S.-Canada Free Trade Agreement, recently negotiated, certainly had as one of its purposes the undermining of organized labor unions in Canada, where in recent decades they have been stronger than in the United States.

REFORMING AND RESTORING LABOR LAW

Because labor law presently fails to measure up even as an approximate formulation of justice, a rather large variety of proposals has been presented in recent years with the aim of reforming labor law and, perhaps, of restoring it to the status of workable and well-respected law. A complete listing, of course, would include conservative proposals, but these are not very useful for our purposes because they often fail to accord the right to exist to labor unions. William F. Buckley, Jr., for example, has barely conceded such a right and has proposed a range of strictures such as a two-week limitation on all strikes.[32] The National Right-to-Work Committee seems to have a hard time concealing its animosity to collective bargaining in its magazine ads and lobbying efforts, but it has been successful in outlawing the union-shop contract in twenty low-wage states. Inconsistencies, as well as a lack of good will, abound in such proposals.

Conservatives historically have lustily favored freedom of contract, but often oppose the freedom to negotiate a union-shop contract. In Indiana, I have had the opportunity to watch firsthand the Republican Party's opposition to union-shop contracts on the ground that nonsympathetic employees should not be required to pay union dues. Simultaneously, the party has for many years, though no longer, collected a fee for its coffers from every citizen of the state, Republican or not, who paid for a car license or drivers' license. And former President Reagan's words and actions demonstrated that he thinks unions are good in Poland but not for this country, as he praised Solidarity, the Polish union, and smashed PATCO, the air traffic controllers' union.

Serious conservative scholars continue to make their contributions as well. Though these might be honorably motivated and reasoned out in better and wholly more preferable ways, they too often fail to give much credence to the idea that labor organizations should be allowed to exist or exercise economic and political power. The most recurrent themes of these treatises is that labor unions are too inefficient to be tolerated in a modern economy and that Wagner Act–type protections of unions and prohibitions upon employers might have been good for 1935 but are surely outmoded today.[33]

Such claims must be addressed, and this is an intellectual debate that must be joined, though I have sought to do this elsewhere.[34] After a century or more of debates, assertions, and counterassertions, it appears improbable that union opponents will change their minds. I can only dispense with their arguments here by saying that there is no solid evidence for their views in any writings produced to date, and this opinion is quite widely shared. A likely key to such claims can perhaps be found in Thorstein Veblen's theme of social and psychological satisfaction derived from lording it over the underlings, a kind of pecking-order syndrome. Efficiency, it is safe to say, is often window dressing for the other motivations in economic relationships.

A case in point is that few conservatives or promanagement people write or express their concern about the difficult problem of delay in NLRB elections and unfair labor practice proceedings. Reformers, of course, take a very different stance. This is because Canada, certainly one of the countries more comparable to our own, has experienced growth of the labor movement in recent years. This growth has occurred alongside the decline of union membership and the reduction of economic and political power of unions in the United States. It is therefore no accident that Canada's labor law provides for bargaining elections immediately after a petition is filed. There can be no delays.

Unfair labor practice charges are also given speedier treatment, but they are not allowed to impede the election process or the signing by members and supporters of petition cards, as is the case in the United States. The net effect of this is that "coercion time" is reduced and union sympathies can be registered in the election while "the iron is hot," rather than years later. This is strategically very important and works to a union's advantage, in keeping with the sentiments of the preamble of the NLRA. This advantage should nonetheless be seen as merely a by-product of the fairness wrought by striving for a coercion-free environment. Not surprisingly, this reform is one of the centerpieces of the AFL-CIO's labor law reform program.[35] Practically speaking, however, no such reform is on the immediate horizon, and the AFL-CIO's major labor law reform efforts are currently directed at the banning of replacements for strikers.

MIGRATING IDEAS

This reform, which advocated speed in NLRB processes, is closely associated with Canadian law professor, Paul Weiler, who now teaches and conducts research at Harvard, and who has analyzed its potential impact in this nation and has urged its adoption.[36] Weiler is a fertile source of other proposals for reform as well, but nearly all of them surround his concerns over the problem of delay. He would like to see a requirement of compulsory arbitration in cases of a deadlock in bargaining on the first contract after an election. This would deal with the problem of delay and resolve the great difficulty of ensuring a contract for newly organized workers, something that often is not possible to achieve. Weiler would also loosen restrictions on secondary boycotts, the only economic weapon available to labor other than the strike. It should be added that boycotting power is an increasingly important consideration as the labor movement looks toward effective economic and political action on an international scale. Weiler also favors some reforms on the firing of strikers, although my reading of these is that his outlook is rather ambivalent.[37]

The Weiler proposals are interesting because they demonstrate the results of some clear and hard thinking obviously carried out from a profitably comparative perspective. To a considerable degree, these proposals answer the major concerns of this chapter, the reestablishment of an equitable standard in the law and the enhancement and strengthening of the political power of labor. The incremental changes that restore power to labor in strike and boycott situations would be helpful if they were enacted. But the primary thrust of the Weiler proposals seeks to deal with the problem of justice delayed becoming justice denied. He wants to deal head on with the coercion that is such a decisive factor in the achievement of first contracts, the settlement of unfair labor practice charges, and the all-important representation elections. Weiler even indicates that he would accept petition-card majorities on the latter point in lieu of the election process itself, and those organizers (including, at one time, myself) with practical experience in the field can only applaud this fair proposal.

Most other analysts and writers are considerably more modest than Weiler in their demands for changes. Many of these people state, or at least give the impression, that they would be well-satisfied just to see a return to the principles of the Wagner Act and its preamble and, of course, a return to meaningful enforcement of these.[38] There can be no doubt that this would represent a net gain for labor. A fair shake in the law would be such a novelty that it might indeed have a toniclike effect upon the labor movement. Such a turn of events, alas, is probably as far off as the realization of Weiler's proposals.

OTHER MODELS FOR REFORM

Currently, law reform in general appears to be a distant hope. It might be best, therefore, to formulate an ideal set of changes by picking and choosing among those models that exist or have existed in the world. This would have to be done with care and prudence, because it is easy to make the mistake of trying to transplant institutions into hostile environments in which they can never be expected to grow or prosper. It is equally imprudent to let matters drift so that no ideas have been thrashed out by the time the opportunity arises to implement them. (It could be argued, I suppose, that no such opportunity will arise in the foreseeable future. This could be true, but it is hardly self-evident. I, for one, have the utmost confidence in the ultimate failure, the inescapable tendency to botch or corrupt matters, that eventually occurs with conservatives at the helm. This particularly would be the point if we ever arrive at something approaching a fair national elections system [see Chapter 6]).

It must be underscored that labor law is never static. New changes develop, and for a terribly long time these have been, mostly, to the disadvantage of workers and their unions. The U.S.–Mexico Free Trade Agreement is a major threat; but the unions took a serious setback in the 1988 Supreme Court decision of *Communications Workers of America* v. *Beck,*[39] a decision unquestionably brought about through the agitation of the National Right-to-Work Committee. In this case, the Court ruled that unions must divine, through accounting, the amount of dues money used for purposes *other than* collective bargaining and then charge only this amount to the members who object to their money being used for educational, community service, mutual support, or political activities such as lobbying. It is a picayune amount of money that is at stake, but the result will be to harass unions quite badly and increase their administrative expenses substantially. The analogue for this decision is one in which a court awards trespass damages in a case involving a walk across someone's privately owned land. The damages are probably there, but they are not severe, and nominal damages are the only award usually possible to win. But the lesson is simply this: Unions cannot just sit around and become politically inactive, or else they will be faced with more and more actions of this kind until they must cease to function. Staying on the offensive is the only hope in America, the nation with the record of perhaps the greatest labor oppression of any of the wealthy industrialized societies.

Although those of us interested in reform and restoration of labor law must keep an open mind and must certainly debate and consider a variety of ideas, I believe that a good place to start is with models of the labor movement that are around at the present time or at least in the recent past in nations like Britain, New Zealand, and Israel. All of these have labor movements that are more or less permanent fixtures of the political, social, and economic landscape. More important, all of them have traditionally been built around the idea that if it is possible to have a collective bargaining organization in existence in a given situation, then ipso facto, you have it.

Recent changes in labor law in Britain (and, in fact, the de novo enactment of labor law supposedly to fill voids where they existed) have strongly attenuated this idea in the law if not in the political culture. These changes were the handiwork of the Thatcher governments. New Zealand has likewise seen some scaling back on its so-called compulsory unionism law, although a solid union-shop situation remains in industries such as food freezing and the docks. (These are important elements of the industrial scene in this small country.) Israel, on the other hand, seems to have experienced a very slight, or perhaps no, reduction in the powers or the pervasiveness of its huge and all-encompassing Histadrut labor organization, though some seem to be arguing that this should occur.

The model we should begin with, then, is one in which labor union organization is assumed, a given of industrial and commercial life and of virtually all employer-employee relationships that can be defined as such. This may appear to be a long step for a society such as the United States to take, and it is, at least when the idea is first contemplated. It is not as long a step as it may seem, however, for several reasons.

WHY A NEW MODEL CAN WORK

A new model for the labor movement in the United States can work for a variety of reasons. First, the countries that are the source for such a model are not totally alien to our political culture. They are Western societies and they are democratic nations. In addition, it can be convincingly argued that most Western societies—Canada, Germany, Belgium, and Sweden are good random examples—are closer to this model than they are to the American model, which is probably the freak in the lot. The rates of unionization in these countries are 37 percent, 40 percent, 70 percent, and more than 80 percent, respectively.[40] The American model, with well under 20 percent, is that of a labor movement that frankly does not fit what one might call a norm among these nations. There are some good labor history reasons why this is the case, of course, but this does not change the fact of this low and undesirable number of members.

Second, the United States has already and long ago declared as a public policy, in the preamble of the Labor-Management Relations Act (LMRA), that it is the responsibility of government not only to protect the right to organize, but, in fact, to actively *encourage* it. Our labor law, ironic as it may appear in light of its routine and day-to-day violations, is not supposed to be neutral. The LMRA clearly states in its opening text that it is on the side of unionization whenever or wherever this is possible. It is not such a long leap, in light of the prescriptions of the preamble, to move to an actively presumptive role in support of unionism in place of a passive—or openly thwarted—dedication.

Third, although it is desirable to return to the principles of the Wagner Act and the fair and regular enforcement suggested and called for by this rubric, it is probably impossible in light of the mighty scale of labor law violations that have gone on year after year since the enactment of more lenient—for the employers—amendments in 1947. (Admittedly, violations of labor law by employers did exist before Taft-Hartley, but they were usually dealt with more severely in the Wagner Act era.) Violation of labor law has become not only a given of many or most employer strategies and tactics but also an industry of vested interests for the lawyers and consultants hired by employers.

Returning to the Wagner Act and its protections, which would surely be a gain compared to the present climate, would be analogous to setting up a track meet in which one team has to begin each race 500 meters behind the other. A return to the Wagner Act might be possible, but a return to the Wagner Act *era* is impossible. More precisely, the Wagner Act could not be expected to work well after the wholesale pummelling its principles have endured for several decades. The character of boss-worker relationships in America must be understood within the contexts of illegality, coercion, and oppression. Because no labor movement in the industrialized world has had to endure more repression, in all probability, than America's has,[41] breaking out of this mold of contempt for the law requires a wholly new approach.

TOWARD A MORE PERFECT UNION

A new framework in which unions are in place in every office, shop, factory, terminal, or conceivable center of work would provide an unmistakable, crystal-clear set of assumptions for employers, their lawyers, and their consultants to encounter, experience, and negotiate with. There undoubtedly would be some incentive to relocate offices, factories, and other facilities outside the country, but this trend could be marginally managed by a combination of market forces and legislation. It might be asked whether this new legal framework would come into being because of a forfeiture on the part of employers wrought by their past and present contempt for the law. The answer, of course, is yes. After all, the need for this larger set of assumptions is based upon a track record of the systematic and overwhelming tendency of employers to thumb their noses at both the letter and spirit of labor legislation and rulings.

We already have a precedent in American labor law that rests upon a principle not unlike this one. In *United Dairy Farmers Cooperative Association* v. *NLRB*,[42] a federal appellate court ruled that the NLRB may issue a bargaining order, even in the absence of a union card majority or electoral victory, when an employer's outrageous and pervasively unfair labor practices have destroyed any chance for a free election.[43] This decision is qualified by the consideration that there must be a reasonable possibility that the union would have won the election but for the employer's unfair labor practices. The principle of this case has tremendous potential and can be capably generalized if it can be revived, but the Dotson-led NLRB has seen fit to invalidate it.

We know for a fact that many bargaining elections could have been won and that many first contracts could have come into being were it not for the pervasively unfair practices of employers. How many elections and how many contracts would have been won is of course conjectural. It hardly seems fair, however, to limit the doctrine in the *United Dairy Farmers* case to circumstances of unique and extreme import, for it is just as likely that other employers have resorted to pervasively unfair practices, some of which are the subject of NLRB hearings and court cases and most of which, given the disincentives, probably are not. Our guideline on the generalization of this principle can be taken from the preamble of the LMRA, which calls not for neutrality but for the encouragement of labor union organization. This case therefore stands for a principle and a potential that are logically supported and reinforced by the preamble.

The goal of a strengthened labor movement would surely be helped greatly by a legal assumption that a bargaining unit exists wherever one may exist. The AFL-CIO federation might have 80 or 90 million members rather than 15 million, but the strength of the labor movement cannot merely be measured in numbers alone. It might truly develop some countervailing political weight against corporations and business groups because its resources would be substantially greater, and, most important, the labor movement's political socialization efforts vis-à-vis its membership would be bound to have a greater effect.

Many problems would have to be ironed out in such a scheme. Quick disaffiliations would have to be prevented in those locations where the workers have been socialized into antiunionism for years or decades. This could be done by establishing a trial period of collective bargaining sufficient to experience its benefits. An appellate procedure outside the union's structure would have to be available to dissident members to ensure union democracy, though this would be a ''last resort'' kind of tribunal. (Some unions already have these.) Admittedly, it might also be necessary to more precisely define just what is a union. For example, should it be involved in hiring decisions as is often the case in the skilled trades? What about organizations like the Teamsters, which has some management characteristics as well as other features that seem to take it outside of the traditional definition of a labor union?

All of these problems are resolvable, but there may be many others, which are presently unanticipated and which should be brought up, worked through, and discussed. In terms of social and economic costs, complexity, and, most important, the cause of justice, the present system—or nonsystem—of labor law in America is much more daunting, much more unfathomable, and, in the long run, destructive to the fabric of the law and the society it is supposed to serve.

NOTES

1. March 10, 1990.

2. A survey by Penn and Schoen Associates in 1989 showed that 65 percent of the sample opposed employers having the right to replace strikers with 28 percent approving of this. A Roper Poll, done at approximately the same time, shows a 2:1 disapproval of the hiring of permanent replacements for strikers.

3. Cass R. Sunstein, ''Rights, Minimal Terms, and Solidarity: A Comment,'' *University of Chicago Law Review* 51 (1984), 1041-60.

4. James B. Atleson, *Values and Assumptions in American Labor Law* (Amherst: University of Massachusetts Press, 1983); Richard B. Freeman and James L. Medoff,

What Do Unions Do? (New York: Basic Books, 1984); Charles Fried, "Individual and Collective Rights in Work Relations: Reflections on the Current State of Labor Law and Its Prospects," *University of Chicago Law Review* 51 (1984), 1012–40; Robert E. Smith, *Workrights* (New York: Privacy Journal, 1983); Paul Weiler, "Promises to Keep: Securing Workers' Rights to Self-Organization under the NLRA," *Harvard Law Review* 96 (1983), 1769–1827, and his "Striking a New Balance: Freedom of Contract and the Prospects for Union Representation," *Harvard Law Review* 98 (1984), 351–421.

5. Committee on Education and Labor, Subcommittee on Labor-Management Relations, *The Failure of Labor Law—A Betrayal of American Workers* (Washington, D.C.: U.S. Government Printing Office, 1984).

6. Robert A. Dahl, "Power to the Workers?"*New York Review of Books* 15 (November 19, 1970), 20–24; Robert A. Dahl, "What Is Political Equality?" *Dissent* 26 (1979), 363–68; Robert A. Dahl and Charles E. Lindblom, *Politics, Economics and Welfare*, 2d ed. (New York: Harper, 1970); Theodore J. Lowi, *The End of Liberalism: The Second Republic of the United States* (New York: W. W. Norton, 1979); Grant McConnell, *Private Power and American Democracy* (New York: Knopf, 1970).

7. Freeman and Medoff, *What Do Unions Do?*

8. Dahl and Lindblom, *Politics, Economics and Welfare.*

9. Kay L. Schlozman, "What Accent the Heavenly Chorus? Political Equality and the American Pressure System," *Journal of Politics* 46 (1984), 1006–32.

10. Jonathan G. Axelrod, "Common Obstacles to Organizing under the NLRA: Combatting the Southern Strategy," *University of North Carolina Law Review* 59 (1980), 147–73; Fried, "Individual and Collective Rights"; Richard A. Posner, "Some Economics of Labor Law," *University of Chicago Law Review* 51 (1984), 988–1011; Weiler, "Promises to Keep"; Weiler, "Striking a New Balance"; Archibald Cox, Derek C. Bok, and Robert A. Gorman, *Labor Law: Cases and Materials*, 6th ed. (Mineola, NY: Foundation Press, 1986).

11. See the two articles by Weiler cited before; also, Robert Kuttner, "Can Labor Lead?" *New Republic* 3608 (March 12, 1984), 19–25.

12. Schlozman, "What Accent the Heavenly Chorus?"

13. Weiler, "Striking a New Balance."

14. James Fiorito and C. R. Greer, "Determinants of U.S. Unionism: Past Research and Future Needs," *Industrial Relations* 21 (1982), 1–32.

15. David Kairys, "Introduction," in David Kairys (ed.), *The Politics of Law: A Progressive Critique* (New York: Pantheon, 1982), 1–2.

16. A. J. Riggs, "National Labor Relations Act—Its Restrictions on the Constitutional Right of Free Speech," *Texas Bar Journal* 46 (1983), 567–71.

17. Laura Cooper, "Authorization Cards and Union Representation Election Outcomes," *Northwestern University Law Review* 79 (1984), 87–141; Stephen B. Goldberg, J. G. Getman, and J. M. Brett, "Union Representation Elections: Law and Reality: The Authors Respond to the Critics," *Michigan Law Review* 18 (1981), 564–93; S. R. Wall, "Representative Bargaining Orders: A Time for Change," *Cornell Law Review* 67 (1982), 950–89; J. Bernstein, "Union Busting: From Benign Neglect to Malignant Growth," *University of California Davis Law Review* 14 (1980), 1–78.

18. See n. 5.

19. "Stickin' It to the Union: Confessions of an Ex-Unionbuster," *UE News*, March 29, 1991, 6–7.

20. Ibid., 6.

21. See n. 5.

22. Weiler, "Promises to Keep."

23. Weiler, "Striking a New Balance"; Kuttner, "Can Labor Lead?"; *Wall Street Journal*, February 16, 1982, and August 3, 1982.

24. Ira Glasser, "You Can Be Fired for Your Political Views," *Civil Liberties* 327 (April 1979), 8.

25. William B. Gould, "The Rights of Individual Workers," *Center Magazine* 17 (July/August 1984), 2–14.

26. See n. 5.

27. Atleson, *Values and Assumptions*.

28. Arthur M. Goldberg (participant/discussant) quoted in Gould, "The Rights of Individual Workers," 8.

29. *Los Angeles Times*, January 24, 1985.

30. Kuttner, "Can Labor Lead?"

31. See n. 5.

32. For a complete list of his labor law proposals, see my *City of the Right*, Chap. 3.

33. Fried, "Individual and Collective Rights."

34. See n. 32.

35. Committee on the Evolution of Work, *The Changing Situation of Workers and Their Unions* (Washington, D.C.: AFL-CIO, 1985).

36. See the various articles written by Weiler and cited in these notes.

37. See the two articles by Paul Weiler listed in n. 4.

38. Kuttner, "Can Labor Lead?"

39. 108 S.Ct. 2641, 56 *Law Week* 4857 (1988); the screws have been tightened even further in *Lehnert* v. *Ferris Faculty Association*, ____ U.S. ___ (1991), and by an administrative order signed by President George Bush in mid-1991. The transparency of politicians on many issues is of course nothing remarkable; all the same, it should be pointed out that though the president claimed a real concern for workers—nonunion workers—in enforcing this decision, he left open the real question of coercion of corporate employees and their "contributions" to the company's PAC; one of my M.B.A. students pointed out from his job experience that his supervisor told him that such contributions were "legally voluntary but actually mandatory." We will probably have to wait a long time to see this matter addressed.

40. A list of work force percentages unionized in various countries is found in James P. Begin and Edwin F. Beal, *The Practice of Collective Bargaining*, 7th ed. (Homewood, IL: Irwin, 1985), 469.

41. Gould, "The Rights of Individual Workers." Most histories of American labor will either state this or demonstrate this point.

42. 633 F.2d 1054 (CA-3, 1980), 89 LC #12,350.

43. "The National Labor Relations Board Has Authority to Order an Employer to Bargain with a Labor Organization When the Employer Has Committed Egregious Unfair Labor Practices, Despite the Absence of a Union Count Majority or Election Victory," *University of Cincinnati Law Review* 50 (1981), 405–14; "The National Labor Relations Board May Issue a Bargaining Order Notwithstanding the Absence of a Union Card Majority When an Employer's 'Outrageous' and 'Pervasive' Unfair Labor Practices Have Destroyed Any Chance for a Free Election, and When a Reasonable Probability Exists That the Union Would Have Won the Election 'but for' the Employer's Unfair Labor Practices," *George Washington University Law Review* 49 (1981), 780–800.

An earlier version of this chapter appears in *Labor Law Journal* 36 (September 1985).

6 Questioning Elections Law

One of the basic questions for the 1990s is . . . the future of democracy in America. Historically, parties have organized our complex government and, in the process, have given the whole enterprise legitimacy among the public. There is no substitute for them.

—Walter Dean Burnham[1]

WALTER DEAN BURNHAM SUMS UP, in a forthright and dramatic way, why American electoral law merits our consideration at the present time. The competitions of parties and candidates must be carried out in an electoral process that relates to the people, many of whom have opted out of it. And, ultimately, this process must again establish links between the governed and those who govern.

It is time to tinker with the system. Some of its mechanics can be improved. It will remain the case, of course, that many of the psychological, ethical, and spiritual troubles of the nation will persist no matter what is done with the electoral process. But a fairer presidential election system will at least afford the opportunities for change that our present state of affairs seems to demand.[2]

This is not merely a question of making some improvements. The need for change is a profound and obvious one. It might be possible for one party and its leaders to serve the nation well while controlling the White House for twenty years of a twenty-four-year period, though it is hardly likely in our somewhat unresponsive fixed-term system. It is also true, moreover, that a variety of demographic, cultural, media, and money factors can be expected to entrench the party in power unless some revolutionary events and changes occur fortuitously. Unless some way or ways can be found to help the process of change, at least at the margins, our whole democratic enterprise can be expected to suffer.

There are several reasons for this. First, it is believed that political change in the United States is axiomatic if new and worthwhile approaches to international and domestic problems are to be undertaken. The conservative case in the post-Vietnam, post-Watergate, post-Irangate era is not strong. Risking more conservative government appears irrational in light of the reckless disregard for national security, for the general welfare, and even for democratic processes that have characterized the past two or more decades. We should not issue a driver's license to those who have crashed time and again. Second, it is clear that only winning executive power will provide respite from these decades. Victories in congressional or state-level races may provide some satisfaction, but recent history indicates they hardly provide much effective check on an administration bent upon its will whatever the stakes may be or whatever the law says. And third, it simply will not do for those who have great cynicism about the system, such as the author, to propose or suggest inaction;[3] at the least, this kind of counsel, which has been so heartily taken up by the general public, should be examined and reexamined before it is set out or continued.

The strategies and tactics available are full of pitfalls, and that is why this must be a cautionary chapter. It is amply clear that, although tactical schema for an election campaign can be useful, it is quite in order—indeed, it is vital—to develop a long-term strategy that will provide advantages in the balance of factors that vitally influence American politics. One can argue that the conservative movement in this country has benefited from thinking long-term and developing its strategies accordingly. No coherent strategy can be found on the other side. The only discernible strategy, if one can call it that, has been to win as many elections as possible and, perhaps, to ensure control of the legislatures in the crucial period after the decennial census. This surely has not been enough.

It should be added that the development of such a long-term strategy falls well within the best traditions of political science. Any assistance rendered in rebalancing a skewered political system can help to provide coherence to and *perhaps* even relegitimize the system. We shall see, of course.

ELECTIONS LAW AND THE ELECTIONS GAME

It is not difficult to demonstrate a connection between electoral law and electoral participation, and it is almost equally possible to show a connection between electoral law and *who* participates in elections. These connections are at the center of the works of Maurice Duverger and V. O. Key, for example, but they also inform the work of Walter Dean Burnham, Earl Black, Merle Black, Herbert E. Alexander, Arend Lijphart, Bernard Grofman, Nelson W. Polsby, Aaron Wildavsky, Douglas Rae, Martin Wattenberg, Richard Rose, Raymond E. Wolfinger, Steven J. Rosenstone, and many others.[4] In short, electoral law defines electoral *constituency*. Electoral law also defines the character of the *ballot*, and although this is an important consideration and can even be determinative of outcomes, it will not be given much attention here simply because no reform of the electoral process in this area seems to have occurred that can be expected to aid in the development of electoral equity and/or new advantages to the forces of political change. A third consideration, however, the electoral *formula*, must be given close attention because it bears directly upon needed changes and the possibility of their precursor, new results.[5]

These considerations will be brought to bear upon three proposed presidential election reforms: (1) the abolition of the electoral college and its replacement with a one-person, one-vote system; (2) the abolition of voter registration as a prerequisite to the exercise of the franchise; and (3) a massive strengthening of labor unions through legislation adapted from other democratic countries that will strengthen the chances of political change and of a profound difference in future election results. The all-important matter of constituency would be affected by all three of these changes, whereas the formula issue is directly linked only to the first two proposed changes and indirectly with the third. It will be appreciated that the proposed reforms are posited in connection with hoped-for political changes much more than any "common good" or "general welfare" considerations; and this is simply because the advantages accruing to society as a whole from such changes, though clearly defensible (and I would say even preferred), are not emphatically defined moral absolutes nor will they appeal to political conservatives and their phalanxes, at which these proposals are aimed.

THE HOPELESSNESS OF CAMPAIGN FINANCE REFORMS

Before taking up the reforms suggested by this agenda, a brief word is in order about campaign finance reform because it is a perennial proposal (and, one may add, a Pandora's box) of lobby groups and activists associated with a progressive perspective. Campaign-reform considerations are most certainly important, but reform of campaign finance does not, at the moment at least, appear to be a likely avenue of meaningful change. A review of the history of these efforts will show that there are significant obstacles.

First, there are important and valid First Amendment objections that can be brought to bear upon any campaign-finance laws, and these cannot be easily dismissed. The Supreme Court notes in *Buckley* v. *Valeo* (1976) that good and valuable civil liberties objections can be mounted against such proposals, even though public financing is constitutional.

Second, the banning of this or that kind of financing, even if it should meet constitutional muster, will ordinarily result in people finding a way around it quite legally. Note the vast array of committees that is organized for candidates in order to qualify under expenditure limitations.

Third, the writing of campaign-finance legislation has been careless enough not to anticipate a variety of problems and circumventions that can arise, often making the object of reform less rather than more likely.

Last, the impact of finance-reform legislation on labor unions, the major financial mainstay of progressive political forces, has often been deleterious. The net effect of this is that corporate ability to finance elections legally through PACs is enhanced, whereas labor is left in the same place or in a worse position.

We cannot and should not foreclose campaign finance reform proposals. For the moment, however, the three avenues of change set out in what follows may be more promising, even taking into account the advocacy, in one instance, of the cumbersome process of constitutional amendment.

THE ELECTORAL REFORM AGENDA I: ABOLISH THE ELECTORAL COLLEGE

> Is the Electoral College stacked against the Democrats? The answer is yes. . . .
>
> —William Schneider[6]

The Electoral College has long been a subject of debate among political observers and especially among political scientists. The arguments against the Electoral College are familiar—that it militates against third parties, that a popular-vote winner can be an electoral vote loser; that some states are given more attention than others by presidential candidates; that the Framers did not foresee its use in a time of well-developed political parties; and that it is simply unfair, mathematically and democratically, to make one person's vote count for more than another person's.[7] Opposition to a one-person, one-vote system is based upon a variety of reasons, including unequal attention given to the states, the "good" two-party system, the simplification of party strategies, and the unlikely prospect of a popular-vote winner actually losing an election.[8] The Electoral College has been defended on the ground that certain interests—and in the past, these have often been liberal, big-state, or minority interests—have benefited from this system.[9] This argument is quickly losing favor today in the face of overwhelming odds against these interests now fostered by the Electoral College. Truth to tell, it never gained much currency. Indeed, it was a liberal Democrat, Senator Birch Bayh of Indiana, who sponsored and ardently labored for a constitutional amendment establishing a popular-vote system.[10]

Whatever the situation may have been in the past, there are two facts about the Electoral College that stand out today that have negative implications for liberals, progressives, the Democratic Party, minorities, feminists, environmentalists, consumerists, labor unions, and allied groups:

1. Population shifts are gradually (and not too gradually at that) working against the northeastern and midwestern states, which have been the mainstays of progressive coalitions in presidential elections. Tables 6.1 and 6.2 clearly demonstrate this, and the situation is one that is well appreciated by political observers.
2. The South has moved from a position of being one-party Democratic to one-party Republican for presidential election purposes. The Rockies, significantly gaining in strength though less important than the South in terms of numbers, have also become one-party Republican for presidential election purposes for a variety of reasons.[11]

TABLE 6.1 Electoral-Vote Distribution Trends, 1960–90

The Democrats have benefited slightly from the loss of electoral strength in rock-ribbed Republican Indiana and the Plains states:

	1960	1970	1980	1990	GAIN OR LOSS
Indiana	13	12	12	12	−1
Kansas	7	7	7	6	−1
Nebraska	5	5	5	5	—
North Dakota	4	4	3	3	−1
South Dakota	4	4	3	3	−1
				NET LOSS	−4

But the Electoral College has overwhelmingly disadvantaged, and will continue to disadvantage, the Democrats because of losses of strength in the Northeast and Midwest:

	1960	1970	1980	1990	GAIN OR LOSS
Connecticut	8	8	8	8	—
Delaware	3	3	3	3	—
District of Columbia	3	3	3	3	—
Illinois	26	26	24	22	−4
Iowa	9	8	8	7	−2
Maine	4	4	4	4	—
Maryland	10	10	10	10	—
Massachusetts	14	14	13	12	−2
Michigan	21	21	20	18	−3
Minnesota	10	10	10	10	—
New Hampshire	4	4	4	4	—
New Jersey	17	17	16	15	−2
New York	43	41	36	33	−10
Ohio	26	25	23	21	−5
Pennsylvania	29	27	25	23	−6
Rhode Island	4	4	4	4	—
Vermont	3	3	3	3	—
Wisconsin	12	11	11	11	−1
				NET LOSS	−35

At the same time, the South, the Border states, and the Rockies have made significant gains:

	1960	1970	1980	1990	GAIN OR LOSS
Alabama	10	9	9	9	−1
Arizona	5	6	7	8	+3
Arkansas	6	6	6	6	—
Colorado	6	7	8	8	+2

(*continued*)

TABLE 6.1 (*continued*)

	1960	1970	1980	1990	GAIN OR LOSS
Florida	14	17	21	24	+10
Georgia	12	12	12	13	+1
Idaho	4	4	4	4	—
Kentucky	9	9	9	8	−1
Louisiana	10	10	10	9	−1
Mississippi	7	7	7	7	—
Missouri	12	12	11	11	−1
Montana	4	4	4	3	−1
Nevada	3	3	4	4	+1
New Mexico	4	4	5	5	+1
North Carolina	13	13	13	14	+1
Oklahoma	8	8	8	8	—
South Carolina	8	8	8	8	—
Tennessee	11	10	11	11	—
Texas	25	26	29	32	+7
Utah	4	4	5	5	+1
Virginia	12	12	12	13	+1
West Virginia*	7	6	6	5	−2
Wyoming	3	3	3	3	—
				NET GAIN	+21

This leaves the Pacific states, which are probably competitive except for Alaska:

	1960	1970	1980	1990	GAIN OR LOSS
Alaska	3	3	3	3	—
California	40	45	47	54	+14
Hawaii	3	4	4	4	+1
Oregon	6	6	7	7	+1
Washington	9	9	10	11	+2
				NET GAIN	+18

*West Virginia is included in this list for the sake of convenience, but its loss of strength should be counted as a Democratic disadvantage.

Against this massive advantage of a bloc of southern and Rockies states, the Democrats have no significant bloc of reliable supporters. Only ten states and the District of Columbia have gone Democratic more than once since 1968 and 1988. The Republicans have, in fact, captured well over 70 percent of all electoral votes since the election of that polarized year.

The numbers tell the story. Table 6.1 shows that although the Republicans have lost four electoral votes in Indiana and the Plains states since 1960, the

Democrats have been saddled with a net loss of thirty-five potential electoral votes in the Northeast and Midwest. At the same time, a "power shift" of twenty-two new votes have been added to the South-Border-Rockies total, a trend that will continue and may even accelerate. The Pacific states, except for Alaska, appear to remain competitive.[12]

The newest studies of polarization in the American body politic emphasize that the most serious problem for the Democrats is the massive rejection of their party by white males in the South and the Rockies and by other groups in these areas of growing strength.[13] It appears unlikely that candidate selection, policy initiatives, platform positions, or any other Democratic Party activity in the near future will turn this situation around. The best way to ameliorate the effects of this rejection, it appears, is to remove the overemphasis upon results in these states that is a concomitant of the Electoral College system.

The best time to begin work on this constitutional amendment is now, because the same factors that reduce the strength of liberals and Democrats in the Electoral College also work to reduce their numbers in Congress.

THE ELECTORAL REFORM AGENDA II: ABOLISH VOTER REGISTRATION

> [R]egistration laws have a substantial effect on the percentage of the population that goes to the polls on election day.
>
> —Steven J. Rosenstone and Raymond E. Wolfinger[14]

> It [nonregistration] is a good system and I am content that voter fraud is virtually nonexistent in our state.
>
> —Carl Kalvelage, Minot State College, Minot, North Dakota[15]

Forty-nine states require voter registration, whereas one, North Dakota, does not. Three states—Maine, Minnesota, and Wisconsin—permit registration on the same day voting takes place, sometimes as late as a minute or two before a vote is cast. Registration is alien to any number of democratic and Western voting systems, such as Britain, Germany, and Ireland.[16]

Easing registration requirements has also enjoyed some momentum in recent years. "Motor-voter" laws, which combine registration activities with driver's license renewal, registration by mail, increased opportunities for the handicapped, and other innovations, have been sanctioned by the states. The results of these efforts indicate limited but nonetheless significant gains in increasing turnout (or, at the least, accessibility) and no development of fraud problems.[17] Facts and experience have not always been pertinent to the perceptions and politics of President George Bush, however, and he cited fraud probability as his reason for vetoing a motor-voter law in May 1992.

TABLE 6.2 New Population Levels: The Basis of Voting Strength

RANK	STATE	1990 POPULATION
1	California	29.84 million
2	New York	18.04
3	Texas	17.06
4	Florida	13.00
5	Pennsylvania	11.92
6	Illinois	11.47
7	Ohio	10.89
8	Michigan	9.33
9	New Jersey	7.75
10	North Carolina	6.66
11	Georgia	6.51
12	Virginia	6.22
13	Massachusetts	6.03
14	Indiana	5.56
15	Missouri	5.14
16	Wisconsin	4.91
17	Tennessee	4.90
18	Washington	4.89
19	Maryland	4.80
20	Minnesota	4.39
21	Louisiana	4.24
22	Alabama	4.06
23	Kentucky	3.70
24	Arizona	3.68
25	South Carolina	3.51
26	Colorado	3.31
27	Connecticut	3.30
28	Oklahoma	3.16
29	Oregon	2.85
30	Iowa	2.79
31	Mississippi	2.59
32	Kansas	2.49
33	Arkansas	2.36
34	West Virginia	1.80
35	Utah	1.73

TABLE 6.2 (*continued*)

RANK	STATE	1990 POPULATION
36	Nebraska	1.58 million
37	New Mexico	1.52
38	Maine	1.23
39	Nevada	1.21
40	Hawaii	1.12
41	New Hampshire	1.11
42	Idaho	1.01
43	Rhode Island	1.01
44	Montana	0.80
45	South Dakota	0.70
46	Delaware	0.67
47	North Dakota	0.64
48	District of Columbia	0.61
49	Vermont	0.56
50	Alaska	0.55
51	Wyoming	0.46

Source: U.S. Bureau of the Census, *Statistical Abstract of the United States, 1991*, 111th edition (Washington, D.C.: U.S. Government Printing Office, 1991), p. 20.

Any regulation or lack of regulation that eases the path of voting tends to increase participation and results in a higher total vote.[18] Wolfinger-Rosenstone, for example, conducted studies in which a variety of conditions were arrayed against turnouts—keeping the polls open later, extending the period of eligibility for registration, and so forth. In virtually all cases, exercise of the franchise was increased by improvements in access to the exercise.[19]

It is reasonable to expect, then, that the absence of a registration requirement will increase turnout. And it does. Ronald Pynn of the University of North Dakota points out that his state had a 71.0 percent turnout in the 1972 presidential election, 67.2 in 1976, and 64.3 in 1980. All of these figures are higher than the national average, and the latter two figures rank fourth and eighth, respectively, in the nation.[20] In addition, the one in-depth study of the North Dakota system of nonregistration reports both high levels of turnout and a general satisfaction of the researcher with the system.[21] What about fraud? Pynn reports it is not a problem, and Carl Kalvelage agrees. A challenge may be made at the time a person votes, but the vote must be permitted to be cast as long as the voter signs an affidavit attesting to her/his residence and the general eligibility accorded citizenship. To attest fraudulently would of course be a crime, but there are few if any prosecutions.[22] An interview with a Republican Party official brought out the view that the Democratic Party engages in fraud, but no cases or instances were offered to support this charge.[23] Fraud is to all intents and purposes impractical in North Dakota, because most communities are very small and the state only has four cities with a population larger than 30,000.[24] Pynn, Kalvelage, and Lloyd B. Omdahl all indicate a confidence in such a system for North Dakota, although they are uncomfortable about extrapolating this system to the nation as a whole.[25]

It appears quite probable that voter turnout would increase in presidential elections if registration was no longer a requirement. And this could help to quell concerns about the continuous decline in turnout in presidential elections (with a very small and unimpressive blip in the 1984 race) that has plagued the psephological scene since 1960. The case against legislative enhancement of voter access to the polls, by contrast, appears to be anecdotally based and is occasionally even ill-informed.[26]

There of course can be no assurance of exactly what character this supposed larger turnout might possess. Indeed, there are some studies and events that indicate that voter registration drives do not bring about much change in election results.[27] Even more distressing, perhaps, is that it can quite persuasively be shown that the act of voting is nearly always cost-inefficient for individuals.[28]

It remains the case that obtaining a high turnout, especially of like-minded liberals, progressives, and Democrats, can yield some positive results. First and foremost, there is the possibility that such efforts will result in the margin between victory and defeat. Second, there is the assurance that the other side, better financed and historically more likely to show up at the polls, will be organized to the hilt; organizing the voters on your side is therefore a defensive act if nothing else. Third, this organizing will be easier to perform if one can dispense with registration drives altogether and simply concentrate upon mobilizing voters. Registration drives, after all, are expensive, and the resources they drain off can well be used for other and better purposes.

How is this to be done? If only national elections are involved, it may be possible to simply pass a federal statute. The vagaries of the law are such, however, that a full-dress constitutional amendment may be required. But it is possible that because residence requirements can no longer be used to prevent voting in a presidential election, registration requirements could likewise be dispensed with. However it is done, it seems certain that turnout will increase after such legislation is enacted. And the Democrats have probably never been known to lose a national election because the turnout was unexpectedly large.

If registration must persist, then election-day signups seem to be the best way to deal with it. Not incidentally, Minnesota and Wisconsin, two of the voting-day registration states, do have large cities, but they do not have any large-scale reports of fraud.[29]

THE ELECTORAL REFORM AGENDA III: STRENGTHEN LABOR UNIONS

Labor unions occupy a unique position in American politics. They are interest groups, to be sure, but unions are much more than that. They are the *only* interest groups that provide, and are capable of providing, large sums of money and people power to liberal and progressive candidates on a sustained and reliable basis. It is true that House leaders such as the powerful (and often conservative) Ways and Means chairperson can independently (should this be the term?) raise large sums of money not just for reelection but for purposes of distribution to other deserving or favored members of Congress, Senators, Senate candidates, and sometimes party officials. Just how far this process can go was illustrated by the activities of resigned House Democratic leaders James Wright and Tony Coelho. But these examples hardly matter, for these kinds of support are neither reliable nor sustainable if officeholders are to be free of privileged influences.

The arguments in favor of a strong labor movement, a vital ingredient for any social order aspiring to democratic principles, are summarized in Chapter 5. The history of labor unions, like the history of all institutions, demonstrates a more than occasional lapse in terms of seeing to the needs of the membership and maintaining the requisite militancy necessary for protection of workers in the antilabor environment that is so uniquely strong in the United States. There has also been corruption, but unions have a better record than many institutions—most certainly business corporations—in adhering to principles of morality. In any event, this is hardly the issue.

The model suggested here has worked in societies of varying levels of prosperity, cultural homogeneity, and international competitiveness. New Zealand has been quintessentially the arena for this model of unionism, but important likenesses can be seen in the labor movements of Sweden, Germany, and other countries, all of which have stronger labor movements than the United States.[30]

It is a long step from the present weakness of the unions and the morass of America's corporations and industry to this model. I am convinced that it is vital for the economic protection of workers, but the political importance of unions to progressive politics is also a paramount concern. The three foundations of this idea outlined in Chapter 5—fealty to the spirit of the law, the practical nature of the idea in light of experience in other countries, and a very salutary blow against the illegality and coercion rife in labor-management matters—are, I believe, compelling; and, in the spirit of fairness, they would do much to restore something approaching a level playing field for the game of American politics.

DOUBTS

Most assuredly, none of us should hold our breath until the three major sets of reforms outlined above are achieved. These are ambitious goals, to say the least. A constitutional amendment, a radical and national change in voting rights law, and a complete overhaul of labor law are each difficult to achieve, though the right time and circumstance (a forthcoming economic crash? a new humane sensibility?) can make any or all of these achievable. It must be candidly admitted, however, that doubts are entertained about making these proposals.

The first and most obvious doubt is whether the right time and circumstances —in other words, the opportunity—for bringing these proposals to fruition will ever come about. A second doubt that must be realized by any rational person is that reforms often fail to achieve their purposes. The best laid plans of politicians or political scientists have certainly been known to founder on this fate, whether we speak of the campaign finance reform of recent years, or of the progressive reforms of the first two decades of this century, or even of the great broadening of the franchise in nineteenth-century England, a broadening that often results in Tory victories. The answer to this dilemma, one must suppose, is to do as best we can, plan carefully, develop an exquisite sense of timing, and anticipate as much as possible the various kinds of fallout that may occur as a result of achievement or even of trying to achieve goals. Would there be some terrible and sweeping reaction to the strengthening of labor unions or to the abolition of voting registration? Would political scientists dislike the loss of certain tracking abilities that would inevitably accompany the end of registration? Would popular-vote selection of presidents really yield any significant changes in the electoral process?

The greatest source of doubt, however, comes from a related but overarching question that must be addressed: the value of the electoral process itself. This does not mean that a different system of choice is advocated; it means instead that we must ask whether *any* electoral system in this country can be insulated in even the least way from elite manipulation. There are great and good reasons for asking this question, because any number of political scientists and other social scientists view the electoral system cynically and because a huge percentage of eligible voters choose not to exercise the franchise. The groups most likely to benefit from the proposals set out in this chapter are the very ones who have most disdained the electoral system—the working class, the poor, and non-white groups.[31] Burnham aptly points out that "the real class polarization in the electoral races is not between Democratic and Republican voters as much as between both and the party of nonvoters."[32]

Nonvoters can hardly be scorned for their failure to participate. The reasons for not voting are many and varied. (One possible explanation, of course, is satisfaction with the system, although the subgroups in the population who abstain, as well as the continual downward movements of participation numbers, seem to work against this argument.) Potential voters may reject the major candidates, may see little prospect of influencing results in one-party states, may see no connection between candidates and policies or perhaps policies and themselves, may be bewildered by the clang of campaigns, or may be simply eliminated from the voting rolls because of a change of residence. Many citizens adhere to the central theme of the "power elite" thesis—that powerful persons and interests make all of the important decisions, regardless of officeholders or parties—and they can hardly be blamed for doing so.[33]

We are only beginning to understand the role of voting in American politics. A study by Kim E. Shienbaum underscores this, arguing that most American voters understand that they are not changing very much by participating in the electoral process. They have developed a ritualized response to campaigns and elections that legitimates the political system and reemphasizes their commitment to parties and perhaps certain candidates. They know in most instances this exercise makes little immediate difference in their lives. Middle-class voters are reconciled to this impotence because they are affiliated with interest groups that, they are fairly certain, will look after their vital interests. Poor people and the "left out," lacking this certainty, are less inclined to participate in a ritual that is by and large designed to preserve the status quo; they may even view the process as a sham. Many of our traditional assumptions and conceptions about the meaning of voting, then, bear further study and should perhaps take into account the premises of scholars like Shienbaum.[34]

Persuasive as such analyses are, the individual citizen is left with little to do on one's own behalf if the electoral system is shunned. Those who wish to maintain the quality of life—who cherish the environment; who are concerned about war, the poor, minorities, and workers; and who want to see a Supreme Court that supports the Constitution against its usurpers—cannot disdain the electoral process. In other times, this may have been possible; but the Far Right attack upon American traditions, values, and institutions that has been carried out from the White House in recent years has galvanized even those of us who were once inclined to nonparticipation or to satisfaction with our disdain. It has been necessary to rethink, to buckle down, and to work on tinkering with the system so that it represents a more level playing field of democratic opportunity.

NOTES

1. "Elections Dash GOP Dreams of Realignment," *Wall Street Journal,* November 26, 1987.

2. Even prominent conservative writers strongly state or imply that change is needed; Kevin Phillips, *The Politics of Rich and Poor: Wealth and the American Electorate in the Reagan Aftermath* (New York: Random House, 1990) (maldistribution of wealth has become excessive and the conservative movement is out of ideas); David A. Stockman, *The Triumph of Politics: The Inside Story of the Reagan Revolution* (New York: Harper & Row, 1983) ("supply side" economics was simply a way of justifying redistribution in favor of the wealthy via tax laws and the budgetary process).

3. This is a slight overstatement; the author has never really suggested inaction but rather a thoughtful approach to the decision of whether or not to vote; Houseman, *State and Local Government*, Chap. 8; H. Mark Roelofs and Gerald L. Houseman, *The American Political System: Ideology and Myth* (New York: Macmillan, 1983), Chap. 14.

4. Maurice Duverger, *Political Parties: Their Organization and Activities in the Modern State*, trans. by Barbara North and Robert North (New York: John Wiley, 1963); V. O. Key, Jr., and Alexander Heard, *Southern Politics in the State and Nation* (New York: Knopf, 1949); Walter Dean Burnham, "Elections as Democratic Institutions," *Society* 24 (May/June 1987), 38–48; Earl Black and Merle Black, *Politics and Society in the South* (Cambridge: Harvard University Press, 1986); Herbert E. Alexander, *Financing Politics: Money, Elections, and Political Reform*, 3d ed. (Washington, D.C.: Congressional Quarterly Press, 1984); Arend Lijphart, *Democracies: Patterns of Majoritarian and Consensus Government in Twenty-One Countries* (New Haven: Yale University Press, 1984); Arend Lijphart and Bernard Grofman (eds.), *Choosing an Electoral System: Issues and Alternatives* (New York: Praeger, 1984); Nelson W. Polsby and Aaron Wildavsky, *Presidential Elections*, 6th ed. (New York: Charles Scribner's Sons, 1984); Douglas Rae, *The Political Consequences of Electoral Laws* (New Haven: Yale University Press, 1969); Martin Wattenberg, *The Decline of American Political Parties, 1952–1980* (Cambridge: Harvard University Press, 1984); Richard Rose, "Elections and Electoral Systems: Choices and Alternatives," in Vernon Bogdanor and David Butler (eds.), *Democracy and Elections: Electoral Systems and Their Political Consequences* (Cambridge: Cambridge University Press, 1983), and "Electoral Systems: A Question of Degree or of Principle," in Lijphart and Grofman, *Choosing an Electoral System*; Raymond E. Wolfinger and Steven J. Rosenstone, *Who Votes?* (New Haven: Yale University Press, 1980).

5. A. Blais and R. K. Carty, "The Impact of Electoral Formulae on the Creation of Majority Governments," paper presented to the 1987 Annual Meeting of the Western Political Science Association, Anaheim, California, March 1987.

6. William Schneider, "Political Change Has Stacked the Electoral College Against Democratic Party," *National Journal*, November 3, 1984, 2110–11.

7. Neal R. Peirce and Lawrence D. Longley, *The People's President* (New Haven: Yale University Press, 1981); John F. Banzhaf III, "One Man, 3.312 Votes: A Mathematical Analysis of the Electoral College," *Villanova Law Review* (Winter 1968), 303–46; Theodore S. Arrington and Saul Brenner, "Should the Electoral College Be Replaced by the Direct Election of the President? A Debate," *P.S.* 17 (Spring 1984), 237–50; R. Gordon Hoxis, "Alexander Hamilton and the Electoral System Revisited," *Presidential Studies Quarterly* 18 (Fall 1988), 717–20.

8. Arrington and Brenner, "Should the Electoral College Be Replaced by the Direct Election of the President?"

9. Ibid.

10. Ibid.

11. Schneider, "Political Change Has Stacked the Electoral College."

12. On the general phenomenon of this change in political power, see Robert Goodman, *The Last Entrepreneurs: America's Regional Wars for Jobs and Dollars* (Boston: South End Press, 1979).

13. See, among other sources, Martin P. Wattenberg, "The Reagan Polarization Phenomenon and the Continuing Downward Slide of Presidential Candidate Popularity," *American Politics Quarterly* 14 (July 1986), 219–46.

14. Steven J. Rosenstone and Raymond E. Wolfinger, "The Effect of Registration Laws on Voter Turnout," paper delivered to the 1976 Annual Meeting of the American Political Science Association, Chicago, September 1976, 32.

15. Letter to the author dated October 19, 1984.

16. "Voter Registration Information" table, *The Book of the States, 1990–91*, Volume 28 (Lexington, KY: Council of State Governments, 1990), 228.

17. Richard G. Smolka, "Election Legislation," in ibid., 226–27; "National Voter Registration Act," *Congressional Digest* 69 (April 1990), 98.

18. See Rosenstone and Wolfinger, "The Effect of Registration Laws"; for a different view, see two interesting short articles: "How More Voters Can Be Fewer Voters," *National Journal*, July 14, 1984, 1374, and "Once They Came, They Voted the Same," *National Journal*, January 19, 1985, 188.

19. Rosenstone and Wolfinger, "The Effect of Registration Laws"; also Wolfinger and Rosenstone, *Who Vote?*

20. Letter to the author dated October 23, 1984.

21. Lloyd B. Omdahl, *Fraud-Free Elections Are Possible without Voter Registration* (Grand Forks: University of North Dakota Bureau of Governmental Affairs, 1971).

22. Ibid; also Pynn letter of October 23, 1984.

23. Telephone conversation, November 13, 1984.

24. Pynn letter of October 23, 1984.

25. Pynn letter of October 23, 1984; Kalvelage letter of October 19, 1984.

26. See the debates offered against the National Voter Registration Act in *Congressional Digest* 69 (April 1990). Representative Pat Roberts, Republican of Kansas, sweepingly asserts: "We could do it [voting] like other countries. In Australia I think they imprison you"; ibid., 119.

27. See the two *National Journal* items in n. 18, for example, but the bulk of the evidence is to the contrary. See the Wolfinger and Rosenstone works cited in n. 19 and also Robert W. Jackman, "Political Institutions and Voter Turnout in the Industrial Democracies," *American Political Science Review* 81 (June 1987), 405–24, and an interesting one-state survey by George Mather, *Lost Votes: Effects of Methods of Voting on Voter Participation, Iowa, 1920–1984* (Iowa City: Institute of Public Affairs, Division of Continuing Education, 1986).

28. Howard L. Reiter, *Parties and Elections in Corporate America* (New York: St. Martin's Press, 1987), Chap. 1.

29. Smolka, "Electoral Legislation," 226–27.

30. Andrew Sharp, "The 'Principle' of Voluntary Unionism in New Zealand: A Political Debate," *Political Science* 38 (July 1986), 1–28.

31. Burnham, "Elections as Democratic Institutions."

32. Ibid.

33. Mills, *The Power Elite*.

34. Kim E. Shienbaum, *Beyond the Electoral Connection: A Reassessment of the Role of Voting in the American Political Process* (Philadelphia: University of Pennsylvania Press, 1984).

This chapter was written without the benefit of knowing the results of the 1992 presidential election. The results of that election do not change any of the arguments presented. The increased turnout figure is duly noted, and this tends to substantiate the case for removal of the impediment of registration.

PART III

ESTABLISHMENT IDEOLOGY

7 Questioning Law and Economics

If economic sophistication is purchased at the price of legal relevance, the bargain is a bad one.

—Bruce A. Ackerman[1]

Economics [has] replaced law as the language of the state.

—Theodore J. Lowi[2]

IT CAN BE SAID THAT LIFE IS LIVED in microeconomic terms, even though the majority of us who are not economists seldom think about our existence in this way. Central to microeconomic thinking is the bargain, the deal that helps to keep the economic engine running. The picture of human behavior usually borne in mind in the world of economics is well known:

> First are the denuded subjects A and B. Each has a preference for something the other possesses. Each would like to satisfy those preferences. The satisfaction of those preferences will increase overall utility; therefore, an exchange between A and B is both mutually and aggregationally advantageous. It would be a shame if they did not exchange![3]

It is therefore the element of *choice* that is at work in any bargain or refusal to bargain.

It is also this element of choice that is basic to an understanding of the school of jurisprudence now operating under the rubric of "law and economics." (It is recognized that writing and speaking about law and economics have long been the habits of social scientists, law professors, and others who may seek to join these disciplines in various ways, but the "law and economics" school, which is the subject of this study, is a phenomenon that is rather more specific.) Building upon the two essential cornerstones of microeconomic modeling and rational choice theory, the law and economics school has made a major impact upon the study of law and upon the process of legal reasoning over the past two decades. As with other trends in the history of American law, most notably realism and sociological jurisprudence, the law and economics movement seeks to impart a scientific approach to the study of law that will provide a good and reliable means of reaching fair results in the courts. A side benefit, presumably, is engagement in an intellectual process that will benefit legal decision making by reforming and reshaping it.

MICROECONOMICS AND THE LAW

The key to the law and economics approach can be found in applying microeconomic models to legal problems; these models, it is asserted, are applicable to both noneconomic and economic phenomena.[4] It is true that comparatively minor adjustments of these applications must be made as one shifts from, say, torts to contracts to property law. It is in these traditional areas of concern, moreover, that law and economics applications are most generally made; constitutional jurisprudence, by contrast, has to date seen relatively little impact.[5] It is also fair to point out that law and economics jurisprudence is closely associated with the law school of the University of Chicago, and this is in keeping with a decades-long commitment to free market economics that has characterized most of the work of the ''Chicago school'' of the discipline led by such eminences as Friedrich von Hayek, Milton Friedman, and George Stigler.[6]

Such thinkers as these bring normative considerations front and center, but it must be acknowledged that microeconomic modeling, in and of itself, hardly suggests a commitment to any particular brand of economics or ideology. Tools of analysis can be, and often are, relatively neutral and objective in their impact and should hardly be shunned when they can provide findings of empirical import. Simultaneously, we must realize that the history of economics is one in which such modeling can be traced back at least as far as Adam Smith, sometimes characterized as the great founding father of capitalist economic theory, more than 200 years ago. The long trail of thinkers, and of supply-demand curves, perfect competition models, and marginal propensities to do this, that, or the other, carries with it whatever advantages and burdens are derived from a normative patina that lends its support to the truisms and shibboleths of capitalist economics.

It is therefore difficult, and at times impossible, to separate findings derived from microeconomic modeling from the normative base that impels economists—and, most decidedly, practitioners in the law and economics school—to carry out their work. In limited ways (though of course to their credit), such free market advocates as James Buchanan and the late Friedrich von Hayek admit their normative premises formed an element of their achievements. Nobel prize winner Buchanan, for example, states that ''my purpose was ultimately normative rather than antiseptically scientific.''[7] It is important to be aware of this when assessing the work of the law and economics school, because it draws very deep draughts from the pools of knowledge—and values—constructed by such free market thinkers and advocates. The mundane point also has to be made that bevies of critics, within and without the discipline of economics, have produced useful studies that have elaborately and exhaustively teased out the normative—and at times even quite irrational—premises of such thinkers; and some of the richest insights along these lines, it is comforting to observe, have been given to us by political scientists.[8]

MARKET ALLOCATION AND THE LAW

The law and economics approach posits the thesis that much of the law, especially as found in common law traditions, is analogous to the free market; or, more precisely, it mimics the market. This can be seen in the following:

1. The law, like the market, uses prices equal to opportunity costs to maximize efficiency. What this means is that an individual is confronted by the costs of his/her act, but the decision to incur such costs is up to this individual. Heavier than compensatory damages are occasionally imposed, but when they are, the purpose is to create necessary and correct economic incentives.[9]
2. Like the market, the law primarily relies for its administration on private individuals who are motivated by economic self-interest "rather than on altruists or officials."[10]
3. The legal system, again like the market, is competitive. The adversary system forces the court into a position similar to that of a consumer who must make choices between competing products. On this point, Richard A. Posner, perhaps the foremost law and economics advocate, states that the common law system has a preferable tradition and structure in comparison with Continental systems, which require a greater amount of judicial involvement, administration, and discretion.[11]
4. In addition, the legal system is strongly characterized by an impersonality —a disinterested aloofness—of the judge that is held to be analogous to the impersonality of the marketplace. This point is buttressed by the belief that the rules of evidence are of substantial aid in promoting this.[12]
5. And ultimately, as such an approach might suggest, the market is assuredly more efficient than the law is; but this is because statutory and administrative law, those great intruders upon the common law system, have introduced inefficient rules that do not mimic the marketplace. Regulatory activity in such areas as banking law, the minimum wage, labor relations, and auto safety can be held to be efficiency-reducing. The common law, then, or what we might call judge-made law, is much to be preferred over statutory and administrative law because of its ability to mimic the market. The work carried out in the other areas is more overtly political in its aims, thereby producing inefficiency.[13]

These points, it is fair to say, represent the kernel of law and economics. Any one of us who is familiar with the history of the law most certainly has the right to be deeply troubled by such a set of analyses. It is difficult to say that statutes and administrative law are inefficient while courts are efficient; it is impossible to say that they are political while judges, schooled in the traditions of American law with all of its presuppositions and prejudices, are not. It is difficult to define efficiency within the framework of law and justice in such a way as to satisfy a consensus of observers. History shows us that judge-made law gave us *Lochner* v. *New York*, *Plessy* v. *Ferguson*, *Dred Scott*, and *Adkins* v. *Childrens Hospital*,[14] all constitutional decisions to be sure, but also reactionary decisions made by judges who sanctioned slavery, child labor, segregation, inhuman working conditions, and absurd assertions of due process. Statutes and administrative law have given labor the right to organize, unemployment compensation for the jobless, Social Security for the elderly, and equal rights protection to women and minorities. Most assuredly, one could cite examples of enlightened court action and reactionary legislation, but this is not the point. The point is that not only is the law and economics case not made but it defies history. That the legal system is competitive and disinterested, is an assertion that does not bear up well under scrutiny.

It is neither fair nor possible, all the same, to judge the law and economics movement merely by glancing at its postulates, for these assumptions have an important set of antecedents and characteristics that must be examined in order to fully understand law and economics. These include (1) the rational-choice tradition found in the social sciences; (2) free market economics (some might say free market ideology), which go back to the seeds planted by Adam Smith; (3) the Coase theorem, an explanatory device often used in law and economics; (4) the centrality of property rights and what this means for the assumptions of this school; (5) the assertion of efficiency and what this exactly means; and (6) the ideological roots of law and economics.

It would also be possible, I suppose, to look at the underpinnings of microeconomics, which of course some writers do. On occasion, they even call for abandonment of this vital branch of economics.[15] I am content to eschew such an exercise, however, in the belief that a set of models that seems to work for a discipline must be accepted for its usefulness.

RATIONAL CHOICE

Rational choice has always been a given of economic theory and analysis. It is a much more recent development, however, that this concept, so central to microeconomic modeling and case studies, has enjoyed the benefit of transplantation to the discipline of political science. There has been an impressive growth in both influence and in number of practitioners in this subfield. A respected journal, *Public Choice*; a host of articles sprinkled rather heavily throughout the journals of political science and public administration; and some landmark books have been brought into being.

Discussions with specialists have led to the assertion that perhaps public choice theory in political science appears as early as in the 1942 work of Joseph A. Schumpeter.[16] But Schumpeter's work is quite obviously a landmark for other reasons; and it is generally held that the work that is considered *the* point of departure for this subfield is *The Calculus of Consent*, written by James M. Buchanan and Gordon Tullock.[17] This, as far as is generally known, is the first study to use microeconomic modeling techniques to describe political institutions, processes, and decision making. Its starting point is individualistic, suggesting value premises to be sure, but this is a likely and logical tack when one seeks to describe the American political and constitutional systems. It is a book of careful logic and of what many readers have said is a fine balance. Among its more important findings is the heralded one that states that income redistribution schemes imposed by governments are futile and bound to fail in their stated purposes because of the costs associated with administration and because of a variety of bureaucratic behaviors that one must reasonably expect.[18] It is probably the work of Buchanan and Tullock, more than that of any other writer, that has made it seem to be the manifest destiny of the rational-choice school to denigrate social welfare programs as well as business regulation. There are many other concerns of these and other public-choice writers, of course: the short-term and long-term definitions and descriptions of self-interest, the many differences that arise between individual preferences and collective policy outcomes, the rational formulation of policy, or perhaps the factor of altruism.

In 1957, Anthony Downs produced *An Economic Theory of Democracy*, an ambitious attempt to describe the political system in economic terms.[19] It was not always well received in graduate seminars, but it was not always well understood, either. Over the years, it has received accolades and it was the focus of a recent and interesting *festschrift*.[20] This collection, which includes work by distinguished rational-choice writers such as Howard Margolis and Kristen R. Monroe, the book's editor, demonstrates that the public-choice school is not wedded to any particular ideology despite its somewhat conservative roots.

Judge Richard Posner's *Economic Analysis of the Law* and his many other works are regarded as conservative in ideology and intent.[21] This does not necessarily mean that he is rigid; indeed, he is acclaimed for his intellectual growth and change, particularly as reflected in his 1990 work *The Problems of Jurisprudence*.[22] The *Economic Analysis of Law*, nonetheless, is grounded upon a line of reasoning that certainly proceeds quite straight back to Adam Smith, the father of modern capitalist enterprise and probably of the economics discipline itself. And it would be only the most undiscerning and unobservant social scientist who would claim either that such premises are value-free or that the case for free market capitalism, as either an economic or moral set of guidelines, has been definitively made or more than temporarily victorious in the political realm.[23]

ADAM SMITH: GREATLY HONORED, GREATLY MISUNDERSTOOD

It is not asserted here that Judge Richard Posner, other law and economics writers, or public-choice social scientists have misunderstood or misinterpreted the work of Adam Smith, though this may occasionally be the case. It is assuredly true that popular understandings of Smith are often totally misleading and, more to the point, that a fair variety of principles established in the work of Smith tends to be ignored by those who claim to partake of his tradition.

One must cringe at the use of Smith's profile as decor for neckties, a popular thing to do within the Beltway during the Bush and Reagan years. The use of Smith as an adornment for the likes of Edwin Meese III, often just half a step ahead of the law he was presumably the enforcer of, is at the least ironic in light of the stern Scot's writings and lectures in his position as a professor of moral philosophy. Even more appalling, however, is the misuse of the great two-volume *Wealth of Nations*[24] in self-serving and inaccurate ways to propound these in support of the unbridled market, the belief that Smith looked kindly upon big businesses, or the weird idea, uttered quite straightfacedly, that greed is okay. None of these, it is safe to say, would win the endorsement of the man Dr. Samuel Johnson called "a dull dog."[25]

Without going into a laborious dissection of the *Wealth of Nations*, it is important to look at least briefly at Smith to demonstrate that his inheritors, including many in the law and economics school, have failed to take sufficient account of his moral beliefs as they chart their lines of economic, political, moral, and sometimes spiritual legacy. If this can be shown, and I am confident that it can, it will strongly suggest that an important portion of the ideological component and of the analytical component of their assumptions and values is wrongly conceived. Unfortunate and embarrassing as this is, an awareness of it will promote clarity of political thought and an understanding of some of the major dimensions of conservatism—and of law and economics—in social and legal policy.

Smith was stern. Anyone who has been in Edinburgh during the short, cold, and gray days of winter can understand some of the ambience in which this teacher of moral philosophy labored in this land of Calvinism. To a very great extent interpreters of Smith have pegged him correctly. The free market, the invisible hand that guides self-interest but leads to a different and socially useful collective result, the entrepreneurial spirit, the division of labor, the promotion of efficiency, and the objections to monopoly pricing are all there. But on a number of specific matters, Smith is not at one with the U.S. Chamber of Commerce, the Bush and Reagan administrations, the late Malcolm Forbes, William F. Buckley, Jr., Senator Jesse Helms, or the *Wall Street Journal*. On greed, for example, which Smith is often unfairly said to support, he writes:

> In the race for wealth, and honours, and preferments . . . [one] may run as hard as he can, and strain every nerve and muscle, in order to out-

> strip all his competitors. But if he should justle, or throw down any of them, the indulgence of the spectators is entirely at an end. It is a violation of fair play, which they cannot admit of.[26]

There is no evidence that shows that law and economics writers like Posner or Frank Easterbrook have missed this point. They may have missed the full weight of Smith's condemnations of profligacy, however, and this shows up in their relative unconcern about how one who wins wealth might use it. Smith was concerned about this. At one point, he asserts that "In Glasgow where almost no body has more than one servant, there are fewer capital crimes than in Edinburgh."[27] Quoting Bernard de Mandeville, author of *The Fable of the Bees*, which influenced his work, Smith avers that

> [f]rugality is like Honesty, a mean starving Virtue, that is only fit for small Societies of good peaceable Men, who are contented to be poor so they may be easy; but in a large stirring Nation you may have soon enough of it. 'Tis an idle dreaming Virtue that employs no Hands, and therefore very useless in a trading Country, where there are vast Numbers that one way or other must all be set to Work. Prodigality has a thousand Inventions to keep People from sitting still, that Frugality would never think of; and as this must consume a prodigious Wealth, so Avarice again knows innumerable Tricks to rake it together, which Frugality would scorn to make use of.[28]

It should be noted in passing that Mandeville's study of bees is the paradigm to which Smith refers throughout his great work. The implications of such a model are manifold, but behavioral scientists, just to name one group, might have problems understanding some of the parallels and analogues developed. It is a striking thought that conservatives today cite an often unlearned understanding of Smith, whose own understanding in turn rests in many ways upon bee behavior. It is fair to suggest that there may be some major problems here.

It is probably in the area of taxation that Smith's views are most surprising to those who hold conventional conservative views or who may be connected with the law and economics school. Smith's views certainly are not in accord with Buchanan and Tullock, for example, in their joint or separate works.[29] Most ironically, Adam Smith clearly disagrees with the Adam Smith Institute, a right-wing think tank in Britain that gave Prime Minister Margaret Thatcher the idea of the community charge, better known as the poll tax. This crude and cruel head tax is condemned by Smith as "arbitrary" and "unequal."[30] The U.S. Chamber of Commerce would also be at odds with Smith on this, because it has for many years favored a federal sales tax as the best means of raising revenue. Such a system penalizes spending, which represents a greater part of the incomes of the poor than of the wealthy. Smith is not merely content to condemn this tax, however. He favors using revenue-raising powers of government to go after the wastrel-like spending of the idle rich, and he recognizes the need to tax rental income and wealthy persons' houses most heavily:

> The proportion of the expence of house-rent to the whole expence of living, is different in the different degrees of fortune. It is perhaps highest in the highest degree, and it diminishes rapidly through the inferior degrees, so as in general to be lowest in the lowest degree. The necessaries of life occasion the great expence of the poor. They find it difficult to get food, and the greater part of their little revenue is spent in getting it. The luxuries and vanities of life occasion the principal expence of the rich, and a magnificent house embellishes and sets off to the best advantage all the other luxuries and vanities which they possess. A tax upon house-rents, therefore, would in general fall heaviest upon the rich; and in this sort of inequality there would not, perhaps, be anything very unreasonable. It is not very unreasonable that the rich should contribute to the publick expense, not only in proportion to their revenue, but *something more than in that proportion*.[31]

Smith, in other words, is for progressive taxation schemes; that is, he favors taxing the rich more than those in middle-income groups and taxing both of these more than the poor. The proportion of wealth taxed should be greater in the case of the rich than in the case of others. This message is not to be found in conservative treatises on economic policy or even in the more learned disquisitions emanating from the Chicago school of law and economics.

It is probably a good exercise, then, to return to Smith for his insights, for they demonstrate well that modern conservative economists, public-choice theorists, and law and economics people have deviated from the "true path" either because they do not understand it, because they have reasoned that Smith was simply wrong on these points, or even because of more expedient reasons.

THE COASE THEOREM

The Coase theorem, which is not a theorem, is centrally important to public-choice literature and, more important for our purposes, to the law and economics school. In circumstances involving economic issues in which government chooses not to intervene, the parties to a dispute can resolve the problem through private negotiations. If this can be done, we members of the public who are not directly concerned, nearly all of us, should applaud the settlement of this matter because we will not be faced with the costs of negotiation. Ronald Coase, who posed this solution in a landmark article, states that such a solution of voluntary settlement between the affected parties is obviously the most efficient way to deal with the matter. He cautions that such a solution is most likely under conditions of well-defined property rights and law settlement costs.[32]

The political and economic relevance of the Coase theorem is that the absence of transaction costs, which would have likely been imposed by government involvement in the decision making, makes this the most desirable method of settlement. Few can quibble with such a proposition, although disputes about applicability might arise in different cases. The implications of the Coase theorem are clearly in tandem with works like Buchanan and Tullock's *Calculus*, although they really do not employ it except to recommend Coase's article as interesting.[33] The implications of the Coase theorem are clear enough for the courts, however, and this is why Judges Posner, Easterbrook, and others find it useful.[34]

Knowing that Professor Coase, presently the Clifton R. Musser Professor Emeritus of Economics at the University of Chicago School of Law (and a recent Nobel prize winner in economics to boot), was in the past (and still may be) committed to far different political views than those associated with the law and economics school, I wrote to him and asked what he thought about his theorem's employment by a group of conservative scholars for their own purposes. His letter answering this query, which was quite straightforward, said that Professor Coase was not sure about the term "ideology" and, for that matter, he was not sure that Judge Posner was aiming at the promotion of ideology. His intention, he iterated, was to provide a mode of analysis with the theorem. It ordains no specific policy solution, he averred, but it does expedite choices between competing policies.[35]

Interesting as this response is—and I would probably find most anything Professor Coase says about this to be worthwhile—it should still surprise no one that the Coase theorem, and the kind of conversation animated by it receives a fair amount of criticism. Talk about economic bargaining, for example, faces barbs that are based upon both aesthetic and practical grounds. Larry Preston points out that, in his view, the skills and values of conversation about public issues are actually blighted by this kind of dialogue.[36] Bruce A. Ackerman spends the greater part of his book, which critiques law and economics, discussing such approaches in sometimes caustic, sometimes satirical ways.[37] Whether the cases made by Preston and Ackerman are in fact persuasive will to a great extent depend upon the values and outlooks of the great variety of individuals who study the law and the methods used to resolve its weighty problems.

THE CENTRALITY OF PROPERTY RIGHTS

> . . . legal protection of property rights creates incentives to use resources efficiently.
>
> —Richard A. Posner[38]

Property rights are a major linchpin in the law and economics approach. True, property law is just one of many subjects that may arise in legal studies, but it is reasonable to assert that this bundle of rights occupies the central place in legal education and therefore tends to remain at the forefront of lawyers' and judges' minds for the remainder of their careers.

Property rights are of course a two-edged sword in questions of law and public policy. Their protection, perhaps overemphasized in the feudal era and therefore in the common law, can be a matter of grave import to anyone, rich, poor, or middle-level. When an American-based fruit company managed, in cahoots with the corrupt Marcos government in the Philippines, to remove small holders from their farms and had these lands conveyed to the firm, a serious act amounting to little more than robbery took place. The fact that these farmers were then given jobs working on the lands they once owned hardly compensates for this unjust action. It is quite simply the case that property rights protection can aid the less privileged as well as the privileged.

It does not seem remarkable, then, to give wide berth to property rights in discussing the methods of law and economics or, perhaps, the methods of any approach to the study of law. Posner's law and economics treatise on property begins, as in the law schools, with the somewhat quaint discussion of the law of ownership of wild animals, *ferrae naturae*, and proceeds, however briefly, through the tapestries of broadcast licensing, future interests in the ownership of land, environmental pollution problems, and the public lands.[39] His approach is informed by the belief, prevalent in American law, that property rights demarcations simplify the processes of justice. This is seen as efficient, and it therefore coincides with a major Posnerian aim. But there is a further force at work here. The task of the courts is one in which it should be approximating what markets do insofar as this is possible, according to Posner. It follows that a studied and steady recognition of property rights will help to shore up a law court's fealty to market forces in a capitalist system.

Given the conservative (but also libertarian) bent of judges like Posner and Easterbrook, it is not remarkable that they should place property rights in so central a position. To Posner's credit, he does not seem to assert property rights in any a priori way. He does not seek to deny, for example, the power of eminent domain that is held by the various governments of this country. His colleague Richard Epstein, by contrast, goes to the edge of such a declaration.[40] Others go right over the brink:

> In contrast to the Supreme Court, I submit that there is no such thing as the power of eminent domain consistent with the law of nature and, therefore, the laws of the United States.[41]

Despite his lack of this particular brand of extremism, it is important not to get too caught up in acceptance of Posner's (and the law's) valuations of the right of property. The birthplace of this right, as far as our legal system is concerned, is England; but England, despite the bloody-mindedness of the Thatcher era, has long since abandoned many of the common law traditions concerning land, for example. An historically recent Labour government adopted the

Community Land Act of 1976, which placed real property development in the hands of local governments. At one time or another, squatters' rights have been protected in order to permit temporary occupancy of vacated property in times of acute housing shortages. Whether such measures are just or worthwhile must be the major concern of any observer or scholar of the law, but these examples are set out here merely to show that from time to time Britain has experienced an evolution in property law that may be progressive in some of its impact.

This kind of evolution is not unknown in this country. The Supreme Court, for example, has occasionally handed down rulings—*Hawaii Housing Authority* v. *Midkiff* (1984) is a good example—that advance property law along progressive lines.[42] In that case, intervention by the state, faced with a shortage of land ownership opportunities for most of its people was able to prevail against some of the more debilitating barriers erected in the names of such rights. Property rights can hardly be allowed to invariably reign over other rights that are just as important or more important, such as rights to social and physical mobility.[43]

For those of us who hope for a better but also more just society, property rights and the vaunted and associated cause of "free enterprise" seem, often as not, to be the primary fetishistic symbols of the great societal evil of inequality. Unless and until some quite different arrangements are made on the subject of property rights, the centrality of this idea will continue to strike many of us as little more than dogma. What about, for example, investing a property right in a job after an employee has faithfully rendered service to her/his employer for a number of years? In recent times, we have been treated to the spectacle of companies moving out of long-term locations or laying off employees with many years of service and, simultaneously, taking no note of this faithful commitment. Such a property right claim to a job, it appears to me, is entirely valid.

Not all changes in property law, however, require breaking new ground. After all, when we think of great aggregations of property, we naturally think of the giant business corporations and, if we are thoughtful, of the evolution of the protections and privileges afforded by the law of corporations. A random recital of the names of some of these powerful "persons"—as they are defined in the law of corporations—will reveal a host of sleazies who, if they were real people, would have to be regarded as cases of recidivist criminality: Exxon, Union Carbide, Shell Oil, General Electric (dozens of times a loser), General Motors, Nestlé, Georgia Pacific, and United Brands, to recite just a few. The traditions of property law were changed in fundamentals ways to accommodate these shining examples of citizenship. Michael W. McCann, whose work on property law is some of the most interesting writing produced in recent years, points out:

> . . . the impersonal, collectivized, bureaucratic, interdependent, and highly public character of most corporate enterprises simply does not fit well within our tradition extolling the value of property entitlements among private individuals. However, the federal judiciary long ago

> chose virtually to ignore those fundamental social changes and simply declared corporations to be judicial "persons." Although thoroughly mystifying the nature of corporate social power, this legal fiction has provided a useful way of applying traditional rules of property rights to the complex economic relations of industrial capitalism.[44]

It is therefore the case that centrality of property rights, as found in law and economics doctrine and method, carries with it a large bundle of injustice, not only because of what we might make the law become but also because of what we have let it become.

Conceivably, the practitioners of law and economics could serve as agents of wholesome and progressive reform. The evidence to date, however, cannot be described as encouraging.[45]

EFFICIENCY

> [It is] a naive belief that the economist's notion of "efficiency" is sufficiently embracing so as to provide a comprehensive touchstone for policy judgements. *Nothing* could be further from the truth than this. Indeed, modern welfare economists have developed a set of more precise concepts designed to pinpoint some of the critical value choices typically masked by vague and question-begging invocations of "economic efficiency."
>
> —Bruce A. Ackerman[46]

Efficiency is probably the preeminent goal of law and economics. This is a direct manifestation, an allusion, or at the very least an unstated premise of every page of Posner's *Economic Analysis of Law*. Efficiency is what economics, and therefore law and economics, is all about; it is no exaggeration to characterize it as the grail, the shrine, the holy of holies. All the same, it is slippery, indefinite, perhaps even a chimera.

The history of this concept is sad. Efficiency has been lusted after by the banalities and injustices of Taylorism, time studies, and efficiency experts. Today, it is associated with such evils as surveillance of workers by both visual and electronic means and with large-scale layoffs that are meant to make a firm more competitive, though of course this is not always the result of such action.

However bad this history may be and whatever evils have been carried out in the name of efficiency, we can all be confident that economists are able to draw up parameters for measuring efficiency within a context of given elements. Indeed, this is often done without questioning the methods or the measures. And although we can be assured that economists—and, by extension, law and economics theorists and practitioners—can develop measures of judgment based upon this criterion, it is at the same time to be realized that in some way or another this is never quite achievable. Vincent Ostrom, a political scientist who often studies and writes within the traditions of public choice, points out that efficiency divorced from individuals' preferences is meaningless. Although this point would surely be conceded by the law and economics writers, it remains the case that we cannot know whether the economy—or even its constituent parts—is responding efficiently until we know what it is that individuals want, that is, just exactly what their preferences happen to be. Given this consideration, a very distorted picture of efficiency can emerge in any private property-based economy because such an economy always falls short of responding to individuals' preferences.[47]

The reason that this is the case is the absurdly simple fact that not everyone has the means to achieve the preferences she or he may desire. We do not mean by this that human wants are unlimited, which they surely are, but rather that individuals enter the marketplace with different bargaining stances based upon differing amounts of leverage. If one is concerned about a reasonable level of equality, meeting this question head on is a concern; if one is not (and the law and economics school is not), the strong tendency is to accept not only the market, but also the relative strengths and weaknesses of the bargainers as givens. This is a value choice, naturally, but it does mean that those who eschew equality are hardly in a position to claim some optimal efficiency for the market, for the trades that take place in it in a capitalist system, or for the policy prescriptions they are likely to set out from the bench or in legal treatises or articles.[48]

Getting down to cases, it is likely, for example, that a law and economics practitioner or, for that matter, a laissez-faire economist is going to equate any number of bargains for elective facelifts with efficiency, because both the buyer and seller of such services clearly want to see them performed. They would likewise regard deals for food purchased by poor persons as efficient. But it seems clear that these two kinds of bargains are hardly on a par; the food purchases are obviously necessary for survival, whereas the facelifts, though they may perform a nice purpose, may in fact not be necessary at all. It might optimally make more sense to tax that portion of income that is used to buy such services and use these revenues for a more worthwhile purpose. (Buchanan and Tullock and others will tell us that such funds are very likely to be wasted, a gross inefficiency, but there is no compelling reason to believe that they are correct either.) It is the case, I confidently assert, that free market economics often appears to be worked out within the confines of a moral vacuum. A questioner asked Milton Friedman, one of the gurus of the free market, whether he thought a chemist should accommodate the economy or a particular firm by helping it to manufacture napalm. His reply was

> [i]f a chemist feels it is immoral to make napalm, he can solve his problem by getting a job where he doesn't have to. He will pay a price. But the ultimate effect will be that if many, many people feel that way, the cost of hiring people to make napalm will be high, napalm will be expensive, and less of it will be used.[49]

This analysis misses some crucial points of moral importance. In like manner, it could be said that the question of fire inspections by the State of North Carolina in chicken-processing plants is a matter of the costs imposed by such inspections against the liabilities that flow from such a disaster as a fire in a plant. Such a tragic event, with injury and loss of lives, did occur in that state in 1991 (and North Carolina, using its own brand of logic, often advertises itself as a good business location state because of the absence of regulation). The centrality of efficiency in such cases quite obviously begs larger questions.

Example after example could be piled on while belaboring this point, but this is not necessary. It is important, however, to register a further objection to the law and economics standard of efficiency by reiterating the very point made by Bruce Ackerman. Modeling cannot be used as a substitute for hard data; and hard data, seldom a friend of any conservative cause whether we are talking about defense contracts, education, or social welfare costs, have indeed been developed with a variety of sophisticated statistical techniques in a broad variety of public policy areas. Much of the data suggest that it is time to go back to the drawing boards to establish models of efficiency that comport more tangibly with human needs.

The value premises of the law and economics school, in the final analysis, appear to be the paramount consideration. These include beliefs that attribute great complexity and spontaneity to the economy, that mistrust reason and ability as severely limited, and that clearly seem to hold that equality upsets the natural order of things. Planning and regulation are taboo; attempts to realize equality, hardly a desirable goal in the first place from their point of view, are doomed to fail; and hope, a vital ingredient if our lives are to have meaning, must be placed in the machinations of the market. All of this is efficiency. We can also call it ideology.

IDEOLOGY

> There is no principle more basic to the conservative philosophy than that of the inherent and absolute incompatibility between liberty and equality.
>
> —Robert Nisbet[50]

To say that law and economics is an ideology that, in the minds of judges and legal scholars, is attuned to a policy agenda is of course not a very remarkable statement. In various ways Posner, Easterbrook, and others will admit this. And while all of us are entitled to our ideologies, the problem is that the law and economics model has found its way to seats of power, namely, the federal bench, and it therefore must be a concern to all of us. The power of this ideology, as most of its critics are bound to observe, rests upon the cosmetics brought to it by its pseudoscientific character.

That is why it is important to examine this phenomenon. I would submit that (1) there are problems with the applicability of microeconomics to questions of choice, policy, and morals; (2) the approach is undergirded with the great prejudices found in law school education and in what we might call legal training—the overemphasis upon property rights, for example; (3) there are further problems wrought by the discipline of economics generally and by the public choice approach in particular; (4) the Buchanan-Tullock theses are overplayed and overdone and, indeed, they often conflict with hard data;[51] (5) a tracing of the inheritance of the free market school back to Adam Smith will show that the great theorist-founder held grave reservations about some of the values and policy positions that might be attributed to him, showing that a flawed perception undergirds free market economics at least at the popular level and that an inconsistent line of policy and values obtain at the intellectual level; (6) use of microeconomic models and concepts in developing discussion and decision making in the law is faulted by some observers on grounds of aesthetics and inappropriateness; (7) the centrality of property rights in the law and economics scheme carries with it both an excess of ideological baggage and a callousness toward those who compete less well, or do not really have the chance to compete, in the economic arena; (8) support for, and advocacy of, property rights mandates an important departure from common law understandings of property (for example, the modern law of corporations) as well as a failure to take advantage of progressive changes that have occurred in this branch of the law from time to time (as in some of the enactments of Labour governments in England); and (9) the attachment to efficiency demonstrates a somewhat myopic fondness for what is, at bottom, a rather messy concept.

This set of considerations necessarily excludes a variety of criticisms directed at law and economics, which, for a variety of reasons, appear less cogent. Some economists, for example, have urged the abandonment of microeconomics altogether in order to move their discipline away from what they believe to be absurdly one-sided and conservative premises.[52] I for one do not feel obliged to join in such a demand, not because I refrain out of professional courtesy—let's face it, there are plenty of things in their realm, from statistical approaches to one-sided narrowness, that cry out for rectification—but because microeconomics seems to work as a useful tool for a rather large number of people. Tools and methods are not evil in and of themselves; it is basically only their misuse and their omissions that really lend themselves to criticism, and this certainly is the case with law and economics. Another criticism I have not followed up on is the common complaint that the law and economics approach seeks to skirt conflicts by not recognizing that they exist. This may well be the case from time to time, but this realization has to be tempered by the knowledge that the law and economics school does seem, after all, to be eminently political; and if this is the case, this appears unlikely. My observation of the law and economics movement and of the Chicago school in general is that they like conflict very much. They seek out conflict; indeed, they relish it. A further criticism that may be valid but that I believe to be relatively unimportant is the claim, made perhaps most strongly by Bruce Ackerman, that the law and economics model is too simplistic and that such simplism is evidenced by the reduction of legal issues to a set of mechanistic formulas. This may well be, indeed probably is, the case; but I find this hard to fault simply because I have tried, successfully at times I hope, to establish certain regular standards of judgment about the law and its application in the belief that consistency of approach will be at least informative and helpful in the cause of discovery.

More serious, it seems to me, are two important matters that are left out of the equations of the law and economics movement: the matters of class status and class issues and the related but woeful denigration of equality as a value. A democratic system of law and governance seems to require equality, not as some vague intellectual construct, not as a slogan about being equal "in the law" or "before the law," which is not the case in any event, but as a societal goal. To eschew such a goal is truly inefficient in terms of the hope for a better world; such a choice, in fact, must probably be seen as giving vent to what Thorstein Veblen regarded as one of the major reasons for inequality: the psychological importance of it for those who see themselves as above the rest of us. Enduring such nonsense is painful enough; abetting it has brought this nation to its present sorry state. Law must therefore be considerably more than the mere product of intellectual fun and games rooted in the follies of elitism. When it does grow out of this, and I believe it will, we can perhaps find ourselves in a better society, a caring society, a land of equality, democracy, and yes, good bargains.

NOTES

1. Bruce A. Ackerman (ed.), "Introduction," *Economic Foundations of Property Law*, xi.

2. "The Pernicious Effects of Economics on American Political Science," *Chronicle of Higher Education*, December 11, 1991, 81–82.

3. Dennis M. Patterson, "A Fable from the Seventh Circuit: Frank Easterbrook on Good Faith," *Iowa Law Review* 76 (March 1991), fn. 2, 504.

4. Richard A. Posner, *Economic Analysis of Law*, 3d ed. (Boston: Little, Brown, 1986).

5. Rogers M. Smith, *Liberalism and American Constitutional Law* (Cambridge: Harvard University Press, 1990), 169–70.

6. See the excellent study by Conrad P. Waligorski, *The Political Theory of Conservative Economists* (Lawrence: University Press of Kansas, 1990); for my own work concerning Friedman, see *City of the Right: Urban Applications of American Conservative Thought* (Westport, CT: Greenwood Press, 1982), Chap. 4.

7. Waligorski, *Political Theory of Conservative Economists*, 20.

8. Ibid.; Bruce A. Ackerman, *Reconstructing American Law* (Cambridge: Harvard University Press, 1983); Fred Block, *Postindustrial Possibilities: A Critique of Economic*

Discourse (Berkeley: University of California Press, 1990). See also, generally, the literature sometimes classified under the rubric of "Critical Legal Studies."

9. Posner, *Economic Analysis of Law*, 491.

10. Ibid., 491–92.

11. Ibid., 492.

12. Ibid., 493.

13. Ibid., 493–99.

14. Respective cites for these cases: 198 U.S. 45 (1905); 163 U.S. 537 (1896); 60 U.S. 393 (1856); 262 U.S. 525 (1923).

15. Block, *Postindustrial Possibilities*, 38–45.

16. Joseph A. Schumpeter, *Capitalism, Socialism, and Democracy* (New York: Harper Brothers, 1942).

17. James M. Buchanan and Gordon Tullock, *The Calculus of Consent* (Ann Arbor: University of Michigan Press, 1962).

18. See Buchanan and Tullock, *The Calculus of Consent*, esp. Chap. 18.

19. Anthony Downs, *An Economic Theory of Democracy* (New York: Harper & Row, 1957).

20. Kristen Renwick Monroe (ed.), *The Economic Approach to Politics: A Critical Reassessment of the Theory of Rational Action* (New York: HarperCollins, 1991).

21. Sanford Levinson, "Strolling Down the Path of the Law (and Toward Critical Legal Studies?): The Jurisprudence of Richard Posner," *Columbia Law Review* 91 (June 1991), 1221–22 (a review of Richard A. Posner, *The Problems of Jurisprudence*).

22. Richard Posner, *The Problems of Jurisprudence* (Cambridge: Harvard University Press, 1990). Though he is a federal appeals judge, Posner is a prolific author and probably regards himself as some sort of iconoclast. His *Sex and Reason* (Chicago: University of Chicago Press, 1991), applies public-choice methodology to sexual and moral policy choices, and obviously promises stimulation. Some critics are bound to say, however, that applications of economic paradigms have their limits.

23. Certainly the most definitive work on law and economics by a political scientist is Kim Scheppele, *Legal Secrets: Equality and Efficiency in the Common Law* (Chicago: University of Chicago Press, 1988).

24. Adam Smith, *An Inquiry into the Nature and Causes of the Wealth of Nations*, 2 vols., R. H. Campbell, A. S. Skinner, and W. B. Todd (eds.) (1776; rptd. Oxford: Clarendon Press, 1976).

25. Barry James, "Will the Real Adam Smith Stand Up?" *International Herald Tribune*, July 17, 1990.

26. Smith, *Wealth of Nations*, Introduction, 10.

27. Ibid., note, 337.

28. Ibid., 337.

29. It is well nigh impossible and it goes well beyond the scope and purpose of this study to provide anything like a complete bibliography of the works of Buchanan and Tullock; key items I would choose are James M. Buchanan and Richard E. Wagner, *Democracy in Deficit: The Political Legacy of Lord Keynes* (New York: Academic Press, 1977); Gordon Tullock, *Private Wants, Public Means: An Economic Analysis of the Desirable Scope of Government* (New York: Basic Books, 1970), and *The Economics of Income Redistribution* (Hingham, MA: Kluwer-Nijhoff, 1983).

This chapter necessarily leaves out much related material contributed by other authors. Kenneth Arrow's equilibrium theorem, for example, though certainly relevant to many of the considerations that are discussed here, falls outside a critique of law and economics.

30. Smith, *Wealth of Nations*, 857.

31. Ibid., 842. Italics added.

32. A concise explanation of the Coase theorem can be found in A. Mitchell Polinsky, *An Introduction to Law and Economics* (Boston: Little, Brown, 1983), Chap. 3.

33. See pp. 346–47.

34. See Posner, *Economic Analysis of Law*, discussions in Chaps. 1 and 2.

35. Letter to the author from Professor Coase dated July 9, 1991.

36. Larry M. Preston, "Efficiency, Philosophy, and Political Economy," paper delivered to the Annual Meeting of the Midwest Political Science Association, Chicago, April 14–16, 1988, esp. p. 10.

37. Ackerman, *Reconstructing American Law*.

38. Posner, *Economic Analysis of Law*, 30.

39. See, generally, ibid.

40. Richard A. Epstein, *Takings: Private Property and the Power of Eminent Domain* (Cambridge: Harvard University Press, 1985).

41. Gerald R. Thompson, "The Unalienable Right of Property: Examining the Fourth and Fifth Amendments," *Journal of Christian Jurisprudence* 8 (n.d., ca. 1990), 202.

42. 104 S.Ct. 2321 (1984).

43. See the arguments in Gerald L. Houseman, *The Right of Mobility* (Port Washington, NY: Kennikat Press, 1979).

44. Michael W. McCann, "Resurrection and Reform: Perspectives on Property in the American Constitutional Tradition," *Politics and Society* 13 (1984), 162.

45. For differing perspectives on this, see the articles by Patterson, "A Fable from the Seventh Circuit," and Levinson, "Strolling Down the Path of the Law."

46. Ackerman, "Introduction," *Economic Foundations of Property Law*, xi.

47. Vincent Ostrom, *The Intellectual Crisis in American Public Administration*, rev. ed. (University: University of Alabama Press, 1974); Preston, "Efficiency, Philosophy, and Political Economy."

48. John Rawls, *A Theory of Justice* (Cambridge: Harvard University Press, 1971); Waligorski, *Political Theory of Conservative Economists*; Mark Kelman, "A Critique of Conservative Legal Thought," in David Kairys (ed.), *The Politics of Law: A Progressive Critique*, rev. ed. (New York: Pantheon, 1990), 436–52.

49. Milton Friedman, *There's No Such Thing as a Free Lunch* (LaSalle, IL: Open Court, 1975), 245.

50. Robert Nisbet, *Conservatism: Dream and Reality* (Minneapolis: University of Minnesota Press, 1986), 47.

51. The point made here is simple enough: The models to which Buchanan and Tullock are given tell us something, but the hard data achieved within the specialist subdiscipline areas of political science and sociology, for example—areas of concern such as social welfare, education, labor studies, housing, and indeed economic regulation of certain industries as well as taxation and income distribution—tell us something else. True, the public-choice theorists and law and economics people never claim that their models are applicable in all cases, but some of this is mere question begging.

52. Block, *Postindustrial Possibilities*, 38–45.

Epilogue

THIS BOOK WAS DEVELOPED, first, in the hope that the reasoning and discussion processes employed will provide food for thought, a measure of intellectual satisfaction that will help to lead to further investigation of the issues and considerations put forward; and, second, in the hope that the law and policy proposals developed, or something approximating them, will at some future time actually see the light of day. Ideas cannot invariably be timely. James McGregor Burns, among others, has said that he knows his proposals usually have little hope of winning immediate favor, but who knows, they might find favor at some point or another in time. In the meantime, I am sure that he and many social science writers believe that they can add something to our dialogues and perhaps to our minds.

I set some store in the fact that I have chosen to even write an epilogue on American law rather than an epitaph for America. The latter exercise too often seems the more appropriate one. The chaos, excess, short-sightedness, and occasional outright savagery of public policy and our leadership over these recent days and years of our lives can be almost debilitating to anyone who spends time in reflection, contemplation, or serious writing.[1]

Perhaps the darkest cloud on the scene in American law is the Supreme Court. No shifts or movements in the American electorate hold any promise against the decades ahead of us in which the Court will be, quite firmly I fear, in the hands of conservative ideologues. So far, the signs are anything but promising: The Court has moved against the victims of capital punishment, has placed its stamp of approval upon coerced confessions, and has allowed southern school districts with segregationist histories to return to their old ways. Women's rights face the possibility of great setbacks, not the least of which may be the making of abortion either illegal or impossible.

Other spectres on the horizon are disturbing. The United States faces a bleak economic future in the short term, at the very least, because of the merger-mania antics of corporations, a loss of competitiveness that is exacerbated by the overstuffed compensation packages of our industrial leadership, and because the Reagan promises of 1980—lower taxes, better employment opportunities, and a balanced budget—were never realized. Well, yes, lower taxes for the wealthy were realized, so much lower in fact that their breaks added a trillion dollars to the national debt, according to a recent study by Citizens for Tax Justice.[2] One of the spin-offs from this dreadful circumstance is that the wealthy, awash in their riches, are using a small part of the government's largesse to deploy even more right-wing think tanks across the nation. Not only will we continue to be plagued with the tax-exempt ideology—dressed up as "studies"—spewing forth in a constant stream from the Heritage Foundation, the American Enterprise Institute, and so forth, but we now will be witnessing the spectacle of the establishment of conservative think tanks (an oxymoron, it is sometimes said) in each and every state.[3] "Many wealthy individuals and corporations believe it is in their long term interests to fund such operations," states Professor William Galston of the University of Maryland, who has pointed out how easy it is for such institutions to obtain funding.[4] Those who know social science know what these institutes are doing; the public and sometimes even the politicians do not.

A catalogue of such developments and worries of course can be virtually endless. Are there any hopeful signs at all on the horizon? Must we always be pessimistic about the future of law and public policy in this country?

Searching through the signs and soothsayings one always finds in American politics, I do find one remarkable and somewhat hopeful fact about our future: Communism is dead. I do not refer to Communism in the Soviet Union or Bulgaria or Poland. That overinflated threat ceased to exist probably quite well before Gorbachev took power in the "evil empire." What I am referring to, however, is that "Communism" as a label, as a smear, or perhaps more likely, as a whispered charge, is done for; those who have used it will have to think of something else, and so far they have not come up with anything that is really zippy. "Politically correct" will not cut it. Eventually, someone will probably come up with something horrific, but it is probably going to require some time and something else that is becoming more difficult to do in these days of domination by electronic media—intensive levels of socialization.

It is true that our history has always had its bogeys and hysteria-mongering of one kind or another. Our paranoia has produced monsters as needed. It is nonetheless true that "Communism" has held a very special place both as a historical force and as a mighty contributor to the bogeyist lexicon, often demeaning and distorting debates over public policy. "Communism" has animated debate for at least a solid third of the existence of the United States as a nation, and all of this history is recent. Its hard-consonant utterance provides it with a fearsome ring of authenticity that is unique among the words of threat and menace. As a force for harm, it has fallen quite unequally upon its many targets:

George C. Marshall, Dean Acheson, Dwight D. Eisenhower, Nelson A. Rockefeller, Millard Tydings, Robert G. Stevens, Walter P. Reuther, Thomas Kuchel, Wilson Riles, Owen Lattimore, John Stewart Service, G. Bromley Oxnam, thousands of public officials, bureaucrats, clergy, labor leaders, academics, and entertainers.

Communism, in short, served as a fright word and an end-of-thought word. It has often been preceded by an adjective such as conscious, unconscious (which was probably even worse), dedicated, systematic, or insidious. People who might have otherwise written some treatises on politics and government, philosophy, sociology, or perhaps popular culture wound up saying ludicrous and even comical things that they would live to regret. Most of these did know, however, that the label would give them, more often than not, a way of winning a suspension of thought without much use of debate, logic, reason, or even fact.

The distortions of political dialogue hardly end there; for aside from besmirching characters or ruining careers, this fear-mongering led to grievous effects upon the right to political expression. People have been quite intimidated through all of these years when discussing concepts such as democratic socialism, communal values, collectives or cooperatives, or changes in the law that adversely affect privilege in any way. An emphasis upon "group" values could be suspect; so, in the main, these subjects were ignored. In addition—and this certainly is no small matter—political dialogue could become as intensely boring as a study from a right-wing think tank. It often seemed necessary, to cite just one example, to "take the pledge" before discussing any issue of moment; so one was required to listen to ardent statements of anti-Communism before any real conversation could take place. In uglier situations, time was spent on the question of the loyalty of one or more participants. A few individuals who still have not received the word about the demise of Communism, such as television inquisitor Robert Novak, still waste our time in this way.

It can be argued that the crudities of "anti-Communism," or at least the grossest of them, are a thing of the past. Whatever way the American political scene might be described today, this is hardly the 1950s, which were probably the most intense period of inquisitorial law enforcement and congressional harassment. This is true because it would be a rare event in American politics in our time, except in isolated instances, to have someone refer to another as an outright Communist. A measure of sophistication and good grace seems to matter at least that much.

Or do they? Almost any casual observer of political life knows that there can be as many variants on this theme as there have been menaces, real or imagined, in the nation's history. Recent election campaigns have demonstrated that the spirit of the 1950s can be found in abundance. A heinous example of the spirit of red-baiting is the phony "pledge of allegiance" issue of the 1988 presidential campaign. That issue, supported by the graphic image of a flag factory locale as well as the solemnities utterd by George Bush's famous lips, resulted in defensive flag-draping antics by Michael Dukakis, his opponent.

Just as irrelevant to any legitimate concerns of policy or purpose was the issue of Dukakis's membership in the American Civil Liberties Union. In a special way, however, this issue pointed up the unity of our time with the 1950s. Bush spent a lot time talking about the "card-carrying" membership of Dukakis, the adjective underlining the ominous and sinister nature of this affiliation. Whether in the 1950s or today, the fact of membership in the ACLU, Americans for Democratic Action, People for the American Way, or any number of other groups can raise questions in the minds of the fearful and uninformed. After all, many people never take out a membership in anything; anyway, Joe McCarthy told us back in the 1950s that the ACLU is a Communist front organization. The Bush implication against Dukakis's loyalty based upon his membership and the sweeping allegation of McCarthy, although widely separated by time, are possessed of a fundamental unity of purpose, spirit, tone, and falsehood.

In many respects, then, the fact that the "Communist menace" has not necessarily been used in the old unsophisticated manner of a direct charge in recent years hardly means that the same psychological dynamic has not been at work. The spirit of red-baiting has been with us on a continuous basis for more than seventy years. The groundwork for the charges made today was laboriously developed during those hysterical days of the past when the excesses of the red-hunters seemed less evident and were much less exposed.

Now "anti-Communism" has taken a decisive new turn. It is more of an abstraction than anything else, referring (if to anything) to political values rather than to any obvious menace. It pales alongside demagogic weapons such as race or homophobia; observe the recent Jesse Helms Senate campaign in North Carolina. The Communist menace tends to invoke a yawn. And it doesn't mean a thing if it doesn't have that zing.

A problem of considerable moment has been created for superloyalists, however. A reordering of monsters will have to take place; and this, at the least, is an inconvenience. At the most, it is a problem of maintaining mental equilibrium, a perpetual problem on the right in some respects. An editorial that appeared in early 1990 demonstrates the depth of this fear of the loss of "Communism." It says that few people realize the "enormously important part played by fear of Russia . . . in keeping America's feet on the ground."[5] It goes on to say that the excesses of liberalism have been placed on a leash because of this fear. Most appreciatively, it says that

> [t]he threat of aggressive Russian communism has been of incalculable value to the cause of Western civilisation in the last 40 years, justifying conservative values and practices which would otherwise have been long ago eliminated by the dominant liberal *zeitgeist*.[6]

We should be thankful for this admission that Communism has been an enormously useful tool, even when it has been necessary to use it quite insincerely. Character assassination and poisoned dialogue have performed important duties in keeping social change and political efforts in check. So, although it has been obvious for a long time that a domestic Communist threat never had anything to do with the urgencies or substance of our politics, it has proved to be one of the all-time great sticks with which to beat the social and political forces of reform. Small wonder that its passing is lamented on the right; some time is bound to pass before a weapon of such weighty fright value is found.

With these observations I hope that it can be said that this set of chapters ends on a somewhat happy note. This gives me the chance to pick up my lance and proceed, for I think I see some windmills over on the next hill.

NOTES

1. "Savagery" may sound too graphic; but it is fair to say that, apart from the fact that policies that produce poverty or just unfairness can be said to be violent, we have seen wars in Grenada, Panama, and Iraq characterized by blood and hoopla; the imposition of impractical family-planning policies on poor nations, the results of which I have had the displeasure of observing in the Third World; and support for capital punishment and other bloodthirsty crime-control policies.

2. *Inequality and the Federal Budget Deficit* (Washington, D.C.: Citizens for Tax Justice, 1991).

3. Fort Wayne *Journal-Gazette*, June 3, 1991 (Scripps Howard wire story).

4. Ibid.

5. This editorial ran in the London *Sunday Telegraph* originally and was reprinted in the *International Herald Tribune*, February 27, 1990.

6. Ibid. An earlier version of the discussion of the end of the "Communist menace" appears in the (London) *Times Higher Education Supplement*, July 12, 1991.

Selected Bibliography

Abel, Richard L. *American Lawyers*. New York: Oxford University Press, 1989.

Ackerman, Bruce A. (ed.). *Economic Foundations of Property Law*. Boston: Little, Brown, 1975.

———. *Reconstructing American Law*. Cambridge: Harvard University Press, 1984.

Adams, Walter, and James W. Brock. *Dangerous Pursuits: Mergers and Acquisitions in the Age of Wall Street*. New York: Pantheon, 1989.

Block, Fred. *Postindustrial Possibilities: A Critique of Economic Discourse*. Berkeley: University of California Press, 1990.

Buchanan, James M., and Gordon Tullock. *The Calculus of Consent: Logical Foundations of Constitutional Democracy*. Ann Arbor: University of Michigan Press, 1962.

Carter, Lief H. *Administrative Law and Policy: Cases and Comments*. Boston: Little, Brown, 1983.

———. *Reason in Law*, 2d ed. Boston: Little, Brown, 1984.

Cox, Archibald, Derek C. Bok, and Robert A. Gorman. *Labor Law*, 10th ed. Mineola, NY: Foundation Press, 1986.

Epstein, Richard A. *Takings: Private Property and the Power of Eminent Domain*. Cambridge: Harvard University Press, 1985.

Essays on Critical Legal Studies. Cambridge: Harvard Law Review Association, 1986.

Friedman, Milton, and Rose Friedman. *Free to Choose: A Personal Statement*. New York: Harcourt Brace Jovanovich, 1980.

Galbraith, John Kenneth. *The Affluent Society*. Boston: Houghton Mifflin, 1958.

———. *The New Industrial State*. Boston: Houghton Mifflin, 1967.

Geoghegan, Thomas. *Which Side Are You On? Trying to Be for Labor When It's Flat on Its Back*. New York: Farrar, Strauss, and Giroux, 1991.

Houseman, Gerald L. *City of the Right: Urban Applications of American Conservative Thought.* Westport, CT: Greenwood Press, 1982.

———. *State and Local Government: The New Battleground.* Englewood Cliffs, NJ: Prentice Hall, 1986.

Kairys, David (ed.). *The Politics of Law: A Progressive Critique*, 2d ed. New York: Pantheon, 1990.

Kelman, Mark. *A Guide to Critical Legal Studies.* Cambridge: Harvard University Press, 1967.

Kolko, Joyce. *Restructuring the World Economy.* New York: Pantheon, 1988.

Lindblom, Charles E. *Politics and Markets: The World's Political-Economic Systems.* New York: Basic Books, 1977.

McCann, Michael W., and Gerald L. Houseman (eds.). *Judging the Constitution: Critical Essays on Judicial Lawmaking.* Glenview, IL: Scott, Foresman, 1989.

McCloskey, Herbert, and Alida Brill. *Dimensions of Tolerance: What Americans Believe about Civil Liberties.* New York: Russell Sage Foundation, 1983.

Mills, C. Wright. *The Power Elite.* New York: Oxford University Press, 1956.

Monroe, Kristen R. (ed.). *The Economic Approach to Politics: A Critical Reassessment of the Theory of Rational Action.* New York: HarperCollins, 1991.

Phillips, Kevin. *The Politics of Rich and Poor: Wealth and the American Electorate in the Reagan Aftermath.* New York: Random House, 1990.

Piven, Frances Fox, and Richard A. Cloward. *Why Americans Don't Vote.* New York: Pantheon, 1989.

Polinsky, A. Mitchell. *An Introduction to Law and Economics.* Boston: Little, Brown, 1983.

Posner, Richard A. *Economic Analysis of Law,* 3d ed. Boston: Little, Brown, 1986.

Rawls, John. *A Theory of Justice.* Cambridge: Harvard University Press, 1971.

Roelofs, H. Mark. *Ideology and Myth in American Politics.* Boston: Little, Brown, 1976.

Samuels, Warren J., and Arthur S. Miller (eds.). *Corporations and Society: Power and Responsibility.* Westport, CT: Greenwood Press, 1987.

Shienbaum, Kim E. *Beyond the Electoral Connection: A Reassessment of the Role of Voting in Contemporary American Politics.* Philadelphia: University of Pennsylvania Press, 1984.

Smith, Adam. *An Inquiry into the Nature and Causes of the Wealth of Nations,* 2 vols., R. H. Campbell, A. S. Skinner, and W. B. Todd (eds.). Oxford: Clarendon Press, 1976; orig. ptd. 1776.

Waligorski, Conrad P. *The Political Theory of Conservative Economists.* Lawrence: University Press of Kansas, 1990.

Index

About the Author

GERALD L. HOUSEMAN, Professor of Political Science, Indiana University at Fort Wayne, is the author of *City of the Right: Urban Applications of American Conservative Thought* (Greenwood Press, 1982), *G. D. H. Cole* (1979) and *The Right of Mobility* (1979), *The American Political System* (co-authored with H. Mark Roeloff, 1983), *State and Local Government: The New Battleground* (1986), and *Judging the Constitution* (co-edited with Michael W. McCann, 1989).